Kinship Foster

0207 9281506

Child Welfare

A series in child welfare practice, policy, and research

DUNCAN LINDSEY, *General Editor*

Kinship Foster Care
Policy, Practice, and Research

Edited by

Rebecca L. Hegar
University of Texas at Arlington

Maria Scannapieco
University of Texas at Arlington

New York   Oxford
OXFORD UNIVERSITY PRESS
1999

Oxford University Press

Oxford   New York
Athens   Auckland   Bangkok   Bogotá   Buenos Aires   Calcutta
Cape Town   Chennai   Dar es Salaam   Delhi   Florence   Hong Kong   Istanbul
Karachi   Kuala Lumpur   Madrid   Melbourne   Mexico City   Mumbai
Nairobi   Paris   São Paulo   Singapore   Taipei   Tokyo   Toronto   Warsaw

and associated companies in
Berlin   Ibadan

Copyright © 1999 by Oxford University Press, Inc.

Published by Oxford University Press, Inc.
198 Madison Avenue, New York, New York 10016
http://www.oup-usa.org

Oxford is a registered trademark of Oxford University Press

Library of Congress Cataloging-in-Publication Data
Kinship foster care : policy, practice, and research / edited by
Rebecca L. Hegar, Maria Scannapieco.
    p.   cm.—(Child welfare)
Includes bibliographical references and index.
ISBN 0-19-510939-2 (cloth).—ISBM 0-19-510940-6 (paper)
    1. Kinship care.   I. Hegar, Rebecca L.   II. Scannapieco, Maria.
III. Series: Child welfare (Oxford University Press)
HV873.K56   1998   97-34877
362.73'3—dc21   CIP

1 3 5 7 9 8 6 4 2

Printed in the United States of America
on acid-free paper

Contents

PART III
KINSHIP CARE RESEARCH

CONCLUSION

List of Contributors

Richard P. Barth, M.S.W., Ph.D., is Hutto Patterson Professor, School of Social Welfare, University of California at Berkeley, where he has taught about child welfare practice, policy, and research. His coauthored books include: From *Child Abuse to Permanency Planning: Pathways Through Child Welfare Services* (Aldine, 1994) and *The Tender Years: Toward Developmentally Sensitive Child Welfare Services* (Oxford University Press, 1998). He has been a Fulbright Scholar to Sweden, a Lois and Samuel Silberman Senior Faculty Fellow, and a winner of the Frank Bruel Prize of the University of Chicago for excellence in child welfare scholarship.

Mary Benedict, Ph.D., is an associate scientist at the John Hopkins University School of Hygiene and Public Health, Department of Maternal and Child Health. She has devoted her professional career in the child welfare arena, with special concentrations in foster care and sexual abuse. Dr. Benedict received her doctorate at John Hopkins University in Maternal and Child Health. Her most recent publication is "Adult Functioning of Children who Lived in Kin Versus Nonrelative Family Foster Homes," in the special edition of *Child Welfare* devoted to kinship care.

Jill Duerr Berrick, M.S.W., Ph.D., is director of the Center for Social Services Research and associate adjunct professor at the School of Social Welfare, University of California at Berkeley. Dr. Berrick received her Ph.D. and M.S.W. from the University of California at Berkeley; her dissertation focused on child sexual abuse prevention policy. She currently teaches courses on social policy, and social sciences research and conducts research on various topics concerning poor children and families. She follows kinship care policy and practice very closely and has coauthored a curriculum for social workers on the topic. She has authored or coauthored five books on child abuse, foster care, and family poverty and has written extensively for academic journals. Her most recent book, *Faces of Poverty: Portraits of Women and Children on Welfare* was published by Oxford University Press.

Howard Dubowitz, M.D., is an associate professor of pediatrics at the University of Maryland School of Medicine where he directs the Child Protection Program. Dr. Dubowitz is involved in clinical work, research, teaching, and child advocacy. His clinical work includes interdisciplinary consultation on cases of suspected abuse and neglect and he is also active in general pediatrics. Dr. Dubowitz's current research activities are in the study of child neglect—its antecedents and outcomes, and in the area of preventing neglect. Dr. Dubowitz does a considerable amount of teaching within his medical school and also at local, state, and national conferences. He has been very active in the area of legislative advocacy at the state and national levels. Dr. Dubowitz chairs the Committee on Child Maltreatment of the American Academy of Pediatrics, Maryland Chapter. He is on the Executive Board of the American Professional Society on the Abuse of Children and he chairs the Public Affairs Committee. He is a member of the Research Committee of the Federal Interagency Task Force on Child Abuse and Neglect.

Joy Swanson Ernst, M.S.W., is a doctoral candidate at the University of Maryland School of Social Work. Currently, she is completing her dissertation on the ecological correlates of child maltreatment in Maryland. She received her bachelor's degree from the University of Chicago in 1980 and her master's degree in social work from Rutgers University in 1984. She has previously worked in New Jersey, Wisconsin and Virginia for nonprofit agencies serving families and children.

This chapter would not have been possible without the help and generosity of many people. The author thanks Leon Fulcher of the Victoria University of Wellington Department of Applied Social Science, Sue Johnson of the National Office of the New Zealand Children and Young Persons and Their Families Services (NZCYPFS), and the staff at NZCYPFS offices in Palmerston North, Masterton, Levin, Nelson, and Wellington. The following people provided valuable information and/or comments: Barbara Allan, John Bradley, Gale Burford, Tamati Cairns, Ella Davis, Faith Denny, Dan Ernst, Robin Facourt, Penelope Hawkins, Ema Jacob, Ron Malpass, Gabrielle Maxwell, Pare Niania, Anne Opie, Miriam Saphira, Darrin Sykes, Sue Taylor, Waereti Tait-Rolleston and Jill Worrall.

Susan Feigelman, M.D., is associate professor of pediatrics at the University of Maryland School of Medicine. She is practicing general pediatrician and educator in an urban pediatric clinic. Her research and clinical interests are in health care utilization of children in foster care, failure-to-thrive, and the prevention of high-risk behavior among early adolescents. She has been an advocate for the improvement of health care among foster children in the state of Maryland.

James P. Gleeson, Ph.D., is associate professor at the Jane Addams College of Social Work, University of Illinois at Chicago. Dr. Gleeson teaches in the Child and Family Concentration of the M.S.W. program and in the Ph.D. programs at Jane Addams. He is Principal Investigator of two federally funded projects: *Innovative Training for Exemplary Practice: Working with Relatives as Foster Parents,* a curriculum development and training project that focuses on exemplary practice in kinship care, and a research project that investigates case planning for children entering state custody as infants in Chicago and New York, *How Decisions to Change the Case Plan Goal are Initiated.* Dr. Gleeson has been principal investigator for several child welfare projects, including a federally funded research and demonstration project, *Achieving Permanency for Children in Kinship Foster Care,* several projects on *How Child Welfare Caseworkers Learn,* and a study of caseworker *Implementation of a Structured Making Model at Child Welfare Intake.*

Donna Harrington, Ph.D., is an assistant professor at the University of Maryland School of Social Work, where she teaches courses in statistics, research, and human behavior in the social environment. She received her Ph.D. in applied developmental psychology from the University of Maryland, Baltimore County, and her research focuses on factors related to child maltreatment.

Rebecca L. Hegar, M.S.S.W., D.S.W., is associate professor at the School of Social Work, University of Texas at Arlington. She has been concerned with issues of child protection and child placement since the mid-1970s, when she was first employed as a social worker in child welfare. She has worked in the public social welfare systems of Texas and Louisiana as a direct-service social worker and supervisor, and she has done extensive staff training and consultation concerning child placement issues. Her areas of teaching expertise include child welfare and family policy. Many of her conference presentations and journal articles concern child welfare placement decisions, and her work have been published in more than thirty journals. She is coauthor, with Geoffry L. Greif, of *When Parents Kidnap* (1993).

Sondra M. Jackson, M.S.W., L.C.S.W., is currently a faculty member and the director of training at the University of Maryland School of Social Work, Ms. Jackson has years of experience in practice and policy development. Prior to coming to the University she was the assistant director for family and children services in the Baltimore City Department of Social Services. Her other positions include interim executive director, deputy director, office director, and family services program manager at the Maryland State Social Service Administration. Ms. Jackson developed the nationally recognized Maryland Intensive Family Services Program. For over ten years she has conducted training sessions and workshops nationally to improve social workers' skills emphasizing a culturally sensitive approach to service delivery. Her thrust toward helping professionals to build on family strengths and increase cultural competence has led her to the development of a kinship care model. Ms. Jackson has presented numerous papers, workshops, and conference keynote addresses. Her recent publications appear in the journals *Social Work* and *Child Welfare*. She is coeditor of the January, 1997, *Child Welfare* issue "Perspectives on Serving African American Children, Youths and Families." Ms. Jackson's professional memberships include The Children's Defense Fund, The Black Community Crusade for Children, Black Administrators in Child Welfare, National Association of Social Workers, National Association of Black Social Workers, National Advisory Committee for Kinship Care, National Advisory Committee for HIV Positive Children, and the American Professional Society for the Abuse of Children. She is also a member of the Howard County Social Services Board of Directors.

Nicole Le Prohn, M.S.W., Ph.D., is the director of practice research for The Casey Family Program headquarters in Seattle, Washington. Dr. Le Prohn joined Casey after three years as an assistant professor at the University of Southern California School of Social Work, where she taught courses in research, social work practice, and human behavior. Prior to that, she served as a research associate for the Family Welfare Research Group at the University of California, Berkeley and as a child welfare worker in Alameda County, California. She has worked with both foster and biological parents, and with children in family and residential placements. While obtaining her doctorate at the University of Washington, she served as program coordinator for the Family Preservation Project. As a director of practice research, Dr. Le Prohn's work focuses on the evaluation of agency programs, and providing research technical assistance to Divisions on Initiative projects. Other work includes the Quality Services Redesign Project, the Specialized Family Care Project, and ongoing research with the Child Behavior Checklist.

John Nasuti, D.S.W., is an associate professor and director of the BSW Program at the University of North Carolina at Wilmington (UNCW). Prior to coming to UNCW, Dr. Nasuti was the chair of the child welfare concentration at the Graduate School of Social Work, Louisiana State University. His teaching and research interests include risk assessment in child protective services and foster care.

Barbara Needell, M.S.W., Ph.D., is a researcher at the Child Welfare Research Center at the University of California at Berkeley. She is coauthor of several articles, chapters, and a curriculum on kinship care, and *The Tender Years* (Oxford University Press, 1998). As project director of the Performance Indicators for Child Welfare Services in California project and senior research analyst for the California Children's Services Archive, she has worked extensively with statewide administrative data.

Peter J. Pecora, M.S.W., Ph.D., has a joint appointment as the manager of research for The Casey Family Program, and associate professor, School of Social Work, University of Washington, Seattle, Washington. Dr. Pecora has provided training in evaluation of family-based services programs, risk assessment, and other areas to child welfare staff in a number of states. Peter is coauthor of a number of articles and books on child welfare practice, administration, and evaluation, including *Quality Improvement and Program Evaluation in Child Welfare Agencies: Managing into the Next Century* (1996), *Evaluating Family-based Services* (1995), *The Child Welfare Challenge* (1992), *Families in Crisis—The Impact of Family Preservation Services* (1991), and *Managing Human Services Personnel* (1987).

He has provided consultation regarding evaluation of child and family services to the U.S. Department of Health and Human Services, the Federal Substance Abuse and Mental Health Administration, and a number of foundations including the Annie E. Casey Foundation, Colorado Trust, Edna McConnell Clark Foundation, McKnight Foundation, and the Stuart Foundation.

Maria Scannapieco, M.S.W., Ph.D., is associate professor at the School of Social Work, University of Texas at Arlington, and director of the Center for Child Welfare. Dr. Scannapieco has worked in the public child welfare arena for more than nineteen years, with seven years of direct child protection experience as well as foster care administrative experience. Since coming into academia, Maria Scannapieco has continued her commitment to the child welfare field in both teaching and scholarship. Dr. Scannapieco has more than thirty publications and presentations competitively selected, many in the area of out-of-home placement. She has been published in such professional journals as *Child Welfare, Child and Adolescent Social Work, Children and Youth Services Review,* and *Social Work.*

Raymond H. Starr, Jr., Ph.D., a developmental psychologist, is on the faculty of the University of Maryland Baltimore County. He has been conducting research on child maltreatment and related issues for more than twenty-five years. He is the author of numerous publications, including the books *Child Abuse Prediction: Policy Implications* and *The Effects of Child Abuse and Neglect: Issues and Research* (with David Wolfe). Honors include a Congressional Science Fellowship and election to Fellow of the American Psychological Association. He was also a founder and president of the National Syndrome Congress.

Marianne Takas, J.D., a lawyer by training, specializes in the area of child welfare law and policy. She has served as the executive director of the National Foster Parent Association, and as a project director for the American Bar Association Center on Children and the Law. As an attorney, she represented parents and children in child welfare and family law cases. She is the author of *To Love a Child* and *Grandparents Raising Grandchildren*, as well as other books and monographs related to child welfare.

Dana Burdnell Wilson, M.S.N., L.C.S.W., CWLA's program director for cultural competence and kinship care services, has over twenty-two years of child welfare experience in direct services, community organization, administration, and program development. Since joining CWLA in 1993, Dana has presented numerous training workshops, keynotes, and discussion groups on kinship care and cultural competence. She is CWLA's leader in the development of best practice and examination of public policy issues related to kinship care and cultural competence. Dana's career includes building partnerships as well as advancing quality social work practice at the local, state and national levels: as a program director for CWLA; as state program specialist for family services in Maryland; as community liaison and as family services administrator for the Department of Social Services in Baltimore city, as director of social services for Planned Parenthood of Southeast Ohio, and in her role as a community organizer. Dana's clinical experience includes in-home family-based services, group therapy and case management services for group home residents, adolescent pregnancy and parenting services, and family planning counseling. Dana has authored several articles on kinship care, coedited the special kinship care issue of *Child Welfare*, developed the cultural competence module of the Foster pride/Adopt Pride training curriculum for foster parents, and is presently developing a cultural competence training program for child welfare administrators, through a grant she secured from the Prudential Foundation. Regarded as a national expert in the area of kinship care, Dana served on the U.S. Dept. of Health and Human Services' Relative Foster Care Workgroup, and their Technical Advisory Panel for the five-year research study of children in formal kinship care. She had primary responsibility for planning the program for a national kinship care conference, *Kinship Care: A Natural Bridge*, co-sponsored by CWLA, the Edgewood Center for Children and Families, the American Association of Retired Persons (AARP), and Generation United, held August 13–15, 1997 in San Francisco, California.

Susan Zuravin, M.S.W., Ph.D., is an associate professor at the University of Maryland School of Social Work where she teaches courses in human behavior and research design. For a number of years, her main area of research interest has been child welfare. Work on this topic has led to many publications and presentations focused on various foster care as well as child maltreatment themes. Currently, she is working on a series of empirical articles focused on such potential long-term sequelae of child sexual abuse as depression and substance abuse.

Kinship Foster Care

Kinship Foster Care in Context

Maria Scannapieco, Ph.D.
Rebecca L. Hegar, D.S.W.

Kinship foster care, the care provided to children and youth in state custody by relatives, has only recently become a major focus of child welfare practice, policy, and research efforts. As recent as 1992, kinship foster care was a mere mention in major child welfare texts (Cohen, 1992; Costin, Bell, & Downs, 1991; Pecora, Whittaker, & Maluccio, 1992). The care provided to children and youth in placement by relative caregivers is the newest phenomenon in the child welfare system. The explanation for the tremendous increase in the number of children in formal kinship care is multidimensional and ranges from an increase in reported child maltreatment and in the number of children entering foster care, to a reduction in the number of traditional foster homes, to an increase in the number of persons with HIV or using drugs, to a growing population of children who are poor (Children's Defense Fund, 1992, 1997; Courtney, 1996; National Commission on Family Foster Care, 1991; Thornton 1991; United States House of Representatives, Select Committee on Children, Youth, and Families, 1990).

It is impossible to know the exact number of children who are in kinship foster care because not all states have been specifically indexing for relative care (e.g., Office of the Inspector General, DHHS, 1991, reports on only twenty-nine states that track relative care). The Child Welfare League of America reported that by 1992 over 31% of all children in legal custody had been placed with extended family members (Child Welfare League of America, 1994, p. 12). That proportion is considerably higher in many urban areas where kinship care has surpassed the use of traditional foster care (Minkler & Roe, 1992; Takas, 1993; Thornton, 1991). As kinship care becomes the fastest-growing funded service provided within the child welfare system (Gleeson & Craig,

1994), the professional knowledge base for working with kinship placements requires development in the areas of policy, practice, and research.

KINSHIP DEFINED

The phrase "kinship care" was inspired by the work of Stack (1974), who documented the importance of extended kinship networks in the African American community. The term "kin" often includes any relative, by blood or marriage, or any person with close family ties to another (Takas, 1993). Billingsley (1992) refers to this latter category as relationships of appropriation, meaning unions without ties of blood or marriage. People can become part of a family unit or, indeed, form a family unit simply by deciding to live and act toward each other as family (Billingsley, 1992).

The term "kinship care" has recently been used by the Child Welfare League of America's (CWLA) Commission on Family Foster Care, which, in cooperation with the National Foster Parent Association, developed goals and recommendations promoting relatives and friends as placement resources for children in foster care (CWLA, 1994; Takas, 1993). It is kinship in this broad sense that informs the statement by the Kinship Care Policy and Practice Committee of CWLA: "Kinship care may be defined as the full-time nurturing and protection of children who must be separated from their parents by relatives, members of their tribes or clans, godparents, stepparents or other adults who have a kinship bond with a child" (1994, p. 2).

Some definitions of kinship caregiving focus on informal or formal child placement with relatives. Takas notes that kinship care includes both private kinship care (entered by private family arrangement) and kinship foster care (care provided for a child who is in the legal custody of the state child welfare agency) (1993, p. 3).

Other authors prefer the terms "kinship care" and kinship caregivers for private care and "kinship foster care" and kinship foster parents for care that falls within the formal child welfare system (Berrick, Barth, & Needell, 1994; Bonecutter & Gleeson, 1997). The majority of empirical research has been conducted with kinship foster parents (Berrick, Barth, & Needell, 1994; Iglehart, 1994; Thornton, 1991).

In this book, some authors consider kinship care in the broadest sense when reviewing its historical context and practice implications. In discussions of research and of social policy, most authors focus on the narrower meaning most commonly encountered in those context, which is out-of-home care provided by relatives to children in the custody of state child welfare agencies, or kinship foster care.

DEMOGRAPHIC TRENDS

Although social policy and social work practice emphasizes permanency planning and family preservation, the foster care census is skyrocketing. Due in part to a 27 percent increase in the number of reports substantiated as abuse or neglect between 1990 and 1994, there has been a rapid increase in the number of children entering foster care during the past several years (Courtney, 1996; Everett, 1995; United States Department of Health and Human Services, 1996), with an estimate of 442,000 children living in foster care (Tatara, 1993). It is disturbing to note that this increase is projected not to decline but only to grow (Child Welfare League of America, 1994). This increase in the foster care census has been accompanied by a decrease in the number of foster parents, from 147,000 in 1984 to 100,000 in 1990 (National Commission on Foster Family Care, 1991).

The increasing number of children in care and the declining pool of traditional foster families, along with the emphasis in the Adoption Assistance and Child Welfare Act of 1980 (P. L. 96-272) on placement in the most family-like setting, are three of the forces that have led to a growing use of kinship care. More than 31 percent of all children in state custody are placed with extended family members, according to a U.S. Health and Human Services report based on data from 29 states (Office of Inspector General, 1992).

In certain states, the percentage of foster children in kinship homes is even higher than the national average, exceeding the number of children in nonrelative foster homes (Gleeson & Craig, 1994). For example, 51 percent of all children in out-of-home placement in Illinois are in kinship care (Wulczyn & Goerge, 1992). California, which serves 20 percent of the nation's children in foster care, places more than 50 percent of these children with relatives (Berrick, Barth, & McFadden, 1992). Two-thirds of that state's increase in foster care placements from 1984 to 1989 involved children placed with providers related to the children (California Child Welfare Strategic Planning Commission, 1991 as cited in Berrick, Barth, & McFadden, 1992).

Many urban centers have seen the largest increases in kinship placements. The number of children in formal kinship care in New York City, for example, increased from 151 in 1985 to 14,000 in 1989 (Thornton, 1991), and a more recent count shows a total of 23,591 (Takas, 1993). In Philadelphia, which began making kinship placements only a few years earlier, relative homes constituted 67 percent of total foster care homes by 1992 (Takas, 1993).

In addition, many children live in informal kinship care and are not included in studies of the foster care system. It is estimated that from 1.3 million to 4.3 million American children live with various relatives in homes where neither parent is present (Everett, 1995; National Commission on Family Foster Care, 1991); among these are three-quarters of a million children receiving Aid to Families with Dependent Children, 10 percent of the total AFDC rolls (National Commission on Family Foster Care, 1991).

CONTINUUM OF PERMANENCY PLANNING AND KINSHIP CARE

In child welfare practice today, there is no standard typology of child welfare services, but many authors use the level of intervention—supportive, supplementary, or substitute care—as a means of categorization (Cohen, 1992;

Costin, Bell, & Downs, 1991; Kadushin & Martin, 1988). Underlying all levels of service, the philosophy of child welfare is the preservation of the family and permanency planning for children. Kinship foster care often falls under the category of substitute care, but out-of-home care provided by relatives to children and youth can be seen as supportive as well as supplementary service in some cases.

Supportive services are generally thought of as a means to strengthen the ability of parents and children to meet the responsibilities of their respective statuses (Kadushin & Martin, 1988, p. 30). In this context, kinship foster care can be a means of extended family preservation. Kinship care placements last longer than and reunification rates are lower than those for traditional foster parent placement (Berrick, Barth, & Needell, 1994; Dubowitz et al., 1993; Scannapieco et al., 1997; Thornton, 1991; Wulczyn & Goerge, 1992), so focus in practice is on ensuring that placements with relatives remain stable. One means of doing this is for the relative to support and relieve the birth parent and his or her child, thereby reducing strain in the parent-child relationship.

Kinship care is one strategy for family preservation. It generally enables children to live with people they know and trust; supports the transmission of children's family identity; supports the child's cultural and ethnic identity; helps children stay connected to brothers and sisters; and helps children retain or build connections to extended family members (CWLA, 1994). Emphasizing the family preservation approach to kinship care recognizes that the most desirable place for children to grow up is in their own families.

Even though relative caregivers often receive AFDC or foster care grants for children in their care, this usually does not cover all the child's needs, and the relative provides food, clothing, and shelter above the state payment. Kinship care as a supplemental service can be considered in loco parentis (in place of parents) with respect to the income-producing responsibilities of parents (Cohen, 1992).

Kinship foster care is also a form of substitute care. When it is necessary for a child to be removed from his or her parent(s), the juvenile courts and the child welfare agency have several options. On the continuum of placement options, from least restrictive to most, children may be placed in a relative foster home, a nonrelative foster home, a group home, residential care, or other institution. Placement decisions and other case plans consider the developmental level of the child, safety needs, educational needs, and cultural factors. According to best practice principles, the practitioner should first consider possible relative caregivers. Placement with known relatives may cause less trauma for the child than placement in an unfamiliar foster home (Chipungu, 1991). In addition, this option may also be more culturally sensitive and meet specific statutory requirements (e.g., Indian Child Welfare Act, 1978).

Guardianship and adoption are also considered forms of substitute service and should also be explored with kin. However, some studies indicate that many kinship caregivers are not willing to adopt children who are already related to them (Berrick, Barth, & McFadden, 1994; Thornton, 1991). They may also be unlikely to assume legal guardianship of the children (Iglehart, 1994). These findings about adoption and guardianship have been disputed in a recent study by Gebel (1996), who found no difference between relative and non-relative caregivers in the length of time they would care for the children or in their willingness to consider adopting a child placed with them. Kinship adoption and guardianship do exist and are areas of practice being explored more rigorously, especially as the number of children in kinship care and their length of stay in placement continue to rise (see also, in this book, chapter 3 by Gleeson and chapter 4 by Takas and Hegar for thorough discussions of options for relative custody).

CONTROVERSIAL QUESTIONS CONCERNING KINSHIP FOSTER CARE

Despite the rapid rise in the use of kinship foster care, or perhaps because of it, a number of controversies challenge child welfare policy and practice in the formal placement of foster children with kin. Seven of these questions are introduced in this section. In most cases, their ultimate answers are still pending further research and future developments in child welfare policy. However, the chapters that follow touch in various ways on the questions and provide partial answers.

Much of the controversy surrounding kinship foster care arises from a single root issue (see Kurtz, 1994; Task Force on Permanency Planning for Foster Children, 1990): How should formal kinship foster care differ from informal kinship care arranged by families themselves? Attempts to address this root issue lead to questions about the selection, certification, supervision, and payment of kinship foster parents, as well as about efforts to effect reunification of children with parents or achieve other permanency plans. These questions are raised in this section, not to provide answers, but to add context to the chapters that follow and to acknowledge the dilemmas posed by the newest patterns in services to families and children in child welfare. It is important to raise these issues early in this book because its editors and chapter authors generally support the use of kinship foster care for the benefits it can offer children. However, no one involved with the writing of this book is oblivious to the contradictions, inequities, and unintended consequences that can attend major shifts in child welfare policy and practice.

Is Kinship Foster Care Out-of-Home Care or Family Preservation?

As mentioned earlier in this chapter, placements into kinship homes are made all along the continuum of child welfare services, as supportive, supplementary, and substitute care. This flexibility and diversity of practice make it difficult to classify kinship care as either out-of-home care or extended family preservation. The most straightforward answer to this question is that kinship foster care is out-of-home care when the child is in court-ordered state custody; otherwise, it is a branch of services to children in their own homes, whether before state intervention in the parent-child relationship (diversion) or after it (informal care, guardianship or adoption by relatives as part of permanency planning) (see chapter 5 by Scannapieco for detailed discussion).

However, from the perspective of family policy, the answer cannot be so straightforward.

Because of the financial benefits that accrue to relatives only when the foster care board rate is paid, we link this question to others concerning children in poverty and the risk of a two-tiered, segregated system of foster care. We are indebted to an anonymous reviewer of this book in manuscript for observing that "one of the key issues that has been debated over the last few years is whether it is better to regard kinship foster care as an 'in-home' service or as an 'out-of-home' placement. Eligibility for federal and state financial benefits turns on the answer to this important question. The fact that many children in kinship foster care are ineligible for federal title IV-E benefits for reasons of nonremoval, i.e., the kinship home existed informally prior to state intervention, illustrates the need to reconsider our use of conventional (and nuclear-family biased) terms like 'out-of-home placement' when talking about kinship foster care" (see also chapter 3 by Gleeson for how these issues have been addressed in Illinois).

Where Would Children in Kinship Foster Care Otherwise Be Living?

The rate of foster care placement is rising nationally, and the rate of placement in kinship foster homes is rising as fast or faster in some jurisdictions, as we have already discussed. The obvious question, to which there is as yet no answer, is whether children in informal kinship placement, or those who might have been placed informally, are instead fueling the explosion in foster care caseloads (see also Kurtz, 1994). Another way of framing this question is to ask whether the availability of kinship foster care 'sucks' children into state custody and placement. Why this might be so becomes clearer as we examine patterns of funding placements in kinship homes, as well as characteristics of the children, parents, and caregivers.

Should Kinship Foster Homes Meet the Same Licensing Requirements as Other Homes?

Licensure or certification is required of foster homes, and standards for approval are promulgated by agencies such as the Child Welfare League of America and set by each state. Most states require kinship foster homes to meet the same standards as other foster homes in order to receive the foster care board rate for that jurisdiction (see chapter 3 for Gleeson's discussion of another model used for a time in Illinois). Standards address housing, finances, family composition, family history, relationships, attitudes about parenting, and a variety of other factors. For a range of reasons, many kinship caregivers and their houses are not approved as foster homes.

In chapter 10, Pecora and colleagues ask: "What variation in licensing and other assessment criteria should be considered to best meet the full range of child needs without sacrificing certain minimum practice standards?" Should the standards be the same? Or should issues such as space and shared bedrooms be addressed differently when the children are related to the caregiving family? Should some housing standards or matters of family background (length of marriage, cohabitation, police record) be adapted or waived when prospective kinship caregivers apply to be foster parents? This is a set of problems about which the editors of this book have written elsewhere (Scannapieco & Hegar, 1996). However, most states have only begun to address the question.

Should Children in Kinship Foster Care Live in Poverty?

Kinship caregivers differ socioeconomically from traditional foster parents, according to consistent findings from the kinship care research (see chapter 9 by Scannapieco for a detailed review of the literature). They are likely to be older women, are less likely to be married or employed outside the home, and average lower educational attainments than other foster parents. Many rely for their own support on government benefits such as social security retirement or disability, SSI, or TANF. If they do so or are marginally employed, the foster care board payment may be insufficient to raise the household out of poverty.

At the same time, many prospective caregivers do not meet foster care certification standards and so do not qualify for the foster care board rate. If they care for relatives' children, they may receive only the children's TANF grants, if the children were eligible in their own homes, or they may receive no financial help. The conclusion is clear that the caregivers who are most in need are least likely to receive adequate financial support when they open their homes to the children of kin. The difficult question is how to address the financial needs of children in kinship care and their caregivers, especially in light of the dilemma poor families may face if children can obtain an adequate standard of living *only* if they are removed from their parents' custody. This dilemma has an obvious relationship with the question about whether the availability of kinship foster care creates an incentive to place children.

What Kind of Efforts Should States Make to End Kinship Foster Care Placements?

Foster care has been defined for decades as a temporary service that should lead to a more permanent resolution, such as return home, termination of parental rights and adoption, or dismissal of state custody and guardianship by an individual. This was the thrust of the permanency planning movement of the 1970s that culminated with the passage of P.L.96-272, the Adoption Assistance and Child Welfare Act of 1980. Yet virtually all research, including that reviewed and presented in this book, shows that children who enter kinship foster care tend to remain for long periods in stable placement with relatives. Reunification services may be neglected by agencies or perceived as unnecessary by parents and kinship foster parents. Financial considerations often make guardianship unfeasible, and there may be legal and personal barriers to adoption by relatives (these are explored in chapter 4 by Takas and Hegar). How long should the state subsidize placement with relatives?

What Do Families Risk or Lose When They Opt for Kinship Foster Care?

When kin opt for providing care as foster parents, there are obvious ways that their autonomy is curtailed by state regulation. These may include their choices of disciplinary practices, sleeping arrangements, and other family matters. There is also a loss of privacy involved in records checks for certification, requirements of training, periodic home visits, and so forth. Although these types of standards possibly should be modified for kinship foster care (see Scannapieco & Hegar, 1996), the associated loss of autonomy is a clear trade-off for the financial benefits of being part of the foster care program.

A much more serious issue is the loss of control by family members over a child's future, once court adjudication and foster care status have been established. Children in kinship foster care and their parents also risk negative outcomes uncommon for children in the informal care of relatives. Kurtz (1994) raises this issue in the presentation of two provocative cases of permanency planning gone awry. She concludes that

> ... by accepting the formalization of kinship foster care, all participants unintentionally move to a point of greater risk in the face of state intervention. The parent assumes a greater risk of having parental rights terminated, the relative a greater risk of an agency decision to transfer the child, and the children a greater risk of losing family. Child welfare laws and policies fail to acknowledge that relationships, behavior, and needs of all family members in kinship arrangements are likely to be different than when children reside in traditional foster care settings. The failure of the legal system and the child welfare system to recognize viable kinship networks which exist independent of foster care and the priority placed by both systems on a narrow conceptualization of permanency may in many cases gratuitously, or unnecessarily, result in the severance of significant family relationships from the lives of children, particularly poor children of color. (Kurtz, 1994, p. 1520–21)

Is a Two-Tiered, Racially Segregated System of Foster Care Developing?

Research shows not only that kinship foster parents are financially less well off but that they, as well as the children and their parents, receive fewer services from child welfare agencies, when compared with the foster parents, children, and parents involved in traditional foster care (see chapter 9 by Scannapieco). If licensing standards are less likely to be met (see earlier discussion), and if training, monitoring, and services such as transportation and mental health counseling are provided less often, is the standard of care in kinship foster homes satisfactory? Do the advantages of being placed with kin outweigh the likelihood of having access to fewer resources?

Add to the findings about the lower levels of support provided to many kinship care homes the reality that African-American children are placed disproportionately in kinship foster care, and questions naturally arise about a two-tiered and segregated system. For decades, the child welfare system met the needs of children of color reluctantly or not at all (Everett, Chipungu, & Leashore, 1991; Stehno, 1988). Is kinship foster care the newest way for society to leave minority, especially African American, children to the care of their own willing but poorly resourced extended families and communities? In the final chapter of this book, Hegar addresses this question in greater detail, including a discussion of what changes are required to make kinship foster care something more than a residual dependence on family and other nongovernmental resources.

PURPOSE AND OVERVIEW OF BOOK

As kinship care has quickly become a significant part of the continuum of child welfare services, the professional literature has expanded from relative silence to growing numbers of journal articles. Most significantly, three special issues of important interprofessional journals have been devoted to writings about kinship care, *Children & Youth Services Review* in 1994, *Child Welfare* in 1996, and *Families in Society* in 1997. In addition, the Child Welfare League of America has published a slim volume devoted to defining kinship care, reviewing its policy history, and making policy recommendations first formulated by its North American Kinship Care Policy and Practice Committee (CWLA, 1994). However, to date no book has gathered professional thinking about kinship foster care into one volume to provide an overview of the service.

The editors of this book invited prominent researchers, policy analysts and advocates, and practice specialists to contribute chapters detailing their work and thinking concerning kinship foster care. The contributors include several who worked on or consulted with the CWLA Kinship Care Committee. As a group, their published articles account for a large share of the previously available literature on the subject. In contributing to this book, this interprofessional group of experts was invited to bring together their work and thoughts concerning the three topics of kinship care practice, policy, and research. In the rest of this chapter, we preview each section and provide a summary of what each author or team was asked to contribute.

KINSHIP CARE POLICY

This section contains three chapters, the first by Rebecca L. Hegar, who delves deep into the history of kinship fostering as a family form with roots in many cultures. The author surveys an interdisciplinary literature that may be unfamiliar to professionals working in kinship care and considers implications for kinship care policy and practice in the United States.

Next in the policy section, James P. Gleeson surveys policy issues and trends in kinship foster care, using events and decisions in Illinois to illustrate stages of policy development. He places kinship foster care in the context of national efforts to reform the U.S. welfare system. Policy recommendations geared to protect children, support kinship networks, and contain costs conclude the chapter.

The final chapter of the first section is coauthored by Marianne Takas and Rebecca L. Hegar. They review the legal custody options available to kinship caregivers, trace how law and policy have been adapted to the changing circumstances and needs of children and their families, and propose a new legal mechanism of kinship adoption, which would differ from traditional adoption in key ways. Case vignettes that introduce and conclude the chapter illustrate how kinship adoption would satisfy an unmet need.

KINSHIP CARE PRACTICE

This section of four chapters begins with Maria Scannapieco's survey of service delivery models for kinship care that are currently in use in the United States. The chapter categorizes service models on the basis of funding source and of where they fall on the continuum of child welfare services: diversion from placement, substitute care, or family preservation.

Next, Dana Burdnell Wilson presents an overview of kinship care practice based on a CWLA survey of agency directors or program administrators in seven public child welfare organizations and eleven private, nonprofit agencies. Participating agencies were located primarily in the mid-Atlantic states, the urban Midwest, and on the West Coast. This chapter summarizes the agencies' missions, definitions of kinship care, agencies' assessment of the service needs of families involved in kinship care, reasons for kinship placement, characteristics of families served, and training needs and resources of staff.

A chapter by Sondra M. Jackson presents a model for teaching child welfare staff how to provide services to each party in the kinship triad. Emphasis is on the significance of the shift from traditional foster care to kinship foster care. This paradigm shift calls on staff to apply familiar concepts and skills in new ways in order to be effective.

Finally in this section, Joy Swanson Ernst provides another national perspective on kinship care. Her chapter is based on several months of field research concerning child welfare and kinship care in New Zealand, where the indigenous Maori culture has had tremendous impact on how services are provided within the public child welfare system under the Children, Young Persons, and Their Families Act of 1989. This unique national experience with the principles and practice of kinship care provides a case study with intriguing implications for other countries.

KINSHIP CARE RESEARCH

This section first offers an extensive review and synthesis of the research literature on kinship foster care by Maria Scannapieco. She draws together what is known about the characteristics of the parents, children, and caregivers involved in kinship care, along with variables related to service delivery and data concerning outcomes of placement. This chapter serves as an introduction to four additional chapters in this section that report original research studies of kinship care from the perspectives of foster parents, child welfare workers, adolescents in care, and adults who experienced either kinship or traditional foster care.

In the first of these, Peter J. Pecora, Nicole S. Le Prohn, and John J. Nasuti report their study of role perceptions of kinship and other foster parents. The study involved kinship and traditional foster parents from Western Casey Family Programs in thirteen states and foster parents with the public child welfare program in Louisiana. Findings from the study and discussion of their implications are given.

The next research chapter comes from Jill Duerr Berrick, Barbara Needell, and Richard P. Barth, who report on their study of child welfare workers' perspectives on kin placement resources for children. Their study encompassed ten California counties selected to reflect the state's range of geography, urbanization, and proportions of children in kinship placements. The authors draw conclusions from the survey results and provide practice suggestions for making placements and providing services.

Adolescents in kinship care are the focus of a study authored by Raymond H. Starr, Howard Dubowitz, Donna Harrington, and Susan Feigelman. They studied a sample of youth and their kinship caregivers, using standardized instruments to compare assessments from different sources of the adolescents' behavior and found a high level of adolescent behavior problems indicated by the youth themselves, their caregivers, and teachers when compared to national norms. The authors also provide discussion of implications for practice and future research.

Finally in this section, Susan J. Zuravin, Mary Benedict, and Rebecca Stallings report on the adult functioning of former foster children, contrasting groups who were placed in kinship care and traditional foster care with each other and with a comparison group that had never experienced placement. The most conclusive findings concern adult self-sufficiency, in that those placed in kinship care appeared be somewhat more self-sufficient than those in traditional foster care, although both groups suffered when compared with adults who avoided placement as children.

CONCLUSION

In the concluding chapter of this book, Rebecca L. Hegar draws from the policy, practice, and research implications of the preceding chapters. She places the rise of kinship care in context as the most recent of the paradigm shifts in child placement practice that have been necessitated by societal and demographic trends, as well as directed by changing professional beliefs and norms. Just as almshouses gave way to child-caring institutions, which in turn were replaced by free foster homes and then by foster boarding homes, extensive use of kinship foster care is replacing earlier models of substitute care for children. This rapid shift has compelling implications for those who use and provide child placement services, as well as for society as a whole.

References

Berrick, J. D., & Barth, R. P. (Eds.). (1994). Special double issue: Kinship foster care. *Children and Youth Services Review, 16* (1/2), 1–140.

Berrick, J. D., Barth, R. P., & McFadden, J. (1992). *A comparison of kinship foster homes and foster family homes: Implications for kinship foster care as family preservation.* Washington, D.C.: Child Welfare League of America North American Kinship Care Policy and Practice Committee.

Berrick, J. D., Barth, R. P., & Needell, B. (1994). A comparison of kinship foster homes and foster family homes: Implications for kinship foster care as family preservation. *Children and Youth Services Review, 16* (1/2), 33–64.

Billingsley, A. (1992). *Climbing Jacob's ladder: The enduring legacy of African-American families.* New York: Simon & Shuster.

Bonecutter, F. J., & Gleeson, J. P. (1997). Broadening our view: Lessons from kinship foster care. *Journal of Multicultural Social Work, 5* (1/2), 99–119.

Child Welfare League of America. (1994). *Kinship care: A natural bridge.* Washington, D.C.: CWLA North American Kinship Care Policy and Practice Committee.

Children's Defense Fund (1992). *The state of America's children: 1992.* Washington, D.C.: Author.

Children's Defense Fund Reports. (1997). *Key facts about children, January,* 6. Washington, D.C.: Author.

Chipungu, S. S. (1991). A value-based policy framework. In J. E. Everett, S. S. Chipungu, & B. R. Leashore (Eds.), *Child welfare: An Africentric perspective* (pp. 290–305). New Brunswick, N.J.: Rutgers University Press.

Cohen, N. A. (Ed.). (1992). *Child welfare: A multicultural focus.* Boston: Allyn and Bacon.

Costin, L. B., Bell, C. J., & Downs, S. W. (1991). *Child welfare: Policies and practice.* New York: Longman.

Courtney, M. E. (1996). Kinship foster care and children's welfare: The California experience. *Focus, 17* (3), 42–48.

Dubowitz, H., Feigelman, S., & Zuravin, S. (1993). A profile of kinship care. *Child Welfare, 72,* 153–169.

Everett, J. E. (1995). Relative foster care: An emerging trend in foster care placement policy and practice. *Smith College Studies in Social Work, 65* (3), 239–253.

Everett, J. E., Chipungu, S. S., & Leashore, B. (1991). *Child welfare: An Africentric perspective.* New Brunswick, N.J.: Rutgers University Press.

Families In Society. (1997). Foster & Kinship Care: A Special Focus. *Families in Society, 78* (5).

Gebel, T. J. (1996). Kinship care and non-relative family foster care: A comparison of caregiver attributes and attitudes. *Child Welfare, 75* (1), 5–18.

Gleeson, J. P., & Craig, L. C. (1994). Kinship care in child welfare: An analysis of states policies. *Children and Youth Services Review, 16* (1/2), 7–32.

Iglehart, A. P. (1994). Kinship foster care: Placement, service, and outcome issues. *Children and Youth Services Review, 16* (1/2), 107–122.

Indian Child Welfare Act of 1978, P.L. 95–608, 92 Stat. 3069.

Kadushin, A., & Martin, J. A. (1988). *Child welfare services.* New York: Macmillan.

Kurtz, M. (1994). The purchase of families into foster care: Two case studies and the lessons they teach. *Connecticut Law Review, 26*(4), 1453–1524.

Minkler, M., & Roe, K. M. (1992). *Grandmothers as caregivers: Raising children of the crack cocaine epidemic.* Newbury Park, Calif.: Sage.

National Commission on Family Foster Care. (1991). *A blueprint for fostering infants, children and youth in the 1990s.* Washington, D.C.: Child Welfare League of America.

Office of Inspector General, United States Department of Health and Human Services. (1992). *Using relatives for foster care.* Washington, D.C.: U.S. Government Printing Office.

Pecora, P., Whittaker, J., & Maluccio, A. (1992). *The child welfare challenge: Policy, practice, and research.* New York: Aldine De Gruyter.

Scannapieco, M., & Hegar, R. (1996). A nontraditional assessment framework for formal kinship homes. *Child Welfare, 75* (5), 567–582.

Scannapieco, M., Hegar, R., & McAlpine, C. (1997). Kinship care and foster care: A comparison of characteristics and outcomes. *Families in Society, 78* (5), 480–488.

Stack, C. (1974). *All our kin: Strategies for survival in a black community.* New York: Harper and Row.

Stehno, S. M. (1988). Public responsibility for dependent black children: The advocacy of Edith Abbott and Sophonisba Breckinridge. *Social Service Review, 62* (3), 485–503.

Takas, M. (1993). *Kinship care and family preservation: A guide for states in legal and policy development.* Unpublished manuscript. Washington, D.C.: ABA Center on Children and the Law.

Task Forces on Permanency Planning for Foster Children. (1990). *Kinship foster care: The double edged dilemma.* Rochester, NY: Author.

Tatara, T. (1993). *Characteristics of children in substitute and adoptive are: A statistical summary of the VCIS national child welfare date base.* Washington, D.C.: American Public Welfare Association.

Thornton, J. L. (1991). Permanency planning for children in kinship foster homes. *Child Welfare, 70* (5), 593–601.

United States Department of Health and Human Services, National Center on Child Abuse and Neglect. (1996). *Child maltreatment 1994: Reports from the states to the National Center on Child Abuse and Neglect.* Washington, D.C.: Author.

United States House of Representatives, Select Committee on Children, Youth, and Families. (1990). No place to call home: Discarded children in America. Washington, D.C.: U.S. Government Printing Office.

Wilson, D. B., & Chipungu, S. S. (Eds). (1996). Special issue: Kinship care. *Child Welfare, 75* (5), 387–664.

Wulczyn, F. H., & Goerge, R. M. (1992). Foster care in New York and Illinois: The challenge of rapid change. *Social Service Review, 66,* 278–294.

PART I

Kinship
Care
Policy

CHAPTER 2

The Cultural Roots of Kinship Care

REBECCA L. HEGAR, D.S.W.

Foster placement of children with relatives is among the oldest traditions in child rearing and the newest phenomena in formal child placement practice. As an organized social service, large-scale kinship foster care is less than ten years old. However, since their beginnings less than 150 years ago, child placement agencies have sent children to live with relatives. Recently, the number of kinship foster care placements has surpassed traditional foster care in many jurisdictions (Berrick, Barth, & Needell, 1994; Illinois Department of Children and Family Services, 1990; Takas, 1993).

The emerging change in the dominant paradigm for child placement, which parallels earlier shifts from institutions to free foster homes and from free foster homes to foster boarding homes, forms a central theme of the final chapter of this book. This second chapter explores kinship care as a traditional pattern of child rearing. It unearths historical roots of kinship care reaching into several of the world's cultures. In order to do so, it draws from the literature of disciplines that may be less familiar to most readers than is the literature of social work and the other helping professions.

In exploring the extent and nature of traditional kinship fostering, motivations for the practice, and what little is known about its outcomes, this chapter draws from literature concerning ancient and mythical cultures, Oceania (the islands and archipelagoes of the Central and South Pacific), Africa, and North America. A final section considers the implications of traditional kinship fostering for contemporary child placement practice.

EXTENT, MOTIVATIONS, AND OUTCOMES OF KINSHIP FOSTERING

Ancient and Mythical Cultures

The rearing of another's child is among the oldest literary themes. Jung's mother archetype, one of the common motifs of the collective unconscious, includes nonbiological mothering relationships (Jung, 1969). The bible contains examples of foster parenting by unrelated individuals, especially in extraordinary circumstances, such as Moses being reared by Pharaoh's daughter. More commonly, children needing care probably stayed within their kinship network. The ancient obligation that men marry the widow of a deceased brother ensured that many children grew up in the home of an uncle-stepfather.

European prehistory also shows the prevalence of fostering through the frequent references to it in the lives of legendary heroes. In Arthurian legend, King Arthur himself was fostered at birth, resulting in a lifelong friendship with his foster brother, Sir Kay (Mallory, 1906). Versions of the Macbeth legend portray him also as having been reared in the home of a kinsman (e.g., Dunnett, 1982).

Other cultures, some of them discussed in more detail later, also preserve myths of parentless (often fatherless) children who eventually claim their heritage. Luomala writes:

> Hawaiians, like other Pacific islanders, narrate prose sagas that incorporate motifs of the quest of a character, almost always male, to learn the identity of and then to locate his biological father. . . . [N]o other archipelago has as many different semi-historical, mythical, and fictitious heros who ask about their unknown father as the Hawaiian Islands. (1987, p.1)

Their prevalence in the mythology of many different cultures led Otto Rank to explore the themes of parental abandonment and foster rearing in *The Myth of the Birth of a Hero* (1914).

In mythical and ancient fostering, motivations often revolve around the child's or the parent's safety, typically the need to hide an heir away from enemies or the belief that the child will come to pose a threat to the father. Naturally, fostering under these circumstances often involved secrecy, even with respect to the child. Another function of fostering, in both European and Hawaiian practice, was to cement an alliance by placing a valued child under the roof and influence of another family, which was expected to nurture the child in order to further the alliance.

In mythology, at least, the outcomes of fostering tend to be mixed. The most negative consequences, though, tend to be reserved for parents who abandon their children. Although fostering may have saved the child's life in one way or another, bringing up a child in ignorance of his or her heritage has predictable unintended consequences. From Oedipus, who unknowingly kills his father and marries his mother, to Arthur, who conceives his own nemesis in unwitting incest with his half-sister, the moral of the fables is: "Disaster stalks those who know not themselves and their families."

Pacific Islands and Rim

Because of the tribal cultures that surround ancient examples of foster care, the substitute parent frequently came from within the kinship network of the child. More contemporary examples of kinship fostering also come from cultures where the family is surrounded and reinforced by extended family and tribal structures, as in the Maori culture of New Zealand, which is the focus of Ernst's chapter in this book. New Zealand is only one of the island cultures where kinship fostering is common. It is a traditional family form throughout Oceania, the term anthropologists apply to Central and South Pacific islands.

For example, Luomala reports that, in traditional Hawaiian culture, "the grandparents' claim to grandchildren took precedence over that of the natural parents, who had to get their consent to keep a child to rear for themselves. The firstborn, if a boy, customarily went to the paternal grandparents; a girl went to the maternal grandparents" (1987, p. 16–17). Both permanent, adoption-like placements and more temporary foster care placements were made among kin and close friends, almost always within the same social stratum. Although prevalent throughout traditional Hawaiian society, fostering was the norm for Hawaiians of rank: "With rare exceptions, a royal or other highborn child was given by its parents at birth or soon after to another high chief or chiefess, usually related in some way, who became its *kahu hanai*" (Luomala, 1987, p. 27).

Although not as normative as it once was in Hawaiian society, fostering of children is still common in Malaysia. Carsten (1991) reports, on the basis of contemporary field research in Pulau Langkawi, that approximately a fourth of children do not live with both biological parents. Some of them live with single or remarried birth parents, but a substantial group live with foster parents, either related or unrelated. Carsten notes that:

> villagers themselves often make a further distinction between fostering a child and bringing up the child of a close relative. Not infrequently, children reside more or less permanently in the house of a close relative. Such residence varies in duration: it may endure for most of a childhood, for a few months or for some years; it may begin when a child is a baby or when he or she is already an adolescent. It may or may not involve visits of varying duration and frequency to the parental household. When a couple bring up their grandchild or a younger sibling they usually do not refer to the child as an *anal angkat*, foster child, but rather say they are "caring for," or "bringing up" the child, and specify the kin relation involved. (Carsten, 1991, p. 431)

Observers note that fostering by kin is common in traditional societies throughout the Pacific islands and rim (Luomala, 1987; Silk, 1987).

In the Pacific region of Oceania, one motivation for fostering is to forge bonds with kin and fictive kin. Carsten (1991) argues that on one Malaysian island, kinship is a construct created by practices such as sharing living space, meals, and parenting responsibilities. Children are both shared in ways that extend family and exchanged as part of the reciprocity between families (Carsten, 1991, p. 438). In traditional Hawaiian culture, adoption and fostering were "intended to reinforce existing alliances and create new ones beneficial to all concerned" (Luomala, 1987, p. 16). Rank was integrally entwined in the process of fostering, and both placing and receiving families sought to enhance their own and their children's status by strategic foster placements.

Africa

In many parts of Africa, as in regions of the Pacific, the fostering of children within extended kinship networks is an established cultural practice. The literature includes descriptions of fostering in Kenya (Umbima, 1991), Botswana in southern Africa (Pennington, 1991), sub-Saharan Africa generally (Page, 1989), and particularly in West Africa, including Mali (Castle, 1996), Sierra Leone (Bledsoe, Ewbank, & Isiugo-Abanihe, 1988; Isiugo-Abanihe, 1985), Nigeria (Cross & Ibru, 1978; Isiugo-Abanihe, 1985), Ghana (Fiawoo, 1978; Isiugo-Abanihe, 1985), and Gambia (Eastman, 1988).

West Africa appears to be one major center of kinship fostering of children. Based on analysis of Ghanaian census data, Isiugo-Abanihe (1985) estimates that close to 20 percent of children younger than eleven were living away from their parental homes. Between a quarter and 40 percent of parents in Ghana, Liberia, and western Nigeria (Ibada) reported one or more children living away from home. Even higher proportions of parents reporting placement are found in Sierra Leone (Bledsoe, Ewbank, & Isiugo-Abanihe, 1988; Isiugo-Abanhe, 1985). In West Africa generally, fostering may be most common after age ten and is reported to affect more girls than boys (Castle, 1996).

Placement rates among the Herero people in Botswana are similar to those in West Africa. A study by Pennington (1991) found that younger children, girls, and children born to unmarried parents were the most likely to be fostered, usually with female relatives past the years of child bearing. Among some tribal groups, fostering is prescribed in certain situations. For example, Herero-speaking mothers who marry or remarry "are expected to find other arrangements for raising children they have had with other men" (Pennington, 1991, p. 101).

Motivations for kinship fostering in Africa are complex and diverse. Children may be sent to live with relatives for purposes of weaning, care when a family dissolves, instruction in a trade, attendance at school, or helping in the home of the caregiver (Castle, 1996). Castle notes that "in West Africa, fostering is rooted in kinship structures and affiliations and unlike its 'Western' connotations, the term is not necessarily perceived to be associated with families that are in some way disjointed or dysfunctional" (1996, p. 193). Bledsoe and colleagues come to similar conclusions: "One of the most striking features of rural West African families is that costs of raising children are rarely borne exclusively by biological parents; rather, they are shared by many people through the extended family and other social networks. This includes cost sharing within households as well as fostering out children to other households" (1988, p. 627).

Nor is kinship fostering in Africa of recent origin. Pennington (1991) notes that, about a century ago, an observer saw fostering as "a form of 'child insurance' in which parents tried to minimize their chances of losing all their children to epidemics by spreading them out among relatives" (1991, p. 86). Another writer, describing kinship care in Kenya, points out that traditional African religion reinforced obligations of blood relatives to extend caregiving and aid (Umbima, 1991).

Several studies have focused on the relationships between African child fostering and maternal fertility, children's nutrition, and their survival, all important concerns on a continent where famine is an ever-present threat (Bledsoe et al., 1988; Castle, 1996; Isiugo-Abanihe, 1984; Pennington, 1991). The results of these studies are mixed and must be interpreted with caution. For example, both somewhat better and poorer nutritional and health outcomes have been reported for foster children in different African nations and under different circumstances (Bledsoe et al., 1988; Castle, 1996).

In reviewing from an anthropological perspective adoption and fostering in diverse human societies, including but not limited to Africa, Silk discerns "some evidence of asymmetries in the care of natural and adoptive children, as adopted and foster children may be required to work harder, be disciplined more forcefully, or allocated fewer familial resources than natural children" (1987, p. 46).

American Colonies and United States[1]

Colonial America offered few alternatives for children whose parents died or became unable to care for them. Under the Poor Law as it was followed in England's American colonies, grandparents became responsible for their grandchildren in cases of dependency (Trattner, 1994). Children were also subject to the Poor Law solutions of almshouses and workhouses, forced apprenticeship, or emigration. English law had developed wardship (guardianship) as a legal mechanism that placed other dependent children, usually heirs to property, in the care of relatives or other adults. Many more must have lived informally with family members acting from affection and a sense of duty to family.

In early U.S. history, the family, and then the larger ethnic community, were the residual lines of defense against social problems (see Wilensky & Lebeaux, 1965). When orphanages began to be established, it was primarily in response to epidemics and wars that decimated whole communities and kinship networks, making family care of children impossible. Most of these early institutions were founded by religious and ethnic groups to serve children from their own communities.

African American children. Several factors worked to exclude African American children from the early orphanages and from the private placing-out societies that introduced formal foster care in the mid 1800s. The most obvious factor was slavery. If the parents died or were incapacitated, or if the child or the parents were sold, slave children often were cared for by actual or fic-

---

1. Much of this section is abstracted or adapted from: R. Hegar, & M. Scannapieco (1995).

tive kin within the slave community (Everett, Chipungu, & Leashore, 1991; Scannapieco & Jackson, 1996). Even after the end of slavery, for more than a century the emerging formal institutions for dependent children served few African American children, although there were exceptions (Stehno, 1988).

Throughout the twentieth century, family and community self-help, sometimes centered on the church, continued to provide for dependent African American children (Billingsley, 1992; Gray & Nybell, 1990; Martin & Martin, 1985; Scannapieco & Jackson, 1996). Some authors have observed that helping patterns seen in African American families echoed earlier African traditions that were not successfully obliterated by slavery and the American experience (Martin & Martin, 1985; Yusane, 1990).

The historical patterns of kinship caregiving in the African American community persist. Census data report that, compared with white and Hispanic children, a consistently higher proportion of African American children live with neither parent. More than 11 percent of African American children were reported to be living in family settings away from parents (including foster care) in both the 1960 and the 1980 U.S. censuses (Saluter, 1989). Lower proportions were reported in 1970 and during the 1980s (Saluter, 1989), and census data from March 1995 show 10.8 percent of African American children living with neither parent (Saluter, 1996). Some believe that U.S. Census data can undercount children living with relatives and others. For example, one study reports that the proportion of African American children in "informal adoptions" has increased in recent years, from 13.3 percent living with extended family members in 1970 to 16.5 percent in 1989 (cited in Billingsley, 1992, p. 30).

Hispanic children.   Other ethnic minorities, particularly Latinos and Native Americans, have also experienced difficulties within formal child welfare structures. Early in the history of the French and Spanish territories, some Catholic children needing care were taken in at missions and convents, and the first separate children's institution in what is now the United States was founded by Ursuline sisters in New Orleans in 1727 (Trattner, 1994). For many French, Spanish, and, later, Mexican American children, the extended family was the only, as well as the culturally preferred, resource. Contemporary observers note the continued importance of kinship care by relatives (Delgado & Humm-Delgado, 1982) and within the family-extending institution of *compadrazgo* (coparenting or godparenting) (Vidal, 1988). U.S. Census data for 1995 show that 4.4 percent of Hispanic children live away from both parents, up from 3.5 percent in both 1980 and 1988 (Furukawa, 1991; Saluter, 1996).

Native American children.   In a pattern unique in U.S. history, many Native American children were placed in institutions, rather than being left to the care of family, kinship network, and ethnic community. This pattern of placement outside the culture became one impetus behind passage of the Indian Child Welfare Act of 1978, the first U.S. policy document to state an explicit preference for kinship placement (Matheson, 1996). Despite a history of Native American children being intentionally removed from their kinship circles, kinship has continued to be a central aspect of Native American culture (Shomaker, 1989).

Contemporary patterns. Today in the United States, between 2.3 million and 4.3 million children live without their parents in the homes of relatives, according to available estimates (Everett, 1995; Furukawa, 1991; National Commission on Family Foster Care, 1991, Saluter, 1996). Almost one and a half million live with grandparents alone (Saluter, 1996). This growing cultural phenomenon is not evenly distributed across racial and ethnic groups. African American children make up 44 percent of those living with grandparents without a parent in the home (Furukawa, 1991; Saluter, 1996). That pattern is about six times more common for African American children and one and a half times more so for Hispanic children than for white, non-Hispanic children (Furukawa, 1991).

However, kinship caregiving is a cultural phenomenon not limited to families of color. Of the approximately three million American children reported by the U.S. Census reports as living with neither parent in 1995, more than half were white (Saluter, 1996). Evidence of the pervasiveness of kinship caregiving is found in the attention of the popular media (e.g., Creighton, 1991), the number of available self-help books for those raising grandchildren and other juvenile relatives (e.g., Chalfie, 1994; DeToledo, 1995; Takas, 1995), and in the existence of support groups for kinship caregivers in many U.S. cities. Although informal kinship care is not limited to families in poverty, in 1990 as many as half the children in the care of relatives received Aid to Families with Dependent Children (AFDC) because they were eligible in the homes of their biological families. Ten percent of the 7.7 million children receiving AFDC did so in the homes of relatives other than their parents (National Commission on Family Foster Care, 1991).

Explanations for the numbers of U.S. children being reared by relatives are varied. Earlier in the century, reasons were more likely to include parental death, the untenable status of single parenthood before the advent of day care centers or AFDC, and the material advantages some relatives might offer children. However, the recent gradual rise in the proportion of all American children living in homes without their parents, from less than 2 percent in 1960 and 1970, to 2.2 percent in 1980 and 1988 (Saluter, 1989), to 3.3 percent in 1991 (Furukawa, 1991) and to 4.3 percent in 1995 (3.9 percent if identified foster children are excluded) (Saluter, 1996), has other explanations. One factor is that some urban areas have lost part of a generation in the young childbearing years to crack cocaine and other drugs, the HIV/AIDS epidemic, and crime and prison (Burton, 1992; Lee, 1994; Waysdorf, 1994). In the language of the streets, the parents are "on the street," and more stable grandparents and other older relatives have stepped into the parental void. Additional causal factors may include economic realities that make it difficult for young parents to succeed without help from older relatives in the forms of money, housing, or relief from parenting responsibilities.

Although kinship caregiving in the United States has never been absent, particularly among minorities of color excluded from the institutionalized sys-

tem of child welfare, its recent rise has caught the professional world somewhat off guard. In comparison with the avalanche of research concerning children of divorce (e.g., Shore, 1989; Wallerstein, 1991; Wallerstein & Blakeslee,
1989), single parenthood (e.g., Greif, 1990; Greif & Papst, 1988), and other recent shifts in family form, little is known about children brought up by kin,
particularly outside the formal mechanisms for child placement. The emerging literature about formal kinship foster care is reviewed by Scannapieco in
the chapter introducing the research section of this book.

IMPLICATIONS OF TRADITIONAL KINSHIP FOSTERING FOR CONTEMPORARY CHILD PLACEMENT

What does a review of traditional kinship fostering around the world suggest
for those involved in formal child placement? Several generalizations that Silk,
a cultural anthropologist, offers about traditional fostering provide some interesting insights. She writes:

> First, in each of these societies, natural parents who give up primary re-
> sponsibility for raising their children typically delegate care of their offspring
> to close consanguineal kin. Second, natural parents are uniformly reluctant to
> give up their children to others permanently, and often express regret at the
> necessity of doing so. Third, parental investment is not necessarily terminated
> when adoption and fosterage arrangements have been completed. Even after
> their children have left their households, natural parents may maintain con-
> tact with them, continue to contribute some resources to their care, and re-
> tain their rights to retrieve their offspring if they are mistreated. Fourth,
> natural parents are often very selective in their choice of prospective foster
> and adoptive parents; they typically prefer adults who can offer their children
> better economic prospects than they can themselves. (Silk, 1987, p. 46)

The striking aspect of these conclusions, which are based on study of traditional family patterns in the diverse regions of the Arctic, Oceania, and Africa,
is their universality and their contemporary applicability to kinship care in the
developed world. What leads parents to place their children, or for society to
intervene with placement, is often some threat to the child or the family.
Whether that threat is famine, enemies, family dissolution, neglect, or abuse,
kinship care is a cultural pattern that has been a normative social response for
centuries. Within some cultures and subcultures, it remains the preferred pattern of substitute care.

In the United States, a range of family forms has become common as more
adults divorce, remarry, cohabit, bear children outside of marriage, adopt, or
rear the children of their relatives (Furukawa, 1991). A broad view of child
welfare requires that society find ways of buttressing the parental role in each
of these family situations. Children and caregivers in kinship placements, like
all families, depend on social acceptance and support. These may accrue most
naturally where kinship caregiving is a cultural norm.

For children in the foster care system, kinship placement can offer advantages similar to kinship caregiving in more traditional societies. These usu-

ally include: continuity of family identity and knowledge; access to relatives other than the kinship foster parents, sometimes including birthparents and siblings; ongoing life within the ethnic, religious, and/or racial community of origin; and familiarity based on preexisting relationships between the kinship foster parents and children. Other potential advantages of kinship foster care are linked to state custody, including: legal safeguards for the rights of the children, their parents, and the related foster parents; public financial support for children in kinship placement; and state standards and monitoring of care. Other chapters of this book explore the extent to which kinship foster care realizes these potential advantages to children and their families.

The history of traditional kinship fostering reveals that the impulse to take in and care for the children of kinsfolk may be as old as the urge to parent one's own offspring. It is one way of satisfying the adult need for generativity, for "establishing and guiding the next generation" (Erikson, 1963, p. 267), and for extending one's influence into the future. In working professionally to place children with relatives, we are adapting an ancient tradition to meet modern needs. The societal implications of kinship foster care for children in state custody, particularly in the United States, are explored further in the final chapter of this volume.

References

Berrick, J. D., Barth, R. P., & Needell, B. (1994). A comparison of kinship foster homes and foster family homes: Implications for kinship foster care as family preservation. *Children and Youth Services Review, 16* (1/2), 33–63.

Billingsley, A. (1992). *Climbing Jacob's ladder: The enduring legacy of African-American families.* New York: Simon & Shuster.

Bledsoe, C. H., Ewbank, D. C., & Isiugo-Abanihe, U. C. (1988). The effects of child fostering on feeding practices and access to health services in rural Sierra Leone. *Social Science and Medicine, 27* (6), 627–636.

Burton, L. (1992). Black grandparents rearing children of drug-addicted parents: Stressors, outcomes, and social needs. *Gerontologist, 32,* 744–751.

Carsten, J. (1991). Children in between: fostering and the process of kinship on Pulau Langkawi, Malaysia. *Man: Journal of the Royal Anthropological Institute, 26* (3), 425–443.

Castle, S. E. (1996). The current and intergenerational impact of child fostering on children's nutritional status in rural Mali. *Human Organization, 55* (2), 193–205.

Chalfie, D. (1994, September). *Going it alone: A closer look at grandparents parenting children.* Washington, D.C.: American Association of Retired Persons.

Creighton, L. (1991, December 16). Grandparents: The silent saviors. *U.S. News & World Report,* 80–89.

Cross, C. P., & Ibru, C. (1978). A portrait of foster care: Private fostering among two generations of Nigerians. *West African Journal of Sociology and Political Science, 1,* 285–305.

Delgado, M., & Humm-Delgado, D. (1982). Natural support systems: Source of strength in Hispanic communities. *Social Work, 27* (1), 83–89.

DeToledo, S. (1995). *Grandparents as parents: A survival guide for raising a second family.* New York: Guilford.

Dunnett, D. (1982). *King hereafter*. New York: Knopf.

Eastman, K. S. (1988). Gambian fostering. *Journal of International and Comparative Social Welfare, 4* (2), 72–81.

Erikson, E. H. (1963). *Childhood and society* (2nd ed.) New York: W. W. Norton.

Everett, J. E. (1995). Relative foster care: An emerging trend in foster care placement policy and practice. *Smith College Studies in Social Work, 65* (3), 239–254.

Everett, J. E., Chipungu, S. S., & Leashore, B. R. (Eds.). (1991). *Child Welfare: an Africentric perspective*. New Brunswick, N.J.: Rutgers University Press.

Fiawoo, D. K. (1978). Some patterns of foster care in Ghana. In C. Oppong (Ed.), *Marriage, fertility and parenthood in West Africa* (pp. 273–306). Canberra: Australian National University Press.

Furukawa, S. (1991). *The diverse living arrangements of children: Summer 1991. Current population reports. Household economic studies*. Washington, D.C.: U.S. Department of Commerce, Bureau of the Census.

Gray, S. S., & Nybell, L. M. (1990). Issues in African-American family preservation. *Child Welfare, 69* (6), 513–523.

Greif, G. L. (1990). *The daddy track and the single father*. Lexington, Mass.: Lexington Books.

Greif, G. L., & Pabst, M. S. (1988). *Mothers without custody*. Lexington, Mass.: Lexington Books.

Hegar, R. L., & Scannapieco, M. (1995). From family duty to family policy: The evolution of kinship care. *Child Welfare, 74* (1), 200–216.

Illinois Department of Children and Family Services. (1990). Executive Summary. Chicago: Author.

Indian Child Welfare Act of 1978, P.L. 95-608, 92 Stat. 3069.

Isiugo-Abanihe, U. C. (1984). Child fostering and high fertility interrelationships in West Africa. *Studies in Third World Societies, 29*, 73–100.

Isiugo-Abanihe, U. C. (1985). Child fosterage in West Africa. *Population and Development Review, 11* (1), 53–73.

Jung, C. G. (1969). *Four archetypes: Mother, rebirth, spirit, trickster*. Princeton, N.J.: Princeton University Press.

Lee, F. (1994, November 21). AIDS toll on elderly: Dying grandchildren. *New York Times*, A1+.

Luomala, K. (1987). Reality and fantasy: The foster child in Hawaiian myths and customs. *Pacific Studies, 10* (2), 1–45.

Mallory, T. (1906). *Le morte d'Arthur*. Vol. 1. New York: E.P. Dutton.

Martin, J. M., & Martin, E. P. (1985). *The helping tradition in the black family and community*. Silver Spring, Md.: National Association of Social Workers.

Matheson, L. (1996). The politics of the Indian Child Welfare Act. *Social Work, 41* (2), 232–235.

National Commission on Family Foster Care. (1991). The significance of kinship care. In *A blueprint for fostering infants, children, and youths in the 1990s* (pp. 89–107). Washington, D.C.: Child Welfare League of America.

Page, H. (1989). Childrearing vs. childbearing: Co-residence of mother and child in sub-Saharan Africa. In R. J. Lesthaeghe (Ed.), *Reproduction and social organization in Sub-Saharan Africa* (pp. 401–441). Berkeley: University of California Press.

Pennington, R. (1991). Child fostering as a reproductive strategy among southern African pastoralists. *Ethnology and Sociobiology, 12*, 83–104.

Rank, O. (1914). *The myth of the birth of the hero*. New York: Vintage Books.

Saluter, A. F. (1989). *Changes in American family life. Current population reports, special studies*. Washington, D.C.: U.S. Department of Commerce, Bureau of the Census.

Saluter, A. F. (1996). *Current population reports: Marital status and living arrangments, March 1995 (update).* Washington: U.S. Department of Commerce, Census Bureau.

Scannapieco, M., & Jackson, S. (1996). Kinship care: The African American response to family preservation. *Social Work, 41* (2), 190–196.

Shomaker, D. J. (1989). Transfer of children and the importance of grandmothers among Navajo Indians. *Journal of Cross-Cultural Gerontology, 4* (1), 1–18.

Shore, M. F. (Ed.). (1989). Special section: Children of divorce. *American Journal of Orthopsychiatry, 59* (4), 557–618.

Silk, J. B. (1987). Adoption and fosterage in human societies: Adaptations or enigmas? *Cultural Anthropology, 2* (1), 39–49.

Spar, K. (1993, September). *Kinship foster care: An emerging federal issue.* Washington, D.C.: Library of Congress, Congressional Research Service.

Stehno, S. M. (1988). Public responsibility for dependent black children: The advocacy of Edith Abbott and Sophonisba Breckinridge. *Social Service Review, 62* (3), 485–503.

Takas, M. (1993). *Kinship care and family preservation: A guide for states in legal and policy development.* Washington, D.C.: ABA Center on Children and the Law.

Takas, M. (1995). *Grandparents raising grandchildren: A guide to finding help and hope.* Brookdale Foundation Group.

Trattner, W. I. (1994). *From poor law to welfare state: A history of social welfare in America* (5th ed.). New York: Free Press.

Umbima, K. J. (1991). Regulating foster care services: The Kenyan situation. *Child Welfare, 70* (2), 169–174.

Vidal, C. (1988). Godparenting among Hispanic Americans. *Child Welfare, 67* (5), 453–459.

Wallerstein, J. S. (1991). The long-term effects of divorce on children: A review. *Journal of the American Academy of Child and Adolescent Psychiatry, 30* (3), 349–360.

Wallerstein, J. S., & Blakeslee, S. (1989). *Second chances: Men, women, and children a decade after divorce.* New York: Ticknor & Fields.

Waysdorf, S. (1994). Families in the AIDS crisis: Access, equality, empowerment, and the role of kinship caregivers. *Texas Journal of Women and the Law, 3,* 145–220.

Wilensky, H. L., & Lebeaux, C. N. (1965). *Industrial society & social welfare.* New York: Free Press.

Yusane, A. Y. (1990). Cultural, political, and economic universals in West Africa in synthesis. In M. K. Asante & K. W. Asante (Eds.), *African culture: The rhythms of unity* (pp. 39–70). Trenton, N.J.: Africa World Press.

CHAPTER 3

Kinship Care as a Child Welfare Service

Emerging Policy Issues and Trends

JAMES P. GLEESON, PH.D.

Prior to the mid-1980s, the care of children by relatives was viewed primarily as a temporary response to crisis or an informal adoption that occurred within families and outside the legal responsibility of the child welfare system (Child Welfare League of America, 1994; Hegar & Scannapieco, 1995; Hill, 1972, 1977; Martin & Martin, 1978; Stack, 1974; Timberlake & Chipungu, 1992). Since 1985, the number of children in state custody and living with relatives who receive foster care payments has increased dramatically, and kinship care has become a central and important policy issue, particularly in states with major urban centers, where the use of kinship foster care and the growth of foster care caseloads have been the greatest (Gleeson & Craig, 1994; Goerge, Wulczyn, & Harden, 1995; Kusserow, 1992a, 1992b).

Studies of states' policies on the use of kinship care as a child welfare service have revealed a lack of clarity regarding purpose and goals, considerable variation across states, and value conflicts regarding policies guiding placement of children with their relatives (Gleeson & Craig, 1994; Hornby, Zeller, & Karraker, 1995; Kusserow, 1992a, 1992b). While most states' policies indicate a preference for placing children with relatives, in some states placement with relatives is primarily a way of diverting children from the child welfare system. In Maryland, on the other hand, placement of children in state custody with relatives is most commonly viewed as a type of home-based service intended to keep families together. Yet, in most states, if a child has been taken into state custody and placed with relatives, this is considered a type of foster care placement. States that emphasize diversion from the child welfare system or conceptualize kinship care as a type of family preservation service discourage relatives from pursuing licensure or approval as foster parents (Gleeson & Craig, 1994; Hornby et al., 1995). When relatives care for children as a diversion from the child welfare system, or when they care for children in state custody but do so without pursuing licensure or approval as a foster parent, they are, in most cases, eligible to receive financial support for the care of the child through AFDC. When relatives are licensed or approved as foster parents, they are eligible to receive foster care board payments that are three to five times higher than the AFDC child-only rate in most states, and the disparity becomes greater as the number of children in care increases (IDCFS, 1995a; Kusserrow, 1992a; Testa, 1993).

With licensure or approval as foster parents, and higher rates of reimbursement, the child welfare system's regulation and control of the placement increases (Hornby et al., 1995). Some states, like Illinois and New York, have made it easier for relatives to become licensed or approved as foster parents through development of approval standards specific to relatives, waiver of foster care licensing standards, and/or expedited approval processes (Gleeson, 1996; Gleeson & Craig, 1994; Hornby et al., 1995; Kusserow, 1992a, 1992b). Where regulatory standards are specific to relatives or can be waived, it is clear that the purpose of modifying these standards is to make it easier for relatives to care for the child and for the child welfare agency to claim federal matching funds. Requirements that relatives be licensed or approved as meeting licensing standards seem to have little to do with concerns about child protection and a great deal to do with maximizing federal matching funds. Policies in most states indicate that children can remain in the care of relatives if the children are considered to be safe, even if licensing standards are not met (Gleeson & Craig, 1994).

The development of policies regarding the use of kinship care as a *formal* child welfare service was first driven by the combination of a rising demand for child welfare services and lawsuits pertaining to the use of kinship care (Gleeson & Craig, 1994). More recent policy developments have been shaped by a policy context that is increasingly residual in nature, shaped by concerns about growth in child welfare caseloads, efforts to reduce or at least contain costs, and conservative values (Gleeson, 1996). The welfare reform movement and efforts to use managed-care mechanisms to contain costs have influenced this context. The next phase of policy development will be influenced by demographic shifts in the U.S. population, the impact of welfare reform laws on children, families, and the child welfare system, and the way managed-care approaches are implemented to contain the cost of social services to children and families.

In this chapter, Illinois is used as an illustrative example of the stages of policy development that define the use of kinship care as a child welfare service. Policy development in Illinois is described specifically because it has been so dramatic and important in defining kinship care as a child welfare service. The policy issues and trends that shaped kinship care policy development and those that continue to shape the use of kinship care as a child welfare service in Illinois are presented. Future trends that will influence the use of kinship care as a child welfare service are also discussed. The chapter closes with a discussion of the possible responses to challenges and opportunities that are inherent in these emerging policy issues and trends.

KINSHIP CARE POLICY DEVELOPMENT IN ILLINOIS

Before the *Miller v. Youakim* (1976, 1979) court decisions, Illinois, like most states, placed children taken into state custody with relatives but did not provide foster care rates to relative caregivers (Gleeson & Craig, 1994). Illinois statutes and administrative laws specifically defined foster parents as adults not related to the children in care. In 1976, the Northern Illinois District Court held that the Illinois practice of excluding relatives from the definition of family foster home conflicted with sections 601 and 608 of the Social Security Act and was therefore invalid under the Supremacy Clause of the United States Constitution (*Miller v. Youakim*, 1976). The plaintiffs in this case were adults who were providing care for relative children in state custody. Although the caregivers were not licensed as foster parents at the time, the Illinois Department of Children and Family Services (IDCFS) used family foster home standards as a screening mechanism to determine if relatives provided an adequate placement option for the child. In 1979, the District Court's decision was affirmed by the U.S. Supreme Court (*Miller v. Youakim*, 1979) in a decision that requires states to provide relatives who are caring for children in state custody with the same financial support as that provided to nonrelated foster parents if they meet the same licensing standards and the case meets all other standards for claiming federal matching funds.

Unlike most states, Illinois interpreted the *Miller v. Youakim* (1979) decision as requiring that *any* relatives caring for children in state custody should receive foster care payments, regardless of the licensing status of that home or the eligibility of the child's placement for federal matching funds (Hornby et al., 1995; IDCFS, 1995a; Testa, 1993, 1995). A small percentage of the children in the legal custody of the Illinois Department of Children's and Family Services (IDCFS) lived with relatives from the creation of IDCFS in 1965 through 1976. After 1976, the number of children in state custody and living with relatives began to increase steadily, although the overall out-of-home care caseload remained relatively constant from 1975 through 1986 (IDCFS, 1995a; Testa, 1993). After 1986, out-of-home care caseloads in several states began to grow at a rapid rate (Goerge et al., 1995). Caseload growth was largest in major urban areas, among children of color, and among children who entered state custody as infants. Illinois, like New York and California, began to rely increasingly on kinship foster care, partly because caseload growth was accompanied by a marked decrease in the number of available licensed foster homes (James Bell Associates & Westat, u.d.; National Commission on Family Foster Care, 1991).

Relative Preference

Changes in statutory and administrative law, driven by the increasing demand for placement resources and several lawsuits, clearly established relatives as the first placement preference when children were taken into state custody. In

1988, the Illinois Children and Family Services Act was amended to require that relatives "be selected as the preferred caregiver" when placement of children outside the parental home is considered by the child welfare system (IDCFS, 1995a). The statute required that children be placed with close relatives after an immediate preliminary approval process.

On April 20, 1990, in response to a lawsuit filed on behalf of a class of children "who have been adversely affected by IDCFS' practices with respect to the treatment of potential and actual relative caretakers," IDCFS was enjoined from "(1) failing to inform their relatives about the right to become foster parents and receive foster payments; (2) using intimidation, harassment and threats to force their relatives into becoming private guardians rather than foster parents; (3) failing to inform relatives about the right to seek waiver of certain foster home licensing standards; and (4) failing to provide adequate written notice of IDCFS's decisions concerning foster care" (*Reid v. Suter*, 1992).

In 1992, the *Reid v. Suter* consent decree was approved by the Circuit Court of Cook County. IDCFS agreed to make reasonable attempts to identify potential relative caregivers when removal from the parental home is considered; inform relative caregivers about the differences between IDCFS guardianship and private guardianship and tell them that they may apply to become relative foster parents; refrain from any form of coercion to compel potential relative caregivers to become private guardians rather than relative foster parents; and require that all potential relative caregivers referred or considered for approval be informed that they may seek waiver of certain relative home approval standards (*Reid v. Suter*, 1992: 8–10). As part of the consent decree, IDCFS agreed to grant waivers of relative home approval standards unless doing so "would endanger the health, safety or welfare of the child involved" or "would result in a placement for which the federal government refuses to provide funding to IDCFS ... under Title IV-E" or "would pose a substantial obstacle to achieving permanency for the child" (*Reid v. Suter*, 1992: 10). The consent decree specified that "in making placement decisions, IDCFS shall give priority consideration to relatives, in accord with existing law" and strengthened the appeal process for relatives denied approval or placement of a child in their home (*Reid v. Suter*, 1992: 10).

Focusing on Maximizing Federal Matching Funds

In the early 1980s, few of the kinship homes in which children in Illinois state custody lived were licensed as foster homes (Testa, 1993). Title IV-E regulations allowed federal matching funds for placement of children in homes "approved as meeting" the state's foster home licensing standards, as long as the placement of the child met all other IV-E eligibility criteria: (1) the child had been removed from an AFDC eligible home when originally taken into state custody; (2) a judicial determination had been made that "reasonable efforts" had been made to prevent unnecessary placement and taking the child into state custody; and (3) the placement of the child was the responsibility of a state or county child welfare agency (P.L. 96-272). Illinois made two policy changes to increase the number of relative placements eligible for federal matching funds. First, in 1986, IDCFS created standards specific to approval of relative homes for the care of relative children only, not of other state wards. Then, in 1989, private agencies were awarded purchase-of-service contracts to administer home-of-relative programs, which included carrying full case responsibility, monitoring the relative homes, and providing case management services (Schneider, 1993). These agencies were also responsible for conducting home studies and ensuring that the homes in which relative children were placed met the new standards.

Purchase-of-service contracts with private agencies specified limits on the size of caseload carried by caseworkers. By keeping caseloads lower in the private agencies than was common within IDCFS, it was expected that private agencies would be more successful in completing home studies and ensuring that the majority of relative homes complied with home of relative approval standards, thereby increasing the flow of federal matching funds into the state. Also, private agencies had greater flexibility and could add staff positions for program expansion with greater ease than IDCFS.

Delegating responsibility for the majority of children placed in kinship foster care and the creation of home-of-relative standards did not have the expected results. The home-of-relative approval standards were revised repeatedly. Although standards were progressively relaxed to increase the number of approved homes, approval rates remained low, between 40 percent and 60 percent (IDCFS, 1995a; Schneider, 1993; Testa, 1993, 1995). The barriers to approval of relative homes were not fully understood by child welfare policymakers, administrators, advocates, or practitioners. Some blamed kinship caregivers for the low approval rates, claiming that these caregivers were resistant to the approval process. Others blamed the complicated public-private agency bureaucracies for ineptness in completing the home studies and the approval procedures or pointed to inefficiencies in processing criminal background checks as major contributors to the low approval rates.

Private Agency Growth and Private Agency-Public Agency Stalemates

From 1989 to 1995 considerable energy was spent on transferring as many cases as possible to private agencies. Large child welfare agencies that had been providing a variety of child welfare services for many years quickly developed kinship care programs with caseloads that exceeded the size of their traditional family foster care caseloads. Several of these agencies now have program offices that exclusively serve four hundred to one thousand kinship foster care cases. As cases were being transferred to private agencies, children continued to enter state custody, and the IDCFS caseload continued to grow. When existing private agencies could not accept cases fast enough, new community-based agencies emerged, in many cases funded entirely through home-of-relative purchase-of-service contracts with IDCFS.

The state's Child Welfare Advisory Committee, comprising IDCFS and private agency representatives, created a subcommittee for home-of-relative care. Among other issues, this committee debated a "two-tiered" system of reimbursement of relative caregivers—a lower rate until approved, and the full foster care rate when approved—as a possible incentive for kinship caregivers who were viewed as reluctant or resistant to participate in the approval process. The proposal died as a result of strong opposition by private agency representatives and other advocates, who argued that the failure to approve homes was primarily due to bureaucratic inefficiencies and that families should not be made to suffer as a consequence.

Defining Criteria for Service Eligibility

Low rates of licensing or approval of kinship foster homes were not the only problems in accessing federal matching funds. From 1991 to July 1, 1995, approximately 20 percent to 38 percent of children entering state custody and served in kinship foster care were living with the related caregiver when IDCFS intervened (IDCFS, 1995a; Testa, 1995). These "nonremoval" cases did not meet the federal definition of "out-of-home" care and were therefore ineligible for reimbursement under Title IV-E. The high rate of nonremoval cases is partially blamed on interpretations of a 1990 Illinois Appellate Court Decision, *People v. Thornton*. The Illinois Public Guardian interpreted this decision as requiring IDCFS to take custody of children who had been left with relatives by their parents (IDCFS, 1995a; Testa, 1993, 1995). Such children were considered to be "neglected," or receiving "inadequate supervision," by the fact that they had been left with the relative by the parent "without a care plan." Testa (1993, 1995) claims that interpretations of the *Thornton* decision resulted in a "parent-based" definition of neglect that encouraged IDCFS to take custody of children already living with relatives when the state intervened.

Attempts to Facilitate Exits from State Custody

The number of children in home-of-relative placements grew most strikingly in Illinois in the period from March 1990 to March 1995, when it rose from 7,995 children to 26,560 children, an increase of 232 percent (Testa, 1995). During this time period the state's entire caseload of children in out-of-home care grew from less than 21,000 to approximately 47,000 children, and the percentage of these children living in home-of-relative care increased to 57 percent (McDonald, 1995; Testa, 1993, 1995). The growing caseload of children in out-of-home care in Illinois was due not only to increased intake of new cases. The decline in discharges from state custody observed across the rest of the country was a problem in Illinois as well, particularly among children in formal kinship care (Goerge et al., 1995). Consistent with findings of studies conducted in several states, placements with relatives were less likely to disrupt and tended to last longer than nonrelative placements, but they resulted in lower return home and lower adoption rates than those observed for children in nonrelative care (Barth et al. 1994; Goerge, 1990; Testa, 1992, 1993; Thornton, 1991; Wulczyn & Goerge, 1992).

Prior to 1989, children in home-of-relative care, their caregivers, and their parents received infrequent contact and few services in comparison to clients in other types of care provided by unrelated caregivers. This lower level of monitoring and service provision for children in the care of relatives as compared to nonrelatives was not unique to Illinois and has been noted in studies in several states (Berrick et al., 1994; Dubowitz, Feigelman, & Zuravin, 1993; Dubowitz et al., 1994; Iglehart, 1994; Meyer & Link, 1990; Thornton, 1991). It should be no surprise that kinship foster care cases remained open longer than other cases, since permanency planning research conducted in the 1970s indicated that higher rates of caseworker contacts with family members of children in nonrelative foster care are associated with higher rates of reunification and adoption (Stein, Gambrill, & Wiltse, 1978).

One of the expected benefits of purchase-of-service contracts with private child welfare agencies was that private agencies could be required to provide the same level of service to children in kinship foster care as was required for traditional family foster care and that this higher level of contact would facilitate permanency planning. However, the intense focus on transferring cases to private agencies, opening new cases, and approving homes prevented a focus on permanency planning for children in kinship foster care. Also, many practitioners in private agencies and IDCFS questioned whether the permanency goals that had been developed for children in traditional nonrelated foster care were relevant for children in kinship foster care.

Studies conducted in Illinois suggested that adoption was a realistic possibility for a higher percentage of formal kinship care cases than suggested by earlier research (Gleeson, O'Donnell, & Bonecutter, 1997; Testa, 1993, 1995). As the kinship foster care caseload grew, IDCFS placed greater emphasis on ensuring that adoption was discussed with kinship caregivers when return home seemed unlikely. It was clear, however, that a substantial percentage of relative caregivers were willing to care for a child to the age of majority but were unwilling to adopt the child. Private guardianship was a permanency goal that was rarely pursued after the 1990 preliminary injunction in the *Reid* case (IDCFS, 1995a; *Reid v. Suter*, 1992; Testa, 1993, 1995). When caseworkers did discuss private guardianship as an option, they reported that few relatives were willing to consider private guardianship because the only financial subsidy available was the AFDC child-only rate of $102 for the first child, less for each additional child (Gleeson et al., 1997). Continued placement in family foster care, however, was subsidized at an average rate of $350 per month per child, and adoption subsidies were available that were nearly as high as the family foster care subsidy rate.

Researchers at the University of Chicago, in conjunction with the Illinois Child Welfare Advisory Committee, did considerable work on developing an additional permanency option for children in formal kinship care who were unable to be adopted or exit the child welfare system through private guardianship arrangements (Testa, Shook, Cohen, & Woods, 1996). In 1994, the client service planning administrative rules and procedures were amended to create the option of "Delegated Relative Authority" (DRA). DRA was defined as a permanency option for children in safe, stable placements with relatives for whom adoption or guardianship was not possible. The child assigned to DRA status continues to be under IDCFS guardianship and is entitled to receive board payments and medical services, while relatives assume additional responsibilities for the children as delegated to them by IDCFS. DRA status reduces IDCFS intervention to the minimum required by Title IV-E of the Social Security Act (Illinois Department of Children and Family Services & Human Services Technologies, 1994). IDCFS is able to recoup federal matching dollars for children with DRA status if the case meets other Title IV-E eligibility criteria.

The DRA option has not been pursued for the number of children for whom it was projected that it would be appropriate. Private agencies have been reluctant to use the permanency goal of DRA, in part because purchase-of-service contracts reimburse private agencies at a lower level for serving DRA cases than they receive for serving other kinship foster care cases. The lower rate is based on the premise that DRA cases require less frequent monitoring and casework activities; therefore, caseworkers are able to serve a substantially higher number of DRA cases than other kinship foster care cases. Private agency caseworkers were not only reluctant to increase their caseloads; many argued that the majority of cases on their caseloads required ongoing monitoring to ensure that the child's needs were adequately met, and those that did not require this monitoring were heading toward adoption. Also, some IDCFS and private agency staff feared that since DRA cases remained the legal responsibility of the child welfare agencies, reduced monitoring would make them vulnerable to scrutiny by the public, the media, child welfare administrators, and legislators if a tragedy did occur to a child in DRA status (Testa et al., 1996).

Caseload growth continued in spite of attempts to facilitate exits from state custody and in the midst of attempts to reform the child welfare system in Illinois, reform that had been initiated in response to litigation and resulting in a consent decree that was designed to improve service delivery in nearly every area of IDCFS responsibility (*B.H. v. Suter*, 1991). A cornerstone of the reform was a substantial reduction in the average caseload of IDCFS caseworkers. Although the state legislature had previously increased the IDCFS budget substantially to fund many reform initiatives, it did so with the promise that this investment would result in a reduction in the state's foster care caseload and in future costs. At the same time, results of the evaluation of the state's family preservation services revealed that programs funded through this effort were unsuccessful in preventing out-of-home placement (Schuerman, Rzepnicki, Littell, & Chak, 1993). Continued caseload growth angered state legislators, who were frustrated with the results of their investments.

The Illinois Home-of-Relative Reform Plan

The sharp growth in kinship foster care, in the overall IDCFS caseload, and in the IDCFS budget led to the development of the Illinois Home-of-Relative (HMR) Reform Plan. This plan was announced as part of the governor's budget briefing on March 1, 1995, with an implementation date of July 1, 1996. The HMR Reform Plan was one of several initiatives that were driven primarily by the governor's and the General Assembly's mandate to reduce the cost of child welfare services in Illinois (McDonald, 1995). These initiatives attempted to narrow the scope of the IDCFS mission, reduce the growth of out-of-home care, and reduce costs. The general assembly had made it clear that any requests for future supplemental funding requests "may have to be funded with further cuts in the scope of the child welfare mission in Illinois" (McDonald, 1995).

The HMR Reform Plan itself was designed to save the state $44.4 million in FY 96 alone by reducing the number of nonremoval cases taken into state custody, eliminating separate home of relative approval standards, requiring relatives to meet traditional family foster home licensing standards before foster care payments could be received, and creating a reimbursement level for unlicensed relatives caring for children in state custody at the state standard of need—higher than the AFDC child-only payment but lower than the foster care payment (IDCFS, 1995a; McDonald, 1995).

The Illinois HMR Reform plan was initiated through changes in statutory and administrative law. P.A. 89-21, passed by the Illinois General Assembly on May 26, 1995, and signed by the Governor on June 6, 1995, repealed relative preference laws and eliminated the home-of-relative approval standards. It also changed the definition of neglect to a "home-based" definition, preventing children living with relatives from being taken into state custody merely because the biological parents were not providing direct care for the child.

Under the HMR Reform Plan, relatives caring for children in state custody are required to meet the same licensing standards as foster parents in order to receive the same foster care subsidy. Children in state custody can be placed with unlicensed relatives who pass an initial safety check, but these relatives receive a subsidy that is equal to the state standard of need from a combination of Title IV-A and state child welfare funds ($252 for the first child and less for each additional child). Under the HMR Reform Plan, children living with relatives when IDCFS becomes involved are considerably less likely to be taken into state custody; therefore, the AFDC child-only rate is the only financial subsidy for these children unless they are eligible for SSI.

The HMR reform plan also made children in informal kinship care eligible for home-based services through a new initiative, the Extended Family Support Program. Prior to this initiative, children living with relatives and not taken into state custody after a child abuse or neglect investigation were not usually eligible for IDCFS family preservation or other home-based services. The HMR Reform Plan also described other initiatives that were already being developed prior to the plan. These include a family-group conference conducted with extended family members when a child is in danger of being taken into state custody. In a program modeled after a New Zealand program (Connolly, 1994), family support workers meet with extended families to facilitate development of a caregiving plan for a child that avoids taking the child into state custody. A second but related program provides mediation services to extended family members who are considering adoption, guardianship, or delegated relative authority as permanency options for the child (IDCFS, 1994).

Responses from Legal Advocates

The HMR Reform plan was met with two lawsuits. *Youakim v. McDonald* (1995) alleged that the Illinois HMR Reform Plan violated the 1976 judgment order in *Miller v. Youakim* (1976). The *Youakim v. McDonald* lawsuit focused only on children in relative homes who had previously received foster care payments. It did not challenge the state's right to change the eligibility requirements for foster care reimbursements to relatives of children in need of future kinship care. *Reid v. McDonald* (1995) alleged that the Illinois HMR Reform Plan violated the *Reid v. Suter* (1992) consent decree, particularly regarding relative preference and appeal rights for relatives when children are not placed with them or when relatives are denied relative home approval or foster home licensing. The *Reid v. McDonald* (1995) lawsuit was quickly dismissed. However, in *Youakim v. McDonald* (1995), the Northern District Court held that "the transition period established by HMR Reform violates both the Judgment Order and the Due Process Clause of the Fourteenth Amendment" (*Youakim v. McDonald, Memorandum Opinion and Order,* June 30, 1995: 34).

The District Court enjoined IDCFS from reducing foster care payments to all foster children in the care of relatives who were currently receiving foster care payments. The court required IDCFS to modify the planned transition period, giving previously approved relative caregivers and those pending approval more time to submit applications for foster home licensure. IDCFS was required to continue to provide the foster care payments to relative caregivers unless they failed to file applications within the new timeline or until an application filed within the new timeline was denied. The appellate court stayed the order on July 12, 1995, allowing the HMR Reform Plan to be implemented while the court considered the appeal. On February 15, 1996, the Northern District Court ordered IDCFS to restore the foster care payments for the nine thousand children for whom the reimbursement had been lowered under the HMR reform without determination of whether the home met licensing standards (*Youakim v. McDonald, Memorandum Opinion and Order,* July 3, 1996). The U.S. Supreme Court refused to hear an appeal by IDCFS, and on July 3, 1996, a final restoration order was issued by the Northern District Court.

Implementing the HMR Reform Plan

The March 1, 1995, announcement that the HMR Reform Plan was to become effective on July 1, 1996, resulted in a flurry of activity. Foster home licensing regulations were revised, public hearings were held, and a series of meetings was conducted for agencies and staff persons responsible for kinship care cases. The short time frame and the need to learn how the new plan would work required service providers to focus on collecting information and sharing it with their staffs and with relative caregivers. Several private agencies and child welfare advocates encouraged relative caregivers to make applications for foster home licenses. For the first six months of 1995, implementation of the HMR reform plan, licensing studies, and clarification of payment levels consumed the conversations of caseworkers and relative caregivers. Permanency planning once again received little attention.

As time passes, the HMR Reform Plan itself is less the focus of concern. Recent questions have focused on determination of adoption subsidy levels or DRA payment levels when the relative caregiver is not licensed or on clarifying the status of the *Youakim v. McDonald* court case, its meaning for restoration of payments and what documentation needs to be completed for relative caregivers to receive payment restoration. IDCFS has also placed greater emphasis on facilitating kinship adoptions. As time passes, the HMR reform plan is only one of many initiatives that are being simultaneously implemented, all with similar goals of reducing the IDCFS caseload and the cost of child welfare services in Illinois. Among these initiatives are changes in state policy on adoption assistance, a waiver request to use IV-E matching funds to support subsidized guardianship for children in kinship care, and redesign of the purchase-of-service agreements between IDCFS and private agencies that expands the definition of full case responsibility and incorporates a managed care approach referred to as performance-based contracting. Each of these initiatives is briefly described in the paragraphs that follow.

Changes in the state's adoption assistance policy. The same state statute that "reformed" kinship care in Illinois reduced the adoption subsidy for special-needs children from a maximum payment of one dollar less than the foster care payment to $25 less than the foster care payment (P.A. 89-21). The previous policy based the amount of adoption assistance on the child's needs. The new statute and related state regulations require a means test, using the adoptive family's income to determine the amount of the adoption subsidy. The new policy eliminated cost-of-living increases that had previously been awarded each time the foster care payment was adjusted and emphasized that adoption subsidies are not an entitlement, giving IDCFS greater discretion in terminating or reducing adoption subsidies in future years.

IV-E waiver request. IDCFS submitted a IV-E waiver request to the U.S. Department of Health and Human Services, proposing a five-year demonstration project to test the effectiveness of providing subsidized guardianship as a permanency option for children in kinship care (IDCFS, 1995b). The waiver, approved in September 1996, allows IDCFS to use IV-E matching funds to support guardianship subsidies for appropriate families randomly assigned to the experimental condition. At the time of this writing, IDCFS is coordinating efforts to train child welfare staff to facilitate permanency planning efforts to include adoption, delegated relative authority, and subsidized guardianship.

Purchase-of-service redesign. Partly as a mechanism for reducing the caseloads of IDCFS staff and partly to comply with other aspects of the *B.H. v. Suter* (1991) consent decree, IDCFS expanded the definition of full case responsibility required of private agencies awarded purchase-of-service contracts. Prior to the redesign, children in state custody and served by private agency personnel through purchase-of-service agreements also had an IDCFS case manager assigned to their case. The redesign replaced the case managers with liaisons to agencies with purchase-of-service contracts. All tasks previously completed by the IDCFS case managers were delegated to the private agencies.

The purchase-of-service redesign was implemented with little warning and little training of private agency or IDCFS staff. Private agencies protested implementation of the redesign without renegotiation of purchase-of-service agreements to compensate the private agencies for the additional case responsibilities. Several issues continue to be clarified regarding definitions of clients and responsibilities for monitoring the safety of siblings of children in state custody.

Private agency protests did slow down the second part of the redesign of the relationship between IDCFS and purchase-of-service contractors. Referred to as performance-based contracting, this part of the redesign is a managed care approach to contracting for child welfare services. Through performance-based contracting, private agencies will be reimbursed for a specific number of cases. To maintain the funding level, a specific number of new cases must be accepted by these agencies within specified time frames. If these agencies are to be able to serve cases without increasing caseload size, an equal number of cases must be discharged from care as are accepted into care. Performance-based contracting has particular relevance to kinship care, since discharge rates from kinship care have been low, and facilitating exits from state custody for children in kinship care is still a puzzling problem.

Policy Issues and Trends Shaping Kinship Care
Policy Development in Illinois

Policy development defining the use of kinship care as a child welfare service in Illinois has gone through three phases and is entering a fourth. During the first phase of policy development, prior to the *Miller v. Youakim* (1976, 1979) court decisions, kinship care was almost exclusively an informal service operating within families and outside the auspices of the child welfare system. Informal kinship care was used to divert children from the child welfare system, and this diversion was frequently initiated by the child welfare system or the courts. Only a small number of children in state custody lived with relatives. If government funding was received by the kinship caregiver to support the care of the child, it was generally AFDC or SSI.

The second phase of policy development in Illinois was driven by the combination of caseload growth, a declining supply of traditional foster homes, responses to a series of lawsuits addressing eligibility of kinship caregivers for foster care board payments, and efforts to maximize federal matching funds to support the growing costs of this service. These driving forces gave impetus to solutions without the direction that could have been provided by a clear mission and purpose for the use of kinship care as a child welfare service (Gleeson & Craig, 1994). Without clarity of purpose, defining the relationship between the formal child welfare system and the kinship systems of vulnerable children is difficult. Without clarity of purpose, the responsibilities of government and family are defined by default in reaction to driving forces that may have little to do with the needs of children and their families.

In Illinois, the use of kinship care as a formal child welfare service grew without clarity of purpose. IDCFS, private agencies, and legal advocates all reacted to rapid growth of this service without a shared mission, each party with its own narrow vision. As a result, kinship care was defined in a narrow and rigid way. Kinship care as a diversion from the child welfare system through private guardianship was discouraged to the point that this option was not explored with children and families for whom it would have been appropriate and even the preference of the families. Home-based services were generally not available to children living with kin. When children were living with kin and the child welfare system was involved in their lives, this was defined in the vast majority of cases as a type of foster care. The energy of IDCFS and the private agencies was directed toward managing the growth of this "new" child welfare service and attempting to access federal funding to help cover the costs. Staff training emphasized relative home approval studies and standards. The relevance of adoption as a permanency option for children in kinship care was questioned by many, and, with the purpose of kinship care not well defined, a practice model could not be clearly articulated (Gleeson et al., 1997). To further complicate matters, a high percentage of cases in kinship care involved birth parents who were experiencing substance abuse problems that prevented them from adequately caring for their children. Permanency planning for children in kinship care required an understanding of how the birth parents' substance abuse affected the children and the members of the kinship system who were acting as caregivers for the children. The required level of understanding was beyond the capacity of the child welfare system at the time, and this confusion contributed to the blocked exits from state custody for children in kinship care.

Kinship care also grew in Illinois as a service delivered by private agencies, creating a new constituency with vested interests and beliefs about the way the program operated. While it is clear that purchase-of-service contracts with private agencies have resulted in more contact between child welfare caseworkers and children in kinship care, the involvement of private agencies has complicated the policy-making process for IDCFS. The policy-making process was further complicated by a major reform effort shaped by lawsuits and a consent decree, several changes in IDCFS leadership, and initiation of new programs designed to preserve families, prevent out-of-home placement, increase the likelihood of family reunification, and preserve adoptive families. Medicaid funds were tapped for the first time in the state to contract with private child welfare agencies to provide intensive treatment services for children in state custody. The reform efforts effectively lowered the average caseload for IDCFS caseworkers and stimulated improvements in a variety of service areas, yet inadvertently contributed to an emphasis on mandates over mission. Caseworkers in IDCFS and private agencies were trained to implement individual procedures mandated by the reform, but the overall vision of those crafting the reform and the relevance of individual procedures to the overall reform effort was not understood by the majority of caseworkers delivering services. The new services and programs were needed and provided service options not previously available to many children and families, yet each developed separately and divided the attention and resources of IDCFS and private agencies delivering these services.

The third phase of policy development was equally as reactive as the second, this time driven by welfare reform debates and popular rhetoric blaming government intrusion and growth for many of the country's problems (Gleeson, 1996). In Illinois, IDCFS officials reacted to demands of the governor and the General Assembly to dramatically cut the costs of child welfare services. Financial subsidies to relative caregivers and adoptive parents were questioned, and government support for the care of a related child was considered highly suspect and bad policy. Similar pressures are at work in New York, where proposals to limit foster care payments for kinship care to one year were discussed, but not enacted (McLaughlin, 1996). The policy context in which these plans and proposals emerged is one that is more residual and shaped by increasingly conservative values, with increasing shifts toward privatization and an emphasis on cost containment strategies (DiNitto, 1996). In this context, growing caseloads and costs bring public attention, while service recipients and service programs are blamed for the social problems that the service was designed to address (Gleeson, 1996). When growing caseloads are understood to be caused by policies, programs, and participants, the logical solutions include restricting access to programs and services, eliminating entitlements, tightening eligibility requirements, restricting the length of time one can receive benefits, and developing programs to divert potential recipients from the program and to facilitate rapid exit from the program (Gleeson, 1996).

Rationales for the Illinois HMR Reform Plan included claims that the growth in the out-of-home care caseload could be attributed primarily to the placement of children in formal kinship care; unnecessary incorporation of informal kinship care arrangements into the formal child welfare system; and needless intrusion into the lives of many families, particularly African American families (IDCFS, 1995; Testa, 1995). Growth in the out-of-home care caseload and child welfare expenditures was blamed on Illinois's interpretation of the *Miller v. Youakim* (1976, 1979) and the *Thornton* decisions and on relative preference policies (IDCFS 1995a; Testa, 1993, 1995). Comparisons were made with other states, both to indicate that Illinois was not required to reimburse all relatives caring for children in state custody at the same level as nonrelated foster parents and to point out that some other states with different policies have not had the upward caseload spurt experienced by Illinois.

It is not possible to determine to what extent Illinois policies contributed to caseload growth and to what extent the growing need for formal kinship care may have been due to increasing conditions of risk for children and families, particularly for impoverished children and for families of color (Testa, 1992). The child poverty rate in the United States increased from 19 percent in 1989 to 22.7 percent in 1993 (Annie E. Casey Foundation, 1995; Children's Defense Fund, 1995). AFDC benefits have eroded significantly since the 1970s, even when food stamps and Medicaid benefits are considered. Also, the percentage of families headed by single parents increased from 21.6 percent in 1986 to 25.3 percent in 1992 (Annie E. Casey Foundation, 1995). Single-parent families headed by females are the poorest in our country, and poverty has consistently been shown to be a strong predictor of child abuse and neglect and rates of child placement (Lindsey, 1992; Pelton, 1994).

Research conducted in New York City demonstrates that the poorer the community in which children live, the greater the chances that a child will be born at a low birth weight to a mother who did not receive prenatal care, will be placed in foster care during the first year of life, and will remain in state custody longer than children who enter state custody later in their lives (Wulczyn, 1994). In recent years, infants have constituted the fastest-growing age group among those entering state custody, and a high percentage of these children were placed with kin (Goerge et al., 1995). A study conducted by the U.S. General Accounting Office (GAO) revealed that in New York City, Los Angeles County, and Philadelphia County, the total population in out-of-home care increased by 66 percent between 1986 and 1991, while the number of children under three years of age in care in these cities increased by 110 percent (Ross, 1995). In California and New York, the placement of children under three years of age with relatives increased by 379 percent between 1986 and 1981, while the number of children placed with nonrelative foster parents increased by 54 percent (Ross, 1995). The GAO study also revealed that very young children were more likely to enter state custody because of some form of neglect, to come from families where at least one of the parents was abusing drugs, to have serious health-related problems, and to be at risk for future problems as a result of prenatal drug exposure (Ross, 1995).

People of color, and African Americans in particular, as compared to Caucasians, have considerably higher rates of poverty, single-parent households, and out-of-home placement, and they are more likely to be placed in formal kinship care than in other forms of out-of-home care, at least in major urban areas. Of the 26,500 children in formal kinship care in Illinois in March 1995, 87 percent were African American (Testa, 1995). Also, in seven predominantly African American communities in Chicago, 14 percent to 16 percent of all children were under IDCFS supervision, and 54 percent to 63 percent of out-of-home placements were in formal kinship care. Given the rising conditions of risk for African American children and families and the increase in placement rates of African American children in general and in formal kinship care placements in particular, it is difficult to rule these conditions of risk out as a major "cause" of caseload growth. These conditions of risk and the shortage of licensed nonrelative foster homes are at least as plausible as explanations for the growth in the number of children being placed in formal kinship care as may be the influence of kinship care policies.

The Home-of-Relative Reform Plan in Illinois attempted to reduce costs by tightening eligibility requirements and reducing reimbursement rates to relatives caring for children in state custody when the relatives are not licensed as foster parents. Yet it does expand options available for serving children in kinship care arrangements. Some of the new initiatives contained in the Illinois HMR reform plan may be quite effective in reducing the need for protective intervention. Offering home-based services to relatives caring for children at risk of out-of-home care is likely to be effective in strengthening, supporting, and preserving many kinship families. Also, conducting family group conferences is likely to avert the need for child welfare services for some families, and providing mediation services will facilitate exits from state custody for some children through kinship adoptions, delegated relative authority, private guardianship arrangements, and, perhaps, reunification with birth parents.

Also, the subsidized guardianship demonstration project is likely to result in the achievement of legal permanency for an increasing number of children in kinship care. However, the increased number of service options for children in kinship care are accompanied by exits from care that are uncertain and possibly unstable, since our society's willingness to support poor children and families financially is on the decline.

THE NEXT PHASE: WELFARE REFORM, DEMOGRAPHIC SHIFTS, AND MANAGED CARE

The next phase of policy development defining the use of kinship care as a child welfare service will be heavily influenced by implementation of the 1996 welfare reform law, demographic shifts in the U.S. population, and implementation of a managed care approach to cost containment and child welfare service delivery. The impact of each of these policy issues and trends is discussed in this section.

After vetoing two similar welfare reform bills, President Clinton signed the Personal Responsibility and Work Opportunity Reconciliation Act of 1996 into law on August 22, 1996. The law repealed the Aid to Families with Dependent Children program (AFDC), the Job Opportunities and Basic Skills Training program (JOBS), and the Emergency Assistance program, replacing them with a Temporary Assistance for Needy Families (TANF) block grant to states (National Clearinghouse for Legal Services [NCLS], 1996). A five-year lifetime limit is placed on TANF funds provided to families, exempting no more than 20 percent of state's caseloads from this five-year limit due to hardships. The federal entitlement to cash assistance for poor children and families was eliminated with this welfare reform law, leaving states free to determine their own eligibility criteria for families to receive assistance. Federal funding will no longer increase automatically during times of economic downturn and increased need (NCLS, 1996). States must steadily increase the percentage of TANF recipients who are working to 50 percent by the year 2002, and the number of hours of work required increases to 30 per week for single parents by the year 2000. States are no longer required to provide families the first $50 of child support collected on behalf of a child receiving TANF. The law allows states to implement waivers submitted prior to August 22, 1996, and approved prior to July 1, 1997. For example, Illinois may continue to impose a family cap that bars increases in cash assistance for AFDC recipients who give birth to another child. In addition, an eleventh-hour addition to the law permanently bars persons convicted of a drug-related felony from receiving TANF funds or food stamps unless the state affirmatively opts out of this provision or limits its scope. A high percentage of women in prison were incarcerated for drug-related crimes and many of these women are mothers (Hairston, 1996).

The Personal Responsibility and Work Opportunity Reconciliation Act also tightened eligibility requirements for SSI disability funds and reduces food stamp benefits for eligible households. This law barred legal immigrants from receiving food stamps and SSI benefits until they become U.S. citizens and allowed states to bar legal immigrants from receiving TANF, nonemergency Medicaid, programs funded by the social services block grant, and programs funded entirely by state funds.

The welfare reform law cut funding for the Food Stamp program by more than $27 billion over six years. Reductions in food stamp benefits will average 18 percent, with elderly recipients losing an average of 25 percent and working poor families losing approximately 20 percent (NCLS, 1996). The law also repealed existing requirements that states provide written materials in the language of non-English speaking households and allows states to determine how to best serve those with special needs. Funding for child nutrition programs was decreased by $3 billion over the next five years, reducing funds for the Summer Food program and subsidized meals and snacks served at child care homes and after-school programs, except for day care facilities operated by low-income persons or located in the lowest-income areas (NCLS, 1996). Pregnant women in prisons and juvenile detention facilities are no longer eligible for the Special Supplemental Nutrition program for Women Infants and Children (WIC). The law also allows states to bar undocumented immigrant children from these nutrition programs.

The Balanced Budget Act of 1997 amended some of the harshest provisions of the Personal Responsibility and Work Opportunity Reconciliation Act, amending the law to extend by six months the deadline for certain childhood disability redeterminations, continue Medicaid eligibility for disabled children who lose benefits under SSI, and restore SSI eligibility for legal aliens who are blind or disabled. Even with these amendments, persons likely to be hit hardest by welfare reform are the fastest growing part of the population: immigrants, people of color, single-parent families, and older persons (Murdock & Michael, 1996; Sarri, 1996). The Urban Institute estimates that the welfare reform law will push 1.1 million children into poverty (NCLS, 1996). It is likely that the demand for child welfare services, and kinship care in particular, will be even greater as a result of the implementation of the welfare reform law alone. Recent funding cuts in the Social Services Block Grant, low-income housing subsidies, and drug abuse treatment, and increased incarceration rates resulting from mandatory sentencing laws for drug-related crimes that were passed in the 1990s are likely to substantially increase the impact on vulnerable children and families and the child welfare system (Hairston, 1996).

In 1992, approximately 4.3 million children lived with relatives (CWLA, 1994). While the mothers of the majority of these children also lived in these extended family living arrangements, 878,000 children lived with their grandparents, apart from their birth parents. In addition, an unknown number of children are living with aunts, uncles, and older siblings. The overwhelming majority of these situations are informal kinship care arrangements that occur outside the auspices of the child welfare system. Economic resources vary for kinship caregivers, and it is not known what effect welfare reform will have on the financial supports currently in place that allow extended families to care for children in these informal kinship care arrangements, effectively diverting these children from child welfare caseloads. To what degree will the increased economic vulnerability of older persons as a result of the welfare reform law weaken the informal kinship care arrangements that rely on grandparents and great grandparents? To what degree will tightened eligibility requirements weaken informal kinship care arrangements previously supported with SSI subsidies for disabled children?

Also, it is not yet known how the welfare reform law will influence the use of kinship care as a child welfare service for children in state custody. Clearly, most states have relied heavily on Title IV-A funds to help support kinship care arrangements for children in state custody and living with relatives not licensed as foster parents. The Illinois Home-of-Relative Reform Plan relies heavily on these funds to support families diverted from the child welfare system and to provide a subsidy equal to the state standard of need. With the federal entitlement eliminated, will states continue to provide support for these families? Which kinship caregivers will be exempt from TANF work requirements and time limits? When kinship caregivers are exempt from work requirements and time limits, will these their exemption count as part of the 20 percent exempt from the five-year limit? Kinship caregivers who receive TANF funds for themselves and their biological children are not likely to be exempt from the new requirements; therefore, employment, work requirements, day care, and TANF time limits become concerns of child welfare caseworkers who are considering placing other related children with these kinship caregivers (E. Wattenberg, September 28, 1996, personal communication). The elimination of AFDC and the uncertainty of what income supports states will provide, and to whom, makes reunification, diversion to informal kinship care, and unsubsidized guardianship even more questionable exits from state custody. If children exit state custody to the care of a parent or guardian supported by TANF, it is not known what impact work requirements, availability of good quality day care, and time limits will have on family stability and re-entry rates.

The welfare reform law left Title IV-B child welfare services and IV-E adoption assistance and foster care intact. If the demand for child welfare services does increase, IV-E eligible placements are likely to grow. Even with greater emphasis on short-term services, facilitating appropriate exits from state custody remains a problem. States like Illinois are no longer providing assurances that subsidies will continue to support special-needs adoptions. The maximum adoption subsidy in Illinois has been reduced, a means test has been instituted, cost of living adjustments have been eliminated, and it has been made clear that the adoption subsidy is not an entitlement. The tentative nature of the commitment to adoption subsidies in Illinois has already discouraged some kinship caregivers and some caseworkers from pursuing adoption for some children in kinship care.

Subsidized guardianship is also viewed by some as an uncertain exit from state custody in states where IV-E waivers have been awarded. In Illinois, concerns have been expressed that children and families may be left unsupported when the demonstration project ends in five years. IDCFS officials state that the guardianship subsidy will continue beyond the five years for those children who exit state custody through subsidized guardianship during the demonstration project and that these children will remain eligible for Medicaid. However, recent policy directions in Illinois have left many families and caseworkers doubtful that these commitments will be honored in the future. Strong assurances will need to be made, or it is likely that families and caseworkers will be reluctant to pursue this option.

Managed-care approaches to contracting with private service providers are also likely to play a major role in the next phase of policy development. It is probable that managed-care approaches will push more children toward exits from state custody. However, without a clear purpose and a shared mission, it is not clear that the exits pursued will be those of greatest benefit and most likely to ensure safety, permanency, and well-being for children. Managed-care approaches will stress approaches to service delivery that are time limited. If welfare reform does result in a greater demand for child welfare services, it is also likely that this heavier emphasis on time-limited service will be accompanied by tighter eligibility criteria for accessing child welfare home-based and out-of-home care services. Any efforts to reduce caseloads and costs are likely to be evaluated with measures of case status. However, lower caseloads, shorter length of service, and higher discharge rates are not necessarily measures of success, unless the only goal is to reduce costs. Success should not be equated with merely providing less service, to fewer recipients, for lower costs. Costs of services are interpretable only in relationship to the safety, permanence, and well-being experienced by children and families affected by cost reduction policies.

Responding to the Policy Issues and Trends

The next phase of policy development regarding the use of kinship care as a child welfare service is likely to be as reactive as the first three phases, unless we choose to take this opportunity to clearly define the purpose of kinship care within a mission of facilitating safety, permanence, and well-being for our most vulnerable children. This is a mission that exceeds the reach of the child welfare system working by itself. The child welfare system has long been blamed for the failure to protect children and to ensure that children leave the foster care system for permanent homes in a short time period. For too long the child welfare system has accepted this responsibility and has pursued increased funding to assist in the pursuit of these goals; yet, the child welfare system has no ability to control the conditions of risk that increase the flow of children and families coming to the attention of the child welfare system. In effect, different parts of the child welfare system have been fighting with each other over problems they cannot solve. If our shared mission as a society is to reduce conditions of risk and to increase safety, permanence, and well-being for our most vulnerable children and families, then a much broader vision is required, and child welfare agencies become key in presenting this challenge to others in society who are much further removed from those who are most vulnerable.

Child welfare practitioners have detailed information about the needs of children and families, about factors that contribute to family dissolution, and about factors that strengthen and support families. Sharing this information broadly can be very helpful in articulating a shared mission for all members of society and in shaping policy development by identifying the needs of children and families who come to the attention of the child welfare system, and in identifying the community services and supports that would effectively strengthen and support families, whether these families are headed by birth parents or by informal kinship caregivers. Child welfare practitioners are in an ideal position to identify the need for these community services and supports, while proclaiming the inability of the child welfare system to solve the most fundamental problems that bring children and families to the attention of the child welfare system.

Clearly, if welfare reform is to reduce rather than increase the risks of family dissolution, major investments in job creation, employment training, day care, and a variety of other supportive services are needed in the most depleted communities across the country. In addition, family preservation and support services that states have recently put in place need are needed now more than ever. Efforts to expand Head Start programs, to ensure that poor children receive adequate health care and nutrition, and to integrate services provided to children and families across service systems should continue. It is vitally important that these family preservation and support efforts target informal kinship care arrangements as well as birth families of children at greatest risk of harm and entry into state custody.

One of the best lessons from the history of kinship care policy development in Illinois is the need for creative and multiple approaches to ensuring safety, permanence, and well-being for children who come into contact with the child welfare system. Lessons from Illinois and other states suggest that taking children into state custody unnecessarily should be avoided and that diversion efforts can be facilitated through family conferences, mediation, and other nonadversarial approaches to assisting families with decision making. This is not to say that all informal kinship care arrangements are safe or permanent or support the child's well-being. It is clear, however, that if the only service available to vulnerable children and their families is formal kinship care, demand for this placement service will grow. If, on the other hand, a wide array of services and supports is available to strengthen and support families, including extended families and kinship systems, it is likely that some of these children will be safe, will find permanence, and will demonstrate healthy growth and development, without ever coming into state custody. Given the demographics of children in kinship foster care, it is important that diversion efforts are not used merely to justify refusing needed services to children and families of color, a practice all too common in our country's history (Chipungu, 1991; Hill, 1977; Stehno, 1988).

Clearly, in the current political climate, diversion from the child welfare system and short-term interventions for those entering state custody are preferred over long-term kinship foster care. Diversion and short-term interventions are possible, without losing sight of a mission of safety, permanence, and well-being, if vulnerable families can be supported through family support, family preservation, and basic safety net programs. The success of our efforts must be measured not only with case status variables that measure caseload reduction or growth, length of service, cost of service, and rates of diversion or discharge. Advances in computer information systems and creative use of administrative data have increased reliance on case status and cost variables as outcome indicators (DiNitto, 1996; Hairston, 1996). However, case status and cost are better measures of decisions to open cases, to close cases, and to provide given levels of service than they are measures of child safety, permanence, and child well-being. While the work of Wulczyn (1994) in linking public health and child welfare data bases improves our ability to interpret the meaning of case status changes, efforts to evaluate the degree to which we are achieving our mission require direct involvement of the children, parents, caregivers, and other kin involved in the lives of children who come into contact with the child welfare system. Direct measures of child and family well-being are necessary to evaluate our efforts and to maintain our focus (Altshuler, 1996).

While creative community-based family preservation and support programs are likely to be effective in safely diverting some children from the child welfare system, given projections of economic hardships, the relationship between poverty and placement rates, and the limited number of foster homes, it is likely that kinship care will continue to be a major component of the formal child welfare system for our most vulnerable children and families. Financial supports to caregivers are not likely to be increased in the current political climate. Also, if costs of supporting kinship caregivers grow and become noticeable, as occurred in Illinois, it is predicted that new reform efforts will be aimed at reducing these costs. However, particular care must be taken when decisions are made to provide a lower level of financial support for the care of children in state custody by relatives than is provided for nonrelative foster care. Since children being cared for by relatives are more likely to be children of color, the differential payment policy systematically provides less financial support for the care of these children in state custody than is provided for Caucasian children. While higher foster care rates are based on a standard of care not required in birth families or informal kinship care (IDCFS, 1995a), there are many good reasons for providing an even higher level of financial and other supports to relatives who care for children in state custody than is provided to traditional foster parents. These relative caregivers are more likely to be single females and older and to have more health problems, considerably less income, and greater caregiving burdens than traditional licensed foster parents (Berrick et al., 1994).

However, it is clear that providing financial support to family members is not politically popular. Authors of the Illinois HMR Reform Plan report fighting hard to prevent the General Assembly from reducing reimbursement rates to a level lower than the state standard of need for children who are in state custody but living in unlicensed kinship homes. Hornby and her colleagues recommend that states follow the lead of Illinois, indicating that the level of support provided to anyone caring for a child should be in inverse proportion to that person's legal and social obligation to care for the child (Hornby et al., 1995, p. 18). This reimbursement scheme lessens the gaps between current income support levels for economically disadvantaged parents or informal kinship caregivers, unlicensed relatives caring for children in state custody, and licensed foster parents caring for related or unrelated children in state custody. This scheme is consistent with the prevailing political value of personal responsibility before societal responsibility. The flaw in this scheme is that it invests the least in those who need the most support and provides more resources to support the care of children the further they are removed from their parents and other kin.

The Illinois kinship care funding scheme recommended by Hornby and her colleagues does not provide any guidance to child welfare practitioners regarding their role in helping relatives pursue licensure as foster parents. Clearly, a strong advocate for the child and family could invest a great deal of energy in helping kinship caregivers improve their living arrangements, attend foster parent training, or address other issues that would increase the chances of having their home licensed. When is this the appropriate intervention, and does it contribute to the safety, permanence, and well-being of the child? Should efforts to license kinship homes as foster homes be accompanied by time limits for the receipt of foster care payments for kinship caregivers who are unwilling to adopt or become the legal guardian of the child? When relatives care for children in state custody, is the mission of the child welfare system shared with the kinship caregivers—and how are their roles described in relationship to this mission? How can these roles be described using a model of successful informal kinship care as a model, rather than attempting to redefine these families in the image and likeness of nonrelated foster families? How can society bring its resources to bear to strengthen and support informal and formal kinship care, not to replace or destroy the functioning of these extended family systems?

Some of the most important questions to be addressed in the next phase of kinship care policy development can be addressed with research that focuses specifically on kinship caregivers, children, and parents of children in kinship care (Cimmarusti, 1996; Petras, 1996). The child welfare system has relied heavily on kinship caregivers in recent years. While substantial research has been conducted on adaptation, burden, and supports for spousal caregivers, family caregivers of the frail elderly, and parents caring for disabled children, similar research pertaining to kin caring for abused, neglected, or dependent children is sparse. Clearly, more research is required to determine what is needed to support both informal and formal kinship care arrangements that are essential to the safety, permanence, and well-being of children.

Research is also needed that focuses on birth parents of children in kinship care and their involvement in decision making and planning on behalf of their children (Harris, 1997; O'Donnell, 1995). Some of the more creative work on facilitating kinship adoptions involves birth parents in nonadversarial processes for surrendering their parental rights, redefining family roles and responsibilities, and remaining involved in their child's life in a positive way (Gleeson et al., 1997). Research is also needed that describes the experiences of children living in informal and formal kinship care arrangements (Altshuler, 1996). Ultimately, the best measure of our success as a society will be measured by the well-being of all children and families, including those that come to the attention of the child welfare system.

Perhaps the most important step in creating a shared vision for societal response to vulnerable children and families is to clarify the definition of permanence and to achieve consensus on this definition. The use of kinship care as a child welfare service has highlighted the lack of specificity of this term. If permanence means that a child grows up in a family headed by adults who make a commitment to raise the child to the age of majority, then a very high percentage of formal kinship foster care arrangements qualify as permanent homes. However, inherent in the definition of permanence, and not always articulated, is the intention that permanent homes function without the intrusion and supervision of the child welfare system. Living with birth parents, adoption, and guardianship are preferred permanency goals because they require that legal responsibility for the care of the child exists with the caregiver, not with the child welfare system or the state. If our shared societal mission should be to ensure safety, permanence, and well-being for all children, then the resources assigned to the child welfare system are focused on the most vulnerable children and families, and needed for brief time periods for the majority of children and families that come to the attention of the child welfare system.

Creating a shared mission that focuses on safety, permanence, and well-being for all children, including the most vulnerable in our society, is a challenge in a political climate that emphasizes personal responsibility and minimizes social responsibility. However, this political climate is not the only barrier to creating this shared mission. The history of kinship care policy development in Illinois provides an excellent example of the stalemates that occur when well-meaning persons with different, narrow visions advocate to improve the societal response to vulnerable children and families. Advocacy efforts that are adversarial and focus exclusively on reimbursement rates for kinship caregivers, birth parents, agencies, or taxpayers are likely to prevent the creation of a shared mission. The real challenge of the next phase of kinship care policy development is considerably more challenging. What is needed is a process of consensus building that involves the child welfare system, other government-supported social safety net programs, the business and larger taxpaying community, and the families and communities that are most vulnerable and most likely to be in need of child welfare services.

References

Altshuler, S. J. (1996). *The well-being of children in kinship foster care.* Unpublished doctoral dissertation, University of Illinois at Chicago.

Annie E. Casey Foundation. (1995). *Kids count data book: State profiles of child well-being.* Baltimore, Md.: Author.

Barth, R. P., Courtney, M. E., Berrick, J. D., & Albert V. (1994). *From child abuse to permanency planning: Child welfare services, pathways and placements.* New York: Aldine de Gruyter.

Berrick, J. D., Barth, R. P., & Needell, B. (1994). A comparison of kinship foster homes and foster family homes: Implications for kinship care as family preservation. *Children and Youth Services Review, 16* (1/2), 33–63.

B.H. v. Suter. (1991). No. 88 C 5599 (N.D. Ill.).

Children's Defense Fund. (1995). *The state of America's children yearbook 1995.* Washington, D.C.: Author.

Child Welfare League of America. (1994). *Kinship care: A natural bridge.* Washington, D.C.: Author.

Chipungu, S. S. (1991). A value-based policy framework. In J. E. Everett, S. S. Chipungu, & B. R. Leashore (Eds.), *Child welfare: An Africentric perspective* (pp. 290–305). New Brunswick, N.J.: Rutgers University Press.

Cimmarusti, R. A. (1996). *Caregiver burden of kinship foster care caregivers: Impact of social support on emotional distress.* Doctoral dissertation proposal submitted to the Jane Addams College of Social Work, University of Illinois at Chicago.

Connolly, M. (1994). An act of empowerment: The Children, Young Persons and their Families Act (1989). *British Journal of Social Work, 24,* 87–100.

DiNitto, D. M. (1996). The future of social welfare policy. In P. R. Raffoul & C. A. McNeece (Eds.), *Future issues for social work practice* (pp. 254–265). Needham Heights, Mass.: Allyn & Bacon.

Dubowitz, H., Feigelman, S., Harrington, D., Starr, R., Zuravin, S., & Sawyer, R. (1994). Children in kinship care: How do they fare? *Children and Youth Services Review, 16* (1/2), 85–106.

Dubowitz, H., Feigelman, S., & Zuravin, S. (1993). A profile of kinship care. *Child Welfare, 72,* 153–169.

Gleeson, J. P. (1996). Kinship care as a child welfare service: The policy debate in an era of welfare reform. *Child Welfare, 75* (5), 419–449.

Gleeson, J. P., & Craig, L. C. (1994). Kinship care in child welfare: An analysis of states' policies. *Children and Youth Services Review, 16* (1/2), 7–31.

Gleeson, J. P., O'Donnell, J., & Bonecutter, F. J. (1997). Understanding the complexity of practice in kinship foster care. *Child Welfare, 76,* (6) 801–826.

Goerge, R. M. (1990). The reunification process in substitute care. *Social Service Review, 64,* 422–457.

Goerge, R. M, Wulczyn, F. H., & Harden, A. W. (1995). *Foster care dynamics 1983–1993—California, Illinois, Michigan, New York, and Texas: An update from the multistate foster care data archive.* Chicago: Chapin Hall Center for Children at the University of Chicago.

Hairston, C. F. (1996). Foster care trends and issues. In P. R. Raffoul & C. A. McNeece (Eds.), *Future issues for social work practice* (pp. 151–158). Needham Heights, Mass.: Allyn & Bacon.

Harris, M. S. (1997). *Factors that affect family reunification of African American birth mothers and their children placed in kinship care.* Unpublished doctoral dissertation, Smith College School for Social Work.

Hegar, R. L., & Scannapieco, M. (1995). From family duty to family policy: The evolution of kinship care. *Child Welfare, 74,* 200–216.

Hill, R. B. (1972). *The strengths of black families.* New York: Emerson Hall.

Hill, R. B. (1977). *Informal adoption among Black families.* Washington, D.C.: National Urban League Research Department.

Hornby, H., Zeller, D., & Karraker, D. (1995). *Kinship care in America: A national policy study.* Portland: Edmund S. Muskie Institute of Public Affairs, University of Southern Maine.

IDCFS. (1994, September 1). *Kinship permanency planning project.* Springfield: Illinois Department of Children and Family Services.

IDCFS. (1995a, February 27). *Illinois HMR Reform Plan.* Springfield: Illinois Department of Children and Family Services.

IDCFS. (1995b, July 31). Illinois Title IV-E Waiver Request. Springfield: Illinois Department of Children and Family Services.

Iglehart, A. (1994). Kinship foster care: Placement, service and outcome issues. *Children and Youth Services Review, 16* (1/2), 107–127.

Illinois Department of Children and Family Services & Human Services Technologies. (1994). *Delegated relative authority training manual.* Springfield: Author.

James Bell Associates & Westat (n.d.). *The national survey of current & former foster parents.* Washington, D.C.: U.S. Department of Health and Human Services, Administration for Children and Families, Administration on Children, Youth, and Families.

Kusserow, R. P. (1992a). *Using relatives for foster care.* Washington, D.C.: U.S. Department of Health and Human Services, Office of the Inspector General, OEI-06-90-02390.

Kusserow, R. P. (1992b). *State practices in using relatives for foster care.* Washington, D.C.: U.S. Department of Health and Human Services, Office of the Inspector General, OEI-06-90-02391.

Lindsey, D. (1992). Adequacy of income and foster care placement decision: Using an odds ratio approach to examine client variables. *Social Work Research & Abstracts, 28* (3), 29–36.

Martin, E. P., & Martin, J. M. (1978). *The black extended family.* Chicago: University of Chicago Press.

McDonald, J. (1995, June 14). Written correspondence to the child welfare community regarding FY96 budget appropriations.

McLaughlin, M. E. (1996, September 27). *Response from New York City.* Presented to the Kinship Care Forum, Hunter College School of Social Work.

Meyer, B. S., & Link, M. K. (1990). *Kinship foster care: The double-edged dilemma.* New York: Task Force on Permanency Planning for Foster Children.

Miller v. Youakim. (1976). 431 F. Supp. 40, 45 (N.D. Ill).

Miller v. Youakim. (1979). 440 U.S. 125.

Murdock, S. H., & Michael, M. (1996). Future demographic change: The demand for social welfare services in the twenty-first century. In P. R. Raffoul & C. A. McNeece (Eds.), *Future issues for social work practice* (pp. 3–18). Needham Heights, Mass.: Allyn & Bacon.

National Clearinghouse for Legal Services (NCLS). (1966, September) The federal welfare reform bill: Power, money and responsibility—focus shifts to Springfield. *Illinois Welfare News, 2* (1), 1–20.

National Commission on Family Foster Care. (1991). *A blueprint for fostering infants, children, and youths in the 1990s.* Washington, D.C.: Child Welfare League of America.

O'Donnell, J. M. (1995). *Casework practice with fathers in kinship foster care.* Unpublished doctoral dissertation, University of Illinois at Chicago.

P.A. 89-21. (1995). Illinois Rev. Statutes, June 6.

Pelton, L. H. (1994). The role of material factors in child abuse and neglect. In G. B. Melton & F. D. Barry (Eds.), *Protecting children from abuse and neglect* (pp. 131–181). New York: Guilford.

People v. Thornton, Illinois Appellate Court (1990).

Petras, D. D. (1996). *The effect of caregiver preparation and sense of control on adaptation of kinship caregivers.* Doctoral dissertation proposal submitted to the Jane Addams College of Social Work, University of Illinois at Chicago.

Reid v. McDonald. (1995, June 27). No. 89 J 6195, No. 89 J 6196, *Intervening Plaintiff's Motion for Rule to Show Cause and for Preliminary Injunctive Relief.* Circuit Court of Cook County, Chancery Division.

Reid v. Suter. (1992). No. 89 J 6195, No 89 J 6196, *Order Approving Consent Decree; Consent Decree,* May 20.

Ross, J. L. (1995, May 25). *Services for young foster children.* Washington, D.C.: U.S. General Accounting Office (GAO/HEHS-95-114).

Sarri, R. C. (1996). An agenda for child and youth well-being. In P. R. Raffoul & C. A. McNeece (Eds.), *Future issues for social work practice* (pp. 141–150). Needham Heights, Mass.: Allyn & Bacon.

Schneider, J. (1993, January 15). *B.H. v. Suter.* Monitor's Report from July 1, 1992, to December 31, 1992.

Schuerman, J. R., Rzepnicki, T. L., Littell, J. H., & Chak, A. (1993). *Evaluation of the Illinois Family First Placement Prevention Program: Final Report.* Chicago: Chapin Hall Center for Children, University of Chicago.

Stack, C. (1974). *All our kin: Strategies for survival in a black community.* New York: Harper and Row.

Stehno, S. M. (1988). Public responsibility for dependent Black children. *Social Service Review, 62,* 485–501.

Stein, T., Gambrill, E. D., & Wiltse, K. T. (1978). *Children in foster homes: Achieving continuity of care.* New York: Holt, Rinehart & Winston.

Testa, M. F. (1992). Conditions of risk for substitute care. *Children and Youth Services Review, 14,* 27–36.

Testa, M. F. (1993). *Home-of-relative (HMR) program in Illinois: Interim report (rev.).* Chicago: School of Social Service Administration, University of Chicago.

Testa, M. F. (1995, September 22) *Home-of-relative (HMR) reform in Illinois.* Presented to the Kinship Care Forum, University of Illinois at Chicago.

Testa, M. F., Shook, K. L., Cohen, L., & Woods, M. G. (1996). Permanency planning options for children in formal kinship care. *Child Welfare, 75* (5), 451–470.

Thornton, J. L. (1991). Permanency planning for children in kinship foster homes. *Child Welfare, 70,* 593–601.

Timberlake, E. M., & Chipungu, S. S. (1992). Grandmotherhood: Contemporary meaning among African-American middle-class grandmothers. *Social Work, 37,* 216–222.

Wulczyn, F. (1994). Status at birth and infant placements in New York City. In R. P. Barth, J. D. Berrick, & N. Gilbert (Eds.), *Child welfare research review,* vol. 1 (pp. 146–184). New York: Columbia University Press.

Wulczyn, F. H., & Goerge, R. M. (1992). Foster care in New York and Illinois: The challenge of rapid change. *Social Service Review, 66,* 278–294.

Youakim v. McDonald. (1995). No. 73 C 635 (N.D. Ill.).

Youakim v. McDonald. (1995). No. 73 C 635 N.D. Ill. *Memorandum Opinion and Order,* June 30.

Youakim v. McDonald. (1996). No. 73 C 635 N.D. Ill. *Memorandum Opinion and Order,* July 3.

CHAPTER   4

The Case for Kinship
Adoption Laws

Marianne Takas, J.D.
Rebecca L. Hegar, D.S.W.

At age forty-three, May began caring for the two children of her youngest
daughter, Debra. Both of the children were exposed to crack cocaine in utero
and have serious learning, behavioral, and medical needs. Debra, the children's mother, has been trying unsuccessfully to kick her crack habit for about
five years. Debra knows she can't give the children the stability they need, and
she wants May to raise them. The children's father is in prison on drug
charges, and he agrees that the children should be raised by their grandmother. May doesn't want to end the legal relationship between her grandchildren and their parents, but she wants her own legal position to be as secure
and stable as possible.

Ben and Sarah have two children by birth (both now adults), two by adoption (now teens), and Robby, a three-year-old who has been in their foster care
since birth. Welcoming by nature, they made an extra effort to reach out to
Robby's mother, Tina. For the first six months, Tina, age thirteen at Robby's
birth, wouldn't talk with them or her social worker and wouldn't identify
Robby's father. With time, though, Tina began visiting Robby, then became
close to Sarah. With more time, she revealed to Sarah that Robby was conceived when an uncle raped her. Today Tina is sixteen and visits about once
a month, but she's also pregnant again and trying to finish high school. Robby
has a warm, loving personality, cerebral palsy, and a seizure disorder. Tina
wants Ben and Sarah to raise Robby. Her family agrees, and so does the child
welfare agency. Ben and Sarah want to adopt, but they don't want to undo the
trust they've worked so hard to build with Tina.

What do these two families, and perhaps hundreds of thousands of others, have in common? They are among the many families bound by complex

ties of relationship, friendship, and kinship to children in need of permanency. They want and need stability and security for and with the children in their care, but they often find that existing laws do not work for them.

This chapter describes how a new status of "kinship adoption" could appropriately support, formalize, and protect changing family relationships. Kinship adoption could be an appropriate and needed remedy when it is desired by all parties that a child maintain some level of relationship with one or both birth parents after adoption by a relative, family friend, or foster parent. Before exploring the proposed status of kinship adoption in greater detail, it is important to review how the law now regulates parent/child relationships. At the end of this chapter, we return to the case vignettes highlighting the situations of May and her granddaughter and Ben and Sarah and their foster son, Robby.

PARENT/CHILD RELATIONSHIPS AND THE LAW

The concept of parental rights, which is familiar to those who work in the child welfare field, is at the core of the legal changes proposed in the balance of this chapter. In order to set the context for those proposals, this section reviews the evolution of our cultural thinking about parental rights and their assignment to new adults through adoption or guardianship.

Parental rights originated as paternal rights in the Roman legal tradition that influenced most of Europe, and fathers' rights remained superior to those of mothers in the English Common Law that formed the backbone of the U.S. legal system. During the nineteenth century in both England and the United States, mothers' legal position as parents improved, and the state also began to take an active role in the protection of children from a variety of threats and harms. Although the authority of the state to protect the interests of minors and other legally incompetent people had been established much earlier, it was during the nineteenth century that use of the state's "parens patriae" authority expanded in such areas as education, child labor, juvenile justice, and family law, including guardianship and adoption (Krause, 1995; Trattner, 1994).

The original use of guardianship or wardship for minors was to provide children whose parents had died with other adults who would be legally accountable for managing the property of the children until they were of legal age. Actual care of the children themselves was secondary. Adoption, even of orphaned children, was unknown at English Common Law, and the first adoption statutes in the United States were passed in the mid-1800s (Abbott, 1938). Adoption of children who were not orphaned required either their parents' consent or a court's ruling that dispensed with parents' consent because they were unfit as parents. In our legal system, the practice of terminating the rights of living parents, with or without their consent, is less than 150 years old.

It is interesting to reflect on how recently the state has begun intervening in the parent–child relationship. The status of stepparents, relatives acting in place of parents, and foster parents is still evolving. Frequently, these substitute parents find themselves holding some parental rights and obligations, but not others. If parental authority is generally conceived as being "care, custody, and control" of a child, it is clear that many situations in which care is transferred do not carry with them full custody rights. And even when legal custody has been formally removed from parents, there are residual parental rights that they retain unless all such rights are permanently terminated by court action.

Among the rights retained by parents, even when someone else has custody of their child, are the authority to grant or withhold permission to receive medical care, to marry, to join the armed forces, or to be adopted (Krause, 1995). In most situations, children in the custody of the state and in the physical care of relatives or foster parents also have parents who retain these residual parental rights. The same is true of children who have both court-appointed guardians and living parents whose rights have not been terminated.

Reform and Rights Movements in Child Welfare

The past thirty years have brought rapid growth in the number and proportion of children who are adopted, in foster care, and in informal placement with relatives and others. The number of these children and growing professional and public awareness of their needs have led to considerable debate and some significant shifts in social policy concerning children who are not in their parents' care. The permanency planning movement, the adoptee search movement, and the grandparents' rights movement are among the major efforts to effect social change that have direct bearing on the present question of new legal statuses for children in kinship care. Each of these recent social movements is reviewed here.

Permanency planning. In early child welfare practice, it was not unusual for children who entered care to grow up in institutions or foster homes (Mass & Engler, 1956; Theis & Goodrich, 1921). However, beginning in the 1950s, theorists and researchers came to believe that an irreplaceable bond between mother and child made substitute care, particularly institutional care, harmful to children (Bowlby, 1952). Foster care also became less stable as social changes took hold in the 1960s. Some of this lack of stability probably was due to changes in the population of children in foster care. For example, as child abuse became more widely recognized, abused children with serious special needs entered foster care in greater numbers. Other changes in the stability of foster care occurred when more foster families, like other families, moved, divorced, or followed a two-career pattern, sometimes necessitating replacement of children in their care. Then in 1972, the psychiatric and legal team of Goldstein, Freud, and Solnit published a seminal book that proposed that the relationships young children develop with the "psychological parents" who meet their daily needs for care and nurture should receive legal recognition and protection. They also argued that custody matters require resolution within the "child's sense of time," which is shorter than that of adults. Their work indicted a foster care system that had come to involve frequent moves from home to home and that offered little hope of permanence (Goldstein, Freud, & Solnit, 1972).

The permanency planning movement that followed sought ways to move children through the foster care system and back to their own families or into other permanent homes through adoption. It began with federally funded demonstration projects (Emlen et al., 1978) and was institutionalized in 1980 with the passage of Public Law 96-272. As a movement, it produced much of the existing landscape of child welfare practice, including: efforts to avoid placement by preserving families; court adjudication of all children entering public foster care; placement in the least restrictive appropriate setting; periodic court reviews of children in care; family team conferences to plan for children in foster care; and liberalized termination of parental rights statutes.

Adoptee search.   When children were adopted by nonrelatives in early U.S. adoption practice, contact with the birth family ordinarily ended. Sometimes a change of geographic venue ensured lack of contact, as when the Children's Aid Society took children by "orphan train" from East Coast cities to farms and small towns in the Midwest and West (Cook, 1995; Trattner, 1994). Adoption laws that sealed original birth records and reissued birth certificates not only insulated children from birth families but allowed some adoptive families to hide the fact of adoption. Frankness about adoption came slowly as the stigma associated with infertility and illegitimacy declined. Most recently, the search by adoptees for family and roots has broken wide open the unofficial secrecy surrounding adoption, and it has begun to crack official, court-sanctioned secrecy, as well.

Registries that allow willing birth mothers and adult adoptees to contact each other have become common, as have searches outside the protection of registries. "Open adoptions" also have evolved, allowing varying degrees of ongoing contact between birth parents and adopted children. Over a thirty-year period, the efforts of adoptees and birth parents have changed the assumptions and expectations that underlie adoption itself.

Grandparents' rights.   The grandparents' rights movement has been fueled by two social trends: situations where grandparents assume care of children when neither parent is able to provide a home for them, and marriages that end in divorce, potentially limiting contact between children and relatives of the noncustodial parent. The issue of access for extended family members, especially for grandparents, led as far as a series of congressional hearings in 1982 (Hearings, 1982) and a proposed federal "Grandparents Raising Grandchildren Assistance Act of 1993" (Waysdorf, 1994).

In general, access to children is granted by parents to whichever relatives they wish. However, in cases of divorce or death of a parent, courts and legislatures have begun to intervene when the custodial or surviving parent denies visitation to grandparents (McCrimmon & Howell, 1989; Myers & Perrin, 1993). For several years, all U.S. states and the District of Columbia have had statutes addressing access for grandparents (McCrimmon & Howell, 1989). Although the "grandparents' rights" movement has been successful in securing laws permitting grandparents to petition for access to grandchildren in custody disputes, the same is not true in adoption situations (Oppenheim &

Bussiere, 1996). Even in custody disputes, the legal position of other relatives is also much less clear.

Although the national phenomenon of grandparents raising grandchildren has reached the popular press and the self-help book market (Creighton, 1991; DeToledo, 1995; Takas, 1995), as well as being a focus for professional intervention and academic study (Burton, 1992; Chalfie, 1994; Jones & Kennedy, 1996; Minkler & Roe, 1993) and for policy and legal advocacy (Czapanskiy, 1994; Hanson & Opsahl, 1996; Waysdorf, 1994), it has yet to produce much legal change that could help custodial grandparents. One exception is that adoption laws in several states (California, Colorado, Kansas, Minnesota) now express a preference for relatives as adopters (Oppenheim & Bussiere, 1996). However, without changes in the institution of adoption to make it more suited to kinship adoption, the number of formal adoptions by relatives may remain low. Like lack of permanency for children in foster care and the felt need of many adoptees to search for biological kin, the needs of children being raised by grandparents and other relatives continue to challenge the child welfare system and family law to find appropriate solutions.

Existing Options for Relatives Raising Children

Guardianship. Guardianship is a type of legal custody that courts in many jurisdictions can grant to caregiving adults who want some legal protection of their relationship with the children they are raising. Guardianship may work well for some families, but it has several limitations under the laws of most states.

First, guardianship is not as legally secure as adoption. For example, suppose that foster parents Ben and Sarah became guardians and raised Robby for ten years, after which time Tina sought custody as his mother. Ben and Sarah could lose custody, and Robby could lose the family he had had since birth. If Ben and Sarah prevailed, chances are Tina would be further alienated and estranged.

Second, guardianship does not qualify for federally supported adoption subsidies for special-needs children. Welfare reform and decentralization further complicate the financial position of guardians and relatives who are raising children informally (Mullen, 1996). Both of the families described at the beginning of the chapter could face severe financial strain trying to raise their special-needs children without some subsidy and Medicaid coverage.

Third, many group health care providers cover only the birth or adoptive children of the subscriber. For example, if May had health care coverage through her employer, it might not cover her grandchildren, even if she became their guardian.

Finally, guardianship is typically granted in a probate court, with rules and procedures that focus on property concerns rather than child welfare. Depending on the jurisdiction, the family might learn that the probate court would not allow a case to be filed unless the child owned money or property. Or the guardians might be required to come back once a year to file a report about their finances.

Adoption. Adoption is a much more permanent and secure legal option, which typically requires the complete and permanent termination of all legal aspects of the original parent/child relationship. Like guardianship, it may not meet the needs of many relative caregivers.

In many cases, the required termination of parental rights could strain relationships and set back hard-won gains. Grandmother May, for example, would be encouraged to view her daughter's involvement with the children as legally hostile to her own. Ironically, the legal system is imposing a standard that neither of these families may need or want. In addition, termination may unnecessarily sever the child from advantages, however limited, that the family of birth can offer. Perhaps the father of May's grandchildren could, through prison employment or upon release, pay child support. However, the end of the legal relationship between parent and child would also end that obligation. Other benefits through the birth parents, such as health care coverage, social security survivor benefits, or inheritance, could also be lost. And, although the law does not preclude postadoptive visits, current adoption law typically offers little or no legal protection for such contact.

Further, current adoption laws may decrease the likelihood of agreement to the adoption. Robby's mother, Tina, may feel comfortable knowing that Ben and Sarah, who have fostered Robby and welcomed her, will be his family until adulthood. But will she really be able to sign a paper that completely severs her legal relationship with Robby? Quite possibly, the agreement will fall through, Robby will linger in foster care status, and a child welfare agency will spend months or years pursuing a painful, expensive, and possibly unsuccessful action to terminate her rights.

Need for new models. It is not surprising that neither guardianship nor adoption fits the needs of families with ongoing relationships. Both adoption and guardianship evolved as legal remedies to situations quite different from most kinship care cases. As we have discussed, modern adoption law developed primarily to provide permanent care to young children by persons formerly unknown to the child's family of birth. Guardianship law developed primarily to address cases in which the loss of parental care was due to death. Although both adoption and guardianship have been used successfully in many cases, neither is intentionally and optimally designed to meet the needs of families in which one or both parents are living and are important to the child, the parent(s) cannot safely care for the child, and a relative or family friend wishes to provide permanent care.

The law can, however, be adapted to meet changing or newly recognized needs. For example, there is already a major exception to the rule that termination of all existing parental rights must precede an adoption. That exception is stepparent adoption. For example, when a woman marries or remarries and her new husband wishes to adopt her child, we do not require that the mother first relinquish her parental rights. Rather, if the child's father is deceased, relinquishes his parental rights, or has them terminated, the stepfather may adopt in his stead. This simple, sensible adaptation of early adoption law recognized that changing families may require laws that appropriately formalize new relationships, without unnecessarily disturbing existing ones.

Many within the child welfare field recognize that neither guardianship nor adoption is well suited for permanence with kin, but efforts to improve the fit have been limited primarily to improving guardianship. One such proposal, by Czapanskiy (1994), for "co-guardianship contracts" between co-parenting parents and grandparents, would accomplish some of the same goals as the proposals we make later in this chapter.

Other reform proposals and efforts have focused more on the financial drawbacks of guardianship than on its legal and practical shortcomings. It is a widely recognized concern that persons who assume guardianship cannot qualify for federally supported subsides for adoption of children with special needs. A report of the Inspector General of the U.S. Department of Health and Human Services recommended in 1992 that the Administration for Children and Families study the potential costs and benefits of providing such subsidies, noting that the same cost-benefit arguments that apply to adoption subsidies may also apply to subsidized guardianship. At least ten states (Alaska, California, Colorado, Hawaii, Illinois, Massachusetts, Nebraska, New Mexico, South Dakota, and Washington) use their own funds to provide subsidized guardianship to relatives as needed to avoid continued foster care (Schwartz, 1993). Three states (Delaware, Illinois, and Maryland) have requested waivers that would allow them to use federal funds for subsidized guardianship as part of a child welfare demonstration program (O'Connor, 1995).

Adapting adoption to fit relative caregivers has received less scholarly, legislative, and administrative attention. There may be an assumption that family members and friends are not interested in adopting their kin. Yet many relatives do favor the increased legal protections of adoption, at least when reasonably flexible arrangements are offered to them (Testa, 1993). If kinship adoptions could further be supported by more appropriate laws, it appears likely that more families would find them attractive.

Kinship Adoption as a New Alternative

A new legal category of kinship adoption could be legislatively developed to allow all the permanence of adoption, without completely extinguishing every aspect of the relationship between the children and both birth parents. Kinship adoption could involve either or both of two key differences from traditional adoption:

1. relinquishment or termination of the parental rights of **one but not both** parents (as in stepparent adoption), and/or

2. relinquishment or termination of **some but not all** parental rights of both parents (similar to open adoption with enforceable postadoptive visitation)

In either case, the relinquishment or termination of rights would be immediately followed by a full assumption of parental rights and responsibilities by the adopting kin. The child and the adopting kin would have the security of knowing the care arrangement was permanent and legally secure. At the same time, the relationship between the child and birth parent would be disrupted only to the extent actually needed, based on the child's and the family's individual circumstances. The birth parent and the adopting kin would be recognized as having potentially complementary positions, rather than automatically antagonistic ones. This would be the appropriate legal solution to a case presented in the literature by Kurtz (1994) in which the court terminated the rights of an interested noncustodial father in order to provide permanence in the home of the relative who had reared his daughter (the mother was deceased). Kurtz observes that "where eliminating parents who are fit, interested, known to the children, and related to their caretaker is unnecessary, it is an unmitigated harm" (1994, p. 1497).

Although the concept of kinship adoption reevaluates past assumptions about adoption, the sharing of parental responsibility has strong legal precedent. For example, when parents are divorced or live apart, one parent generally assumes the custodial role, with full parental rights and responsibilities. That custodial role coexists, however, with the residual rights and legally defined responsibilities of the noncustodial parent. Stepparents, grandparents, and, sometimes, other relatives also may have legally protected rights to play a role in the child's life, as we have discussed (Victor et al., 1991, p. 19). Most families manage to balance the various roles, which may benefit the child.

By comparison, in a kinship adoption the adopting relative could (like typical custodial parents) provide full parental care, while one or both birth parents could (like noncustodial parents) maintain a more limited role. Although some conflicts would doubtless arise, the kinship adopter would actually have a more secure parental role than a custodial parent after a divorce, because custody would be permanently established.

Because kinship adoption would be statutorily created as a form of adoption, kinship adopters of qualifying special-needs children would be eligible to receive federally reimbursed adoption subsidies.

Kinship adoption by relinquishment or termination of *one parent's* parental rights.　　In many child welfare cases, the two parents of a given child in need of protection have different circumstances, needs, and levels of interest in the child. Frequently, one of the parents, although unable to provide primary care to the child in the foreseeable future, does not wish to relinquish parental rights and may not meet state grounds for termination of parental rights. The other parent may be deceased, unknown, in jail for a period exceeding the child's minority, wish to relinquish parental rights, or meet state grounds for termination of parental rights due to abandonment or continuous abuse or neglect.

In these cases, it would make perfect sense to seek relinquishment or termination of the latter parent's rights, then allow a kinship caregiver to adopt the child in that parent's stead. This form of kinship adoption would closely parallel the already common remedy of stepparent adoption. As in stepparent adoption, there would be two legal parents to the child: the birth parent, who would retain undisturbed rights, and the kinship adopter.

Instead of care responsibilities being shared between, for example, the child's mother and stepfather, they might be shared between the mother and the grandmother. It is true that mother and grandmother might not live together, and the court order granting adoption might need to allocate custodial responsibilities between them. Yet the same would be true in any divorce or separation of two parents.

One-adopter kinship adoption might be particularly well suited to cases of entrenched domestic violence. A common scenario involves a father with a long history of violence and/or sexual abuse toward the child, violence toward the child's mother, and threats or violence to other family members. The mother, who may not be abusive, may be only marginally capable of caring for and protecting the child. In such a case, termination of only the violent parent's rights might be entirely appropriate. Securing such termination, maintaining the mother's parental rights, and allowing a kinship adoption might be precisely the steps needed to provide care, protection, and healing for the child.

Kinship adoption by relinquishment or termination of some *but not all* parental rights.   Another typical case profile involves two parents, neither of whom will be able to resume primary care of the child, at least within any time frame that respects the child's need for timely permanence. Yet the child and the parents may have emotional ties that it would be beneficial to preserve. The parents, not wanting to abandon the child, may refuse to relinquish full parental rights. The judge, seeing that the parents are trying, may hesitate to terminate parental rights. This standoff ultimately hurts the child, who needs a permanent, secure relationship with a person who can provide daily parental care.

This common situation may be ideal for kinship adoption by relinquishment of some but not all parental rights. It would require, at a minimum, the permanent relinquishment or termination of the custodial rights of both parents. Other parental rights and responsibilities, however, could be relinquished or terminated according to the agreement of the parties and the needs of the child. The adopting kinship caregiver would assume full parental rights and responsibilities, as in any other adoption.

A kinship adoption would thus involve the permanent creation of a new parental relationship, while leaving in effect some aspects of the relationship between birth parent and child, such as appropriate visitation and access to school records. In effect, the kinship adopter would become the child's permanent legal parent, while the birth parent(s) would remain noncustodial parent(s) with legally defined roles.

This approach could be used to afford legal protection in some of the situations in which children who have always lived with their grandmother regard their birth mother as they might an aunt or older sister. The stigma, conflict, and potential loss entailed in termination of all parental rights could be avoided when it is unnecessary (Garrison, 1993; Hardin & Dodson, 1983, pp. 128–134).

The remaining rights of birth parents would have the full force of nonextinguished parental rights. Judicial remedies for enforcement, however, would not involve a disturbance of the adoptive relationship. More traditional remedies such as supervised visits and contempt powers could be used.

The parental responsibility of child support should be carefully considered in any kinship adoption legislation. Although retention of a child support obligation might provide a benefit to the adopters, it could provide a disincentive to voluntary agreement by the birth parent. A possible compromise might be to include in the kinship adoption statute special authority to specify in a kinship adoption agreement, if desired by the parties, a limited child support obligation, exempt from current or future state child support guidelines.

Under kinship adoption legislation, counsel could assist the parties to formulate a workable kinship adoption plan. For example, a parent might agree to relinquish custodial rights permanently, to retain rights to monthly visits and access to school records, and to retain a limited child support obligation of $50 per month. If acceptable to the kinship adopters and appropriate to the child's needs, the agreement could then be submitted for court approval as part of a kinship adoption. Counsel for each party should take care to ensure that the client is fully informed and understands the agreement and its implications to the limits of age and ability. Informed consent of older children being adopted should be required. In child welfare cases, the child welfare agency would be involved in negotiations about the plan, either through their legal counsel who is negotiating with counsel for the parties or by the caseworker who works directly with the parties.

A completed kinship adoption would not prevent the adopters or a child welfare agency from later seeking the complete termination of parental rights, if required for the continuing safety of the child within the kinship adoptive home. In that event, rights already surrendered or terminated would be foreclosed from further contest, and the only issue before the court would be whether to terminate any remaining parental rights.

How "Kinship Adoption" Differs From "Open Adoption"

Many families, and some child welfare agencies, currently make use in kinship cases of the practice known as open adoption. Family members may adopt a child, while encouraging one or both birth parents to visit, even after the adoption is completed. It may be asked, therefore, how "kinship adoption" differs from "open adoption," and why new legislation is needed.

Although open adoption can be used effectively in many cases, it has major limitations. Postadoption visitation, the key feature of open adoptions, is in most states either unenforceable or of unclear enforceability. Parties can agree in writing to allow such visitation and may even persuade a judge to incorporate the written agreement into the adoption decree. In all but a few states, however, if there is a later conflict, the birth parent who wishes to exercise the agreed visitation has no clearly enforceable right.

In a typical case that illustrates the problem, *Hill v. Moorman* (1988), the parties agreed in writing to permit postadoption visitation, and the court that granted the adoption appended the agreement to the adoption decree. Later, the adoptive parents changed their minds and denied a birth parent access to the child. The birth parent contested, and an appellate court held that the birth parent had no legal standing to seek visitation under state adoption law, which, like most states today, extinguished all birth parent rights upon an adoption.

In a few states, postadoption visitation is legally established and apparently enforceable. Indiana has particularly clear language that allows parties to incorporate a written agreement into an adoption decree (much as separation agreements are routinely incorporated into divorce decrees) and also allows a court, at a later time, to enforce, not enforce, or modify the provisions, on the basis of the best interests of the child (Annotated Indiana Code, Chap. 31, Sec. 3-1-13). New York's provisions are considerably less clear, with the term "conditional consent to adoption" raising at least some risk that a later visitation conflict could actually jeopardize a completed adoption (N.Y. Social Services Law 383-(2)).

Even if open adoption is firmly, clearly, and appropriately established by state law, it still differs significantly from the concept of kinship adoption described here. The most obvious differences concern one-parent kinship adoption, as described, which is more similar to stepparent adoption than to open adoption. Although perhaps the most logically compelling form of kinship adoption and the least difficult to render in enabling legislation, one-parent kinship adoption is currently unknown in state law.

Kinship adoption with termination of some but not all parental rights is also distinct from open adoption, in that it is more flexible and offers a wider range of possible parental roles. It allows a birth parent to remain a parent, legally and perhaps psychologically, to the degree and in a manner that may benefit the child. It could, for example, allow a limited child support obligation to continue, or it could provide that a birth parent will care for the child each day after school. For some birth parents, the mere fact that it does not require the parent to say legally "You are no longer my child" may render it more acceptable than other adoption options. While clearly not for every family, kinship adoption may both facilitate agreement and allow for pooled resources in some situations.

Focusing on these differences, the basic distinction becomes clear. Open adoption is designed to keep alive, in some small way, a birth bond that would otherwise be lost. Kinship adoption's primary purpose is to maintain those parental bonds that are working, end those that work against the child, and supplement others with a new or additional parental relationship.

Open adoption, as shaped by any of the means currently available, can be an innovative, creative, and caring way for kinship families to adopt. It remains, however, a band-aid on a serious legal rupture. Although it may be the best available choice for an individual family today, it is not an adequate substitute for specific, carefully drafted kinship adoption legislation.

CONCLUSION

Sound laws can be powerful tools to preserve and protect families. Like any other tools, they must fit the job. Adoption laws designed primarily for families unknown to one another, or guardianship laws designed primarily for cases of parental death, cannot adequately serve many of today's kinship families. Kinship adoption legislation can provide a more appropriate tool. It can be designed to assist families who need both more protection than guardianship law offers and more flexibility than current adoption law allows.

Kinship adoption would be a natural adaptation to trends and forces that have shaped child placement for some time: conviction that relatives are natural caregivers for children who are kin to them; recognition of children's need for permanence and stability; understanding of the importance to adoptees of information about their birth families, and knowledge of the key role played by grandparents and other relatives in the lives of many children, particularly when parents are absent or troubled.

Kinship adoption would extend well-established legal problem solving into a new realm. Parental rights are recognized to be a bundle of responsibilities and claims that can, when necessary, be divided between separating parents or between the state and parents of children in foster care. Kinship adoption following partial termination of parental rights would allow similar division of parental rights between custodial relatives and birth parents. Similarly, one-parent kinship adoption would extend the logic of stepparent adoption to permit a relative or friend to step into the place of a parent who relinquishes rights or has them terminated.

Although every family is different, the legal needs of the families profiled in this chapter are typical. Unfortunately, endings to such familiar family stories rarely involve legal solutions that are both durable and flexible. Such endings could become more common. Enacting kinship adoption legislation would be reasonably straightforward, and it is the right thing to do for many children and their caregiving relatives and friends. The families discussed at the beginning of this chapter benefit from a kinship adoption law as follows.

May, who has limited income, talked to a legal aid lawyer about the needs of her two grandchildren. She learned that, by using her state's new kinship adoption statue, she could adopt her grandchildren without completely severing their relationship with their parents. May would be able to do anything a parent could: enroll them in school, consent to medical treatment, obtain social security benefits for them in her name, and make family decisions without having to go back to court. Because the children qualify under the special-needs adoption rules of the state, she could also obtain an adoption supplement and Medicaid coverage for them. May decided that, because neither parent was violent or abusive, she was comfortable with their continued involvement. Each parent would agree only to the permanent termination of custody rights; all other rights would remain in force. Both parents agreed, and the matter was quickly and quietly settled by filing a written agreement with the state's court for family cases. Debra is still trying to kick her crack habit, but at least she has more motivation. Her children are permanently with her mother, but she has a recognized role in their lives.

Through the intervention of the child welfare agency, the criminal actions of Tina's uncle were duly reported to law enforcement. He plead guilty to statutory rape and child molestation under a plea bargain arrangement, and he willingly relinquished all parental rights to Robby. Under the state's new kinship adoption law, this extinguishment of the father's rights would have been sufficient, if Tina consented, to allow adoption by at least one kinship adopter. Yet Ben and Sarah, after discussing their needs with an attorney provided through a prepaid legal plan for foster parents, decided they wanted more security. They asked that Tina also agree to give up custody permanently, making it possible for both of them to adopt. Tina would retain all other rights, and they hoped she would continue to visit regularly. The caseworker, on behalf of the agency, agreed and talked with Tina about the request. After talking with her court-appointed attorney, Tina also agreed. The agreement was made in writing and submitted to the juvenile court, which formalized the adoption. Because of Robby's medical condition, he qualified for a special-needs adoption subsidy and Medicaid coverage. Tina has since had her new baby, whom she sometimes brings to her visits with Robby. "Ben and Sarah are sort of like parents to us all," she says. "I'm glad that Robby can have them, without us all losing each other."

References

Abbott, G. (1938). Adoption introduction. In G. Abbott (Ed.), *The child and the state,* vol. 2 (pp.164–171). Chicago: University of Chicago Press.

Bowlby, J. (1952). *Maternal care and mental health.* Geneva: World Health Organization.

Burton, L. (1992). Black grandparents rearing children of drug-addicted parents: Stressors, outcomes, and social needs. *Gerontologist, 32,* 744–751.

Chalfie, D. (1994). *Going it alone: A closer look at grandparents parenting grandchildren.* Washington, D.C.: American Association of Retired Persons.

Cook, J. F. (1995). A history of placing-out: The orphan trains. *Child Welfare, 74,* 181–197.

Creighton, L. (1991, December 16). Grandparents: The silent saviors. *U.S. News & World Report,* pp. 80–89.

Czapanskiy, K. (1994). Grandparents, parents, and grandchildren: Actualizing interdependence in law. *Connecticut Law Review, 26*(4), 1315–1375.

DeToledo, S. (1995). *Grandparents as parents: A survival guide for raising a second family.* New York: Guilford.

Emlen, A., Lahti, J., Downs, G., McKay, A., & Downs, S. (1978). *Overcoming barriers to planning for children in foster care.* Washington, D.C.: U.S. Government Printing Office.

Garrison, M. (1983). Why terminate parental rights? *Stanford Law Review, 39,* 423–496.

Goldstein, J., Freud, A., & Solnit, A. (1972). *Beyond the best interest of the child.* New York: Free Press.

Hanson, L., & Opsahl, I. (1996). Kinship caregiving: Law and policy. *Clearinghouse Review, 30*(5), 481–501.

Hardin, M., & Dodson, D. (1983). *Foster children in the courts.* Boston: Butterworth Legal Publishers.

Hearings Before the Subcommittee on Human Services of the Select Committee on Aging, House of Representatives, 97th Congress, 2d Session. (1982). *Grandparents: The other victims of divorce and custody disputes.*

Hill v. Moorman, 525 So.2d 681 (La. Ct. App. 1988).

Jones, L., & Kennedy, J. (1996). Grandparents united: Intergenerational developmental education. *Child Welfare, 75* (5), 636–650.

Krause, H. (1995). *Family law in a nutshell.* (3rd ed.). St. Paul, Minn.: West.

Kurtz, M. (1994). The purchase of families into foster care: Two case studies and the lessons they teach. *Connecticut Law Review, 26*(4), 1453–1524.

Maas, H. S., & Engler, R. E. (1959). *Children in need of parents.* New York: Columbia University Press.

McCrimmon, C. A., & Howell, R. J. (1989). Grandparents' legal rights to visitation in the fifty states and the District of Columbia. *Bulletin of the American Academy of Psychiatry and the Law, 17* (4), 355–366.

Minkler, M., & Roe, K. M. (1993). *Grandmothers as caregivers: Raising children of the crack cocaine epidemic.* Newbury Park, Calif.: Sage.

Mullen, F. (1996). Public benefits: Grandparents, grandchildren, and welfare reform. *Generations, 20,* 61–64.

Myers, J. E., & Perrin, N. (1993). Grandparents affected by parental divorce: A population at risk? *Journal of Counseling and Development, 72* (1), 62–66.

O'Connor, M. (1995). Federal legislation update. *The National Advocate* (publication of the National Foster Parent Association).

Office of Inspector General, U.S. Department of Health and Human Services. (1992). *Using relatives for foster care.* Washington, D.C.: U.S. Government Printing Office.

Oppenheim, E., & Bussiere, A. (1996). Adoption: Where do relatives stand? *Child Welfare, 75,* 471–488.

Schwartz, M. (1993). *Reinventing guardianship: Subsidized guardianship, co-guardians and child welfare.* New York: Vera Institute of Justice.

Takas, M. (1995). *Grandparents raising grandchildren: A guide to finding help and hope.* New York: Brookdale Foundation Group.

Testa, M. (1993). Home of relative program in Illinois: Interim report. Chicago: School of Social Work, University of Chicago.

Theis, S., & Goodrich, C. (1921). *The child in the foster home* (Series in social work, child welfare series, no. 2). New York: New York School of Social Work.

Trattner, W. I. (1994). *From poor law to welfare state: A history of social welfare in America* (5th ed.). New York: Free Press.

Victor, R., et al. (1991). Statutory review of third-party rights regarding custody, visitation, and support. *Family Law Quarterly, 25,* 19–57.

Waysdorf, S. (1994). Families in the AIDS crisis: Access, equality, empowerment, and the role of kinship caregivers. *Texas Journal of Women and the Law, 3,* 145–220.

PART II

Kinship
Care
Practice

CHAPTER 5

Formal Kinship Care Practice Models

MARIA SCANNAPIECO, PH.D.

Kinship care has become an integral program option along the continuum of service options in the child welfare system. This chapter presents the current kinship care service delivery models used by public child welfare institutions. Among the "new" practice principles that have been promulgated recently, some are sensitive and informed for working with kinship care networks (see special edition of Child Welfare [1996], 75, 5; chapters 6 and 7 in this book), but these are not universally employed by child welfare programs. And although states are beginning to address the different needs of kinship care, kinship care is not usually viewed as a separate program. State policies and practices vary widely (Gleeson & Craig, 1994; Kusserow, 1992), and, as evidenced by this book and prior special journal issues, child welfare professionals are struggling to institute guidelines to promote the appropriate use of kinship care as a viable resource for families and children.

Kinship care, as a formal placement option, gained acceptance and usage so quickly that practice models have not been able to keep pace and meet the unique needs of relatives. States typically view kinship care in three ways: as a diversion from out-of-home care, as a type of foster care, or as a means of ensuring family preservation. Most states have not yet defined kinship care as a separate, unique program.

This chapter presents the current state of practice for children who reside with relatives and are involved with the child welfare system, and it discusses some of the more intriguing practice principles circulated in the kinship care literature. It is estimated that between 31 percent and 57 percent of foster parents are kinship caregivers (Takas, 1993; Testa et al., 1996). (It is important to note that this chapter does not discuss programs designed for the large number of kinship caregivers and the children residing with them that are outside the formal child welfare system.) The Census Bureau estimates that in 1993, approximately 3.4 million children in the United States lived with grandparents, a 44 percent increase since 1980 (Saluter, 1993). Many live in or near poverty, since 10 percent of the 7.7 million children on Aid to Families with Dependent Children (AFDC) in the United States live with relatives (National Commission on Family Foster Care, 1991).

CONCEPTUAL FRAMEWORK

The child welfare system provides services to kinship families through one of two federal funding programs: the program formerly known as AFDC, and the foster care program. Kinship care programs are placed in a framework defined primarily by the funding source and secondarily by the continuum of services: diversion, foster care, or family preservation. The decision-making process that takes place within this framework should be based on an assessment of the families' and the children's needs, permanency planning issues, risk and safety issues, and family preservation concerns. Not all kinship care situations need to involve the formal foster care system, if the extended family circumstances are such that they need an income transfer but not services, then a diversion program is appropriate. On the other hand, if there are risk factors associated with the case, then the more formal foster care program would be appropriate. In the discussion on conceptual framework, it is recognized that case decision making should distinguish among the different programs and select the most appropriate for the specific family.

The Program Formerly Known as AFDC

Prior to October 1, 1996, Aid to Families with Dependent Children (AFDC) was the funding source for many kinship caregivers in the child welfare system. AFDC was the oldest federal public assistance program, enacted in 1935 as part of the larger Social Security Act. The Personal Responsibility and Work Opportunity Reconciliation Act of 1996 (PRWOR) will now begin to replace AFDC. The provisions of this new welfare law bear the title *Part A—Block Grants to States for Temporary Assistance for Needy Families (Conference Report. HR 3734)*. With the enactment of PRWOR, kinship caregivers must now rely on states to be compassionate and responsive in making policy decisions about the distribution of funds through the block grants.

The welfare reform debate neglected kinship caregivers in its analyses of public policies concerning AFDC. It remains to be seen what implications there are for kinship caregivers in the welfare reform, but the PRWOR does specifically address relatives. Two examples are: ". . . parent or caretaker receiving assistance under the program to engage in work . . . once the State determines the parent or caretaker has received assistance under the program for 24 months (whether or not consecutive), whichever is earlier . . ." (Sec.402(a)(1)(a)(ii); and ". . . parents and caretakers engage in work activities . . ." (Sec.402(a)(1)(A)(iii).

Clearly, there are inconsistencies between the requirements of the new welfare reform and the needs of kinship caregivers and the children in their care (Mullen, 1996). The two-year limit on benefits is in direct opposition to the child welfare permanency planning and family preservation philosophy. Long-term and permanent living arrangements may be in the best interest of children in kinship care. Often children come to live with grandparents, aunts, and uncles after a parent has died of AIDS, has continued to chronically abuse drugs, or has been incarcerated. In these circumstances, it is hoped that the child will remain with the kinship caregiver for many years. The programs described in this section are currently using welfare money in support of kinship care.

Foster Care Program

The second federal funding program is foster care though the Adoption Assistance and Child Welfare Act of 1980, P.L. 96-272, for which relative caregivers who meet licensing standards are eligible (*Miller v. Youakim*). Under 96-272, children must be placed in the least restrictive, most family-like environment. Although the federal foster care statute does not mention relative or kinship caregivers as potential options for out-of-home care for children, kinship care has been interpreted as embodying the values of the law. The *Miller v. Youakim* decision gives relatives the same rights as nonrelatives to foster care payments.

States have a dual system of funding foster care. The first system involves joint payments by the federal and the state governments; the second is a state-only financed system (Killackey, 1992). The federal-state system provides payments known as Aid to Families with Dependent Children–Foster Care (AFDC-FC). Kin may be eligible for AFDC-FC payment if the following criteria are met:

- The child must have been receiving or eligible to receive AFDC benefits prior to placement in the kinship care home.
- The child must have been removed from the home as a result of a judicial determination that his or her safety needs and well-being were being jeopardized in the biological home.
- The placement and care of the child is the responsibility of the state and the child welfare agency.
- The home meets the foster care licensing requirements of the state.

AFDC-FC–financed foster care covers about half of the children in out-of-home care (Courtney, 1996), while state-funded programs cover the payments for the children who are not eligible for benefits under the federal program. It should be noted that *Miller v. Youakim* covers only the AFDC-FC financed program. State-only funded foster care programs are not required by the Supreme Court to compensate relatives and nonrelatives equally.

KINSHIP CARE PRACTICE MODELS

The first set of case management models for kinship care is defined by financial support through the welfare system (Personal Responsibility and Work Opportunity Reconciliation Act of 1996). Kinship care in this group is used in all three areas of child welfare services: diversion, family preservation, and out-of-home care. As will become evident, these programs are not always clearly defined.

Kinship Care Programs Supported by the Program Formerly Known as AFDC

The relative caregiver may receive welfare funding for the child if the following four criteria are met:

1. "The kinchild is under age 18 or, at the state's election, age 18 and a full-time student in a secondary or vocational program that the child will complete by age 19."

2. "The kinchild is deprived of parental support or care by the death, continued absence, unemployment, or incapacity of his or her parents. Parents are considered to be incapacitated if their ability to support a child is reduced by physical or mental defect, illness, or impairment that is expected to last more than 30 days."

3. "The kinchild's income and resources do not exceed the eligibility standard."

4. "The relative is a 'caretaker relative.' This term is defined by federal law to include a child's parents, grandparents, siblings, stepparents, stepsiblings, uncles, aunts, first cousins, nephews, and nieces; persons of preceding generations as denoted by prefixes of grand-, great-, or great-great; and the spouses of any of these relatives, even if the marriage has been terminated. A child in the care of a guardian does not qualify for welfare payment if the guardian is not one of the statutorily defined caretaker relatives." (Mullen, 1995, p. 7)

In addition, if a kinship caregiver is caring for a brother or sister or cousin in the same family, the caregiver receives an incremental increase in her or his welfare payment based on the standard welfare increases. For the purposes of welfare payments, this configuration is included as one family unit.

To receive welfare benefits, the relative caregiver must establish the existence of a familial connection, as defined earlier, but there is no statutory requirement to obtain legal custody to qualify for welfare payments. The relative caregiver has only to prove that the child is residing in the caregiver's home.

Kinship care as a diversion from foster care is the first program model under this type of support. Child welfare professionals have seen relatives as a resource for children for many years. If a report of abuse or neglect has been substantiated and the child has been assessed as not being safe in his or her own home, kin are sought out before the state takes custody of the child. Under these circumstances, the relative takes custody of the child, and, if the state determines it to be necessary, the state will provide protective supervision. In this way, the child welfare system remains formally involved with the kinship care network.

Protective supervision is the least intrusive option along the continuum of court-ordered child welfare services. In this model, the juvenile court retains jurisdiction over the child, but the child remains with the kinship caregiver by court order. The child cannot be removed without a further court hearing, but the kinship care network must cooperate and submit to the supervision of the child welfare agency, as specified in the court's disposition order (Hardin, 1985). Supervision usually entails monthly visits to the relative home by a social worker, the provision of services to the biological parent, and the overseeing of the child's well-being and safety. Once the agency is assured that the relative will look after the needs of the child, the case is closed. If, however, the agency determines that the relative is not meeting the needs of the child, it will assume custody, bringing the child into the foster care system.

Kinship care as family preservation is the second program model supported through welfare funding. Family preservation services may be provided to relative caregivers at two different times in order to meet two distinctive program goals: at the time the child enters the kinship home as a diversion to foster care, and at the time of family reunification to meet permanency planning goals. Both options are similar to protective supervision, but they differ in the intensity of services provided. Although there are many variations in family preservation programs, the models all tend to share certain features. These features are:

- Use of ecological perspective for assessment and intervention
- Assessment and use of strengths as a means of helping
- Maintenance by a primary social worker of a nurturing, supportive partnership with the family
- Designation of one or more colleagues as team members or back-up for the primary worker, these professionals may meet regularly with the worker and the family
- Imposition of substantially lower caseloads than are common in other similar units
- Use of the home as the primary service setting
- Conceptualization of the family system as the service unit
- Acknowledgment of the family as expert in defining its own needs
- Greatest possible use of family resources, extended family, and the community
- Active involvement by relatives in charge of their families as educators, nurturers, and primary care providers and in setting program priorities, planning, and decision making
- Provision of concrete services along with psychosocial services; and
- Limited service duration, ranging from one to six months. (Scannapieco, 1991)

The major objectives of family preservation services are to stabilize the family and to enhance family and child well-being. In both circumstances, the relative caregiver receives welfare payments for the kin children in his or her care and also receives family preservation services to help establish the children in the home. Once stability and continuity are established and the safety and well-being of the child are ensured, the formal child welfare involvement is discontinued. The relative can continue to receive welfare benefits whether or not the child welfare system is involved.

Kinship care as out-of-home care is the final program model under welfare support. The major difference from the programs already discussed is that the child is in the custody of the state but in the care of a relative.

Children who are in the custody of the state while placed with kinship caregivers should be considered children in out-of-home care. Even when the caregivers are receiving welfare payments instead of the federal foster care funding, these children are in the custody of the state, not of their family. The state is ultimately responsible for the child's protection and well-being, and the caregiver does not have primary legal responsibility under these circumstances. Some states do not include these children in their foster care statistics, which is misleading. One example of a program in which relatives receive welfare payments for caring for kin who are in the custody of the state is a program in the state of Maryland called Services to Extended Families with Children (SEFC).

SEFC was developed by the Baltimore City Department of Social Services (DSS), and it began operations in 1983 (Circular Letter # SSA 83-6). It was not until 1988, however, in response to a class action foster care law suit (*L.J. v. Massinga*) and a subsequent consent decree, that the program began to grow significantly. In 1990, 550 children, 20 percent of the foster care population in Baltimore City, were in kinship care homes. By November 1993, this number had grown to 2,701, or 45 percent of the city's foster care population (Baltimore City DSS, 1993). The SEFC program is now typical of statewide approaches to kinship care.

SEFC approaches case management of kinship care cases primarily through specialized units. Based on the Supreme Court's ruling in 1979 in *Miller v. Youakim* that relatives are eligible to receive foster care payment rates and on a 1991 consent decree in Maryland (*L.J. v. Massinga*) that requires kinship foster parents to be informed that they can receive such payments if they meet the licensing requirements, all jurisdictions must offer relatives the option of becoming licensed foster parents. Although Baltimore City DSS offers relatives this option, for a variety of reasons, many relatives choose to participate instead in SEFC.

Under the SEFC program, kinship care providers do not undergo the rigorous foster care licensing process, but they do receive casework services. Caseworkers handle all cases of relative placement in which the relative home has not become a restricted foster home (restricted foster homes are those that go through the foster parenting licensing process in order to care for a particular child or children). Families within the SEFC program collect AFDC payments for related children who are eligible. All the children placed in the SEFC program are in state custody and are covered by Medicaid. In addition, some flexible funds are available to help relatives with such costs as fixing up a house or room or buying furniture for the children. Many houses and apartments in the central city do not meet standards for foster homes, so qualifying to become a restricted placement is difficult.

SEFC families do not go through a formalized licensing procedure, but they are assessed for adequacy. Relative families also are assessed for risk of child abuse and neglect, similar to the assessments made in child protective cases. Additional precautions, such as police record checks and abuse and neglect report checks, are taken to ensure the safety of children placed with relatives. In addition, a site visit is conducted by the caseworker. Workers are assigned to families of children, so that brothers and sisters have the same social worker if the children are located in the same home or in more than one SEFC home in Baltimore City.

Baltimore City's Services to Extended Families program has a history that differs from programs in many other states, but its programmatic elements are applied nationwide. In the chapter in this book by James Gleeson, the Illinois experience is outlined and the new Home-of-Relative Reform Plan (HMR) is discussed. Illinois's plan is very similar to Maryland's. Illinois removed the approval standards for placement in the home of a relative (a lesser standard than foster care licensing), and, for those families that cannot meet the higher foster care licensing standards, the level of financial support was dropped from the foster care rate to a lower state standard-of-need rate (Gleeson, 1996). Under this new initiative, children in state custody can be placed with unlicensed relatives who meet initial safety checks, but these relatives are not eligible for foster care payments (Gleeson, 1996). In light of the poor financial situation in many states, and with the impact of welfare reform, it will be interesting to see how many more states move in this direction.

Foster Care Program: Model 3—Standard Foster Care Program

This kinship care program model falls into the federal foster care financial framework. Programs that receive foster care funding, whether financed solely by the state or through the federal-state partnership, fall into one of two primary categories: kinship homes that meet all foster care licensing requirements, and those that meet standards that have been adjusted to meet kinship home differences (i.e., regarding amount of physical space).

The primary difference between the two categories is the licensing process. Kinship foster care programs that do not differentiate between relative and nonrelative homes use the same licensing procedure for unrelated and kinship foster homes. One of the key elements of the process is that the families go through a homestudy, which includes criminal background and child abuse history checks, fire safety and health code inspections, a medical report, reference checks, a financial assessment, and an autobiographic interview and report for each caregiver. In addition, a number of hours of preservice training are required for all potential foster parents.

When a relative is licensed, the family must agree to follow foster care regulations, which require notification prior to out-of-state trips, no physical punishment, periodic meetings with supervising workers, attendance to the children's medical and dental care needs, and set hours of training per year.

The families also must go through an annual reconsideration process, which requires current medical exams of the caregivers, as well as a home visit by the foster home social worker for an update on the family situation and a reinspection.

The social worker and the agency must also meet state requirements once the relative is licensed as a foster home. These requirements, which are mandated by state and federal regulations, include the following: monthly home visits by the social worker, regular case dictation, meeting of all placement review deadlines (six-month case internal reviews and eighteen-month court reviews), maintenance of medical "passports" for the children, supervision of regular dental and medical care for the children, implementation of case plans, provision of services to biological parents, and arrangement of visits between the parent and the child.

States that do not require kinship homes to meet the "standard" foster home licensing approval process vary on the criteria that they alter for relative homes. The bottom line is that the families receive the higher foster care payment rather than the AFDC payment that families in the previously discussed programs receive. The payments do not rise by successively smaller amounts for each succeeding child, as is the case with AFDC payments, but increase by the same amount for each additional kinship care child in the family.

Other than for level of payment, standards and services between the models are not vastly different. The kinship program models have similar standards for case monitoring and service availability for families and children, but there has been no research conducted that compares the levels of compliance with these standards, nor has there been research to assess any difference in child safety, permanency, or child and family well-being among the models.

INTRIGUING PRACTICE PRINCIPLES ACROSS MODELS

Throughout this book, authors have discussed some of the more interesting practice principles and concepts utilized in kinship care (see chapters by Ernst, Jackson, and Wilson). In this section, the use of family decision-making meetings, caregiver support groups, and the need for differential assessment is highlighted.

Family Decision-Making Meetings

Probably one of the most quickly proliferating practice concepts is that of family group decision making. Two primary models of family group decision making are currently in use in child welfare. Ernst, in this volume, details the New Zealand model, the family group conference. This model was developed and implemented legislatively in New Zealand in 1989 and has since been adapted for use in communities in the United States and Canada. The second family decision-making model is the family unity model, which has been selectively used in Oregon since 1990 (American Human Association [AHA], 1996).

The key elements in both models, as applied in the United States, are as follows:

- Family meetings are called if a child welfare agency performs an initial assessment and determines a child is in need of care and protection.
- The meeting is attended by family members who are currently or who could potentially play a role in the child's life. This may include the child's parent(s), extended family members, close friends, godparents, and others whom the family defines as family.
- The child welfare worker, teachers, psychologists, and other professionals who are working with the family also typically attend the meeting (in the New Zealand model, they do not participate in the family's decision-making process, whereas in the Oregon model they can).
- Parents can limit participation by other family members.
- The meeting setting is amiable and provides an opportunity for all members to feel comfortable to express their thoughts and feelings.
- The New Zealand model adaptation varies from place to place, but has as its underlying major principle family decision making about what is in the best interests of the child. In both models, the family brainstorms options for the care and protection of the child.
- Children are given an opportunity to give input about where and with whom they want to be.
- Child welfare workers mediate the decision-making process by helping the family develop a plan for the child. (AHA, 1996; Berrick, Needell, & Barth, 1995; Wilcox et al., 1991).

Family meetings, no matter the configuration, have been found to reduce out-of-home placement and to increase the frequency with which children are placed within their own ethnic, racial, and/or religious group (AHA, 1996). This practice concept is culturally sensitive and is proving to be quite effective in addressing the child's and the family's well-being. It is worthy of further study and implementation.

Caregiver Support Groups

Support groups are not new, or intriguing, until you look at how relatives have organized them to meet their unique needs. Support groups have proliferated nationwide in recent years to help relatives deal with the complexities of raising their grandchildren, nieces, or nephews (Landers, 1994). Relatives in and out of the formal child welfare system have joined together to give one another the support they feel they cannot obtain elsewhere. Kinship care support groups have been created through grassroots efforts from relative caregivers, private and public agencies, and churches. The groups offer emotional and political sustenance to grandparents, aunts, and other relatives who are raising kin children.

Second Time Around Parents, which began meeting in 1990 in Delaware County, Pennsylvania, is an example of a relative support group. The group started as a support group for grandparents who were forced to assume responsibility, in part or in full, for raising their grandchildren because of drug addiction among their children (Samuel, 1990). The group began with fifteen people who met weekly as a means of support. Gradually, the group moved more into advocacy for themselves and their grandchildren; among the issues the group has addressed are policy issues, funding, and services for the children in their care. The stated objectives of Second Time Around Parents are:

- Funding for foster care services provided by grandparents without requiring relatives to relinquish custody to Children & Youth (foster parents funds in Delaware County, Pennsylvania, are $11,000 per year, whereas public assistance funds are $2,500 a year)
- Funding for educational and therapeutic programs for the grandchildren
- Supportive services for grandparents and other relatives (financial and emotional support, as well as assistance with legal rights and custody issues)
- Funding to establish a national grandparent support network

Other examples of agencies that incorporate caregiver support groups are: Grandparents United: Intergenerational Developmental Education (GUIDE), in Michigan; the Philadelphia-based Parent Action Network; and Grandparents United for Children's Rights, in Madison, Wisconsin. The groups' main objectives are similar to those of Second Time Around Parents, and the underlying comonality of all such groups is the difficulty relatives face in trying to cope with the chaos, and often the trauma, that result from children's being placed in kinship care. As one caregiver says, "Just being able to vent your feelings to people who are going through the same thing as you are is helpful . . . the main thing is that they are your children now" (Samuel, 1990, 3.).

Differential Assessments

Research on kinship placements reveals that they are typically quite stable and tend to last for extended periods (Berrick et al., 1994; Dubowitz, 1990; Gabel, 1992; Iglehart, 1994; Scannapieco, Hegar, & McCalpine, 1997; Task Forces on Permanency Planning, 1990; Thornton, 1991; Wulczyn & Goerge, 1992). As discussed earlier, some models of kinship care require less rigorous training and offer less supervision than is true for traditional foster parents (Scannapieco & Hegar, 1995). Research also reveals a low level of services to kinship homes in some jurisdictions (Berrick et al., 1994; Iglehart, 1994). Scannapieco and Hegar (1996) argue that the stability and length of kinship placements, as well as the diminished supervision often offered them, suggest that two kinds of screening—initial approval of the home and a permanency evaluation—should take place before children are placed in kinship homes (except when the placement is made on a strictly emergency, time-limited basis).

The assessment of kinship homes requires, therefore, attention to two sets of factors: those associated with the first use of any home for child placement (including parenting and family aspects, matters of safety and protection of children, and physical environment), and those associated with selecting a permanent placement for particular children (including attachment, permanence, and kinship) (Hegar, 1993). Across all of these factors, kinship placement raises issues that are substantially different from those associated with traditional foster care, suggesting that each criterion for assessment must be adapted for use with kinship homes.

Jackson (1996) also discusses the need to assess the triad of extended family, children, and parent. She states that the assessment process is unique when children are placed with relatives and that there needs to be a shift from assessing the dyad of parent and child to assessing the triad of child, parent, and extended family. The assessment must focus on an understanding of the extended family system and of the strengths and challenges the triad brings to the kinship care placement.

As Jackson outlines, an intergenerational perspective of the triad members, an understanding of a multidimensional assessment of interpersonal family and environmental systems, and the acknowledgment of cultural realities in extended families form the basis for the development of an assessment framework in kinship care placements.

Kinship home assessments clearly need to be approached differently from formal foster care arrangements. The different strengths that families bring to kinship care need to be considered, and issues of permanency must be looked at from the perspective of the kinship network.

CONCLUSIONS

Comparison of the practice models highlights some of the key issues that underlie the goal of placing foster children with relatives. Foster care licensing traditionally has set standards of housing and child care that exceed those in the families from which many of the children come. While these standards have the intent of ensuring that children in state custody live in minimally acceptable surroundings where abuse and neglect are absent, they sometimes promote concern that foster children are placed far out of their family's social and geographic milieu, making return home more difficult. In addition, foster care has been criticized as a program willing to pay money to strangers who care for children, money that, if paid to the child's family, might raise care to an acceptable level. On both of these points, kinship care offers some advantages over traditional foster care.

Although kinship care sometimes results in the transfer of children to more financially stable grandparents or other relatives, the social distance may well be less than in other placements. In the case of the model of kinship care where the state has custody but the relative receives welfare funding, the welfare payment to relatives for eligible children is no more than the parent might also receive, while in the second foster care payment model, the higher foster care board payment at least accrues to the child's extended family.

Kinship care has proliferated over the past decade. Social policy and practice, in relation to kinship care, must be assessed for the extent to which they meet societal goals, including the safety of children, and the goals of P.L. 96-272, including least restrictive placement and contact with biological relatives. Research findings to date leave many unanswered questions about the effects on children of kinship placement, particularly in comparison with other types of placement.

Kinship caregivers deserve and require support, both financial and emotional. How we provide this support is crucial to the well-being of children in care and their families. If the child welfare field is committed to supporting kinship care, new models of service delivery must be explored.

References

Adoption Assistance and Child Welfare Act, P.L. 96-272 (1980).

American Human Association. (1996, July). Family group decision making: A promising new approach for child welfare, *Child Protection Leader*. Washington, D.C.: Author.

Baltimore City Department of Social Services. (1993). Unpublished quarterly program statistics. Baltimore: Author.

Berrick, J. D., Barth, R. P., & Needell, B. (1994). A comparison of kinship foster homes and foster family homes: Implications for kinship foster care as family preservation. *Children and Youth Services Review, 16* (1/2), 33–64.

Berrick, J. D., Needell, B., & Barth, R. P. (1995). *Kinship Care in California: An empirically based curriculum*. Berkeley: University of California, Berkeley, Child Welfare Research Center.

Courtney, M. E. (1996). Kinship foster care and children's welfare: The California experience. *Focus, 17* (3), 42–48.

Dubowitz, H. (1990, August). *The physical and mental health and educational status of children placed with relatives: Final report*. Unpublished manuscript, University of Maryland Medical School, Baltimore.

Gabel, G. (1992). *Preliminary report on kinship foster family profile*. New York: Human Resources Administration, Child Welfare Administration.

Gleeson, J. P., & Craig, L. C. (1994). Kinship care in child welfare: An analysis of states policies. *Children and Youth Services Review, 16* (1/2), 7–32.

Gleeson, J. P. (1996). Kinship care as a child welfare service: The policy debate in an era of welfare reform. *Child Welfare, 75* (5), 419–449.

Hardin, Mark. (1985). Families, children, and the law. In Laird, J., & Hartman, A. (Eds.), *A handbook of child welfare: Context, knowledge, and practice* (pp. 213–236). New York: The Free Press.

Hegar, R. L. (1993). Assessing attachment, permanence, and kinship in choosing permanent homes. *Child Welfare, 72*, 367–378.

Iglehart, A. P. (1994). Kinship foster care: Placement, service, and outcome issues. *Children and Youth Services Review, 16* (1/2), 107–122.

Jackson, S. (1996). The kinship triad: A service delivery model. *Child Welfare, 75* (5), 583–599.

Killackey, E. (1992). Kinship foster care. *Family Law Quarterly, 26*(3), 211–220.

Kusserow, R. P. (1992). *State practices in using relatives for foster care.* Dallas Regional Office, Office of the U.S. Inspector General.

Landers, S. (1994, May 9). Second-time around families find aid. *NASW News,* p. 8.

Maryland Social Service Administration. (May, 1994). *Families taking care of their own, The Report of SSA's Task Force on Services to Extended Families with Children.* Maryland: Author.

Miller v. Youakim, 440 U.S. 125, 99 S.Ct. 957 (1979).

Mullen, F. (1995). *A tangled web: Public benefits, grandparents, and grandchildren.* Washington, D.C.: American Association of Retired Persons.

Mullen, F. (1996). Public Benefits: Grandparents, grandchildren, and welfare reform. *Generations,* Spring, 61–64.

National Commission on Family Foster Care. (1991). *A blueprint for fostering infants, children and youth in the 1990s.* Washington, D.C.: Child Welfare League of America.

Personal Responsibility and Work Opportunity Reconciliation Act of 1996. Conference Report. HR. 3734.

Saluter, A. (1993, March). Marital status and living arrangements. *Current population reports.* Washington, D.C.: U.S. Department of Commerce, Bureau of the Census.

Samuel, T. (1990, May 20). Parents for the second time around. *Philadelphia Inquirer,* p. 13–37.

Scannapieco, M. (1991). *Family-centered, home-based services: Impact of client characteristics on program outcomes.* Doctoral dissertation, Minneapolis: University of Minnesota.

Scannapieco, M., & Hegar, R. L. (1995). Kinship care: A comparison of two case management models. *Child & Adolescent Social Work, 12* (2), 147–156.

Scannapieco, M., & Hegar, R. L. (1996). A nontraditional assessment framework for kinship foster homes. *Child Welfare, 75,* (5), 567–582.

Scannapieco, M., Hegar, R. L., & McAlpine, C. (1997). Kinship care and traditional foster care: A comparison of characteristics and outcomes. *Families in Society, 78* (5), 480–488.

Takas, M. (1993). *Kinship care and family preservation: A guide for states in legal and policy development.* Unpublished manuscript. Washington, D.C.: ABA Center on Children and the Law.

Task Forces on Permanency Planning for Foster Children. (1990). *Kinship foster care: The double-edged dilemma.* Rochester, N.Y.: Author.

Testa, M., Shook, K. L., Cohen, L. S., & Woods, M. G. (1996). Permanency planning options for child in formal kinship care. *Child Welfare, 75* (5), 451–470.

Thornton, J. L. (1991). Permanency planning for children in kinship foster homes. *Child Welfare, 70* (5), 593–601.

Wulczyn, F. H., & Goerge, R. M. (1992). Foster care in New York and Illinois: The challenge of rapid change. *Social Service Review, 66,* 278–294.

Wilcox, R., Smith, D., Moore, J., Hewitt, A., Allan, G., Walker, H., Ropata, M., Monu, L., & Featherstone, T. (1991). *Family decision making , family group conferences: Practitioners' view.* New Zealand: Practitioners' Publishing.

Wilson, D., Chipungu, S. (Eds.). (1996, September/October). Kinship Care [Special Edition]. *Child Welfare, 75* (5).

CHAPTER   6

Kinship Care in Family-Serving Agencies

DANA BURDNELL WILSON

The full-time care, protection, and nurturing of children by kin has tradition-ally been a private family decision about how best to meet the needs of chil-dren. As a practice that is part of the history of most cultures around the world, kinship care has been a common solution for children whose parents could not care for them. Whether the children were orphaned or their parents were ill, incarcerated, or financially unable to provide for their care, throughout his-tory kin have come forward to provide the day-to-day parenting that was needed. Kinship care was family business.

In the past decade, the decision that kin may best provide for children who cannot live with their parents has increasingly involved family-serving agencies. As more parents struggle with substance abuse and physical and mental health problems, more children are orphaned or otherwise affected by HIV/AIDS, and more families are reported to public child welfare agencies for child maltreatment and family violence, decisions that had been family busi-ness have become agency business as well. Increasingly, agencies entrusted with protecting children across the United States are turning to kin to provide ongoing care for children.

KINSHIP CARE PRACTICE

Kinship care practice as a formal service is evolving in a variety of ways across the United States to address the needs of families in kinship care situations. Somewhere between family preservation and support and foster care practice, family-serving agencies are carving out a flexible system of services and sup-ports for kinship families. The growth and development of kinship care practice is a positive response to the trend of increasing numbers of children being reared by kin who need the services and protections of child welfare and family service agencies, often with the involvement and oversight of the judiciary system.

Family-serving agencies are setting goals for kinship care services that will embrace a broad and inclusive definition of family, respect family strengths, build upon family resources, and work to support each family's effort to prevent the unnecessary separation of children from their kin. Family members are viewed as collaborative partners in service delivery, and interventions are offered to strengthen the ability of the family to care for children and achieve family connectedness (Child Welfare League of America, 1994).

In *Kinship Care: A Natural Bridge*, the Child Welfare League of America (CWLA, 1994) presents a framework for kinship care policy and practice that supports kinship care as the first option that should be considered for children who cannot live with their parents. The framework is based on the following set of guiding principles:

- Every child's family, however family is defined (including nuclear, blended, extended, tribe or clan, and adoptive), is unique and has value, worth, integrity, and dignity.
- All families have strengths. Positive change is promoted when family strengths are supported while family needs are addressed.
- The most desirable place for children to grow up is in their own caring families, when those families are able to provide safe and nurturing relationships intended to last a lifetime.
- When children are placed with kin, child welfare agencies should provide services to support the children's safety, growth, and healthy development. Children in formal kinship care are entitled to the same financial support services and protections that all children in the legal custody of the state receive.
- When children are placed with kin, child welfare agencies should support both the birth parents and the kinship parents in their respective roles as nurturers, protectors, and teachers of the children in their care.
- Child welfare agencies should work to ensure kinship families' access to support, enrichment, and crisis intervention services that are comprehensive, coordinated, culturally responsive, and community based.
- Child welfare agency staff members should recognize the different needs of the many racial, ethnic, and religious groups served by the child welfare system and should be competent in working with a racially and culturally diverse population. (CWLA, 1994)

This set of principles is the philosophical basis for an approach to kinship care services that affirms the value of family connections and supports kin in their efforts to keep and care for children within the family.

Describing kinship care as a resilient, natural system of child rearing, Scannapieco and Jackson (1996) state that the lack of adequate kinship care policy formation and program development indicates that there is still limited recognition of the intrinsic value of supporting and empowering families to care for their own. The importance of the extended family can be acknowledged by including them in the development of the plan for services, or "case plan." It is essential that all possible caregivers be involved in the service planning and decision-making process (Scannapieco & Jackson, 1996). Recognition of the importance of establishing this kind of partnership between the family and the worker is growing.

This partnership approach provides us with an added dimension to child welfare and family service work. "While keeping children with their families and reunifying children and families continue to be our primary goals, there is a broader recognition that families come in a variety of forms, that our work must be guided by a thorough assessment of the family, and that our interventions must engage the whole family in order to be successful" (Barbell, 1995, p. 11).

The thinking that has emerged over the past decade points us to a "family-centered" approach that focuses on the needs and welfare of children within the context of their families and their communities. It views the family as central to the child's well-being (Barbell, 1995). This family-centered approach has practical application in child welfare and in family preservation and support services.

Williams encourages child welfare and family services to regard the family as a system, with a unique definition of self, dynamics, values, and ways of operating as the target for change. When the family is looked upon as a system, intervention is focused on recognizing and building up the strengths within the family unit. Empowerment is a common theme in this approach, as opposed to the emphasis on problems in the deficit approach (Williams, 1991).

In a study of state policies on the use of kinship care, it was found that few state legislative statutes, regulations, judicial decisions, or administrative directives contained clearly articulated goals for kinship care. The authors of the study believe that the primary reason for this is that kinship care is not perceived as an independent program (Gleeson & Craig, 1994). The authors conclude that kinship care is most frequently viewed as a diversion from child welfare services, a component of family preservation and support services, and/or a component of the state's foster care program.

The development of kinship care practice in family-serving agencies will require a clearly articulated set of guidelines, with procedural priorities and steps, in order to support the assertion that kinship care is a distinct service program.

How Agencies Serve Kinship Families

Services available to kinship families vary with the family-serving agency involved. In 1995, the Child Welfare League of America had fifty-one member agencies that indicated that they provided kinship care services. Anecdotal information received from members of the CWLA National Advisory Committee on Kinship Care suggests that there was a broad range of approaches to providing services and supports to kinship families. CWLA surveyed the fifty-one member agencies that provide kinship care services in order to determine how kinship care services are provided across the United States by comparing the different approaches. The survey included questions about each program's definition of kinship care, how narrowly or broadly relationships were defined as kinship, and what mission, goals, and objectives were stated for the kinship care programs. The reasons children came into the care of kin were requested, as well as demographic information about the families. The theoretical base used by the agencies to develop the service programs was requested, as was detail about services directly provided and the average length of time these services were delivered. Options for permanence for children with kin were requested, as well as the percentage of children identified in each plan for permanence. The training needs for kinship care service staff was questioned in the survey. Responding agencies were also given the opportunity to state how their program was progressing, to describe innovations of which they were particularly proud, and to provide suggestions for agencies that were just developing kinship care programs.

Eighteen organizations participated in the survey: eleven private nonprofit agencies and seven public child welfare agencies. Agencies were surveyed via one-hour telephone interviews, usually with either program administrators for kinship care services or the agency child welfare directors. The programs represented reflected different value statements, administrative designs, and practice methods. The majority of the participating agencies served the Mid-Atlantic region, the urban Mid-West, or the West Coast.

Most participating agencies identified as their mission ensuring the safety and well-being of children, preserving family relationships, and enhancing family capacity. Most also indicated a theoretical or philosophical approach that was family focused and strengths based. More than half included program goals of permanence for children, two included statements emphasizing cultural and ethnic connections, and one included advocacy as a part of the agency mission.

Kinship care was defined broadly among the agencies surveyed. Rather than requiring a prescribed set of "blood ties" and acceptable degrees of consanguinity, agencies are moving toward an open view of kinship, recognizing emotional ties as well and allowing the families themselves to determine what kin relationships exist. Only two of the eighteen agencies had a restrictive definition of kin (second degree of consanguinity), and one of those allowed godparents to be included as kin.

Many agencies are struggling to plan and provide permanence for children in care. In this category, there were significant differences between the responses of public agencies and private agencies. While the plans of *adoption by kin* (18%) and *legal custody or guardianship to kin* (18%) were at comparable levels for all agencies, there was a large disparity between the goals of *return to parents* (54% in public agencies, 24% in private) and *long-term relative care* (15% in public agencies, 50% in private). While planning for permanence usually applies to children who are in the legal custody of public child welfare agencies, the children and their families are served both by public agencies directly and by private agencies who contract to provide the services. It is essential to acknowledge that permanence and legal stability are important for all children.

Information was requested on the service needs of the kinship family: the child, the parent, and the relative caregiver. *All* of the respondents indicated a need for drug abuse treatment and related services. Sixteen of the eighteen also identified child abuse/neglect-related services and supportive services for relative caregivers, fourteen included mental health and income assistance, thirteen sought services for birth parents, and as many as nine indicated a need for juvenile justice involvement. Two agencies identified medical care as a need. The following needs were each identified only once by responding agencies: school needs, housing, legal services, respite, recreation for children, and advocacy. It is doubtful that the services identified least are unneeded by kinship families; more likely, the agencies gave more weight to their high-priority needs, which brought the families to their attention in the first place.

When asked about factors that contributed to need for kinship care, all eighteen of the agencies responding identified parental substance abuse, and eleven included children's exposure to drugs. Child abuse and neglect was the second most common contributing factor indicated by sixteen agencies, and as many as thirteen agencies included mental health problems as contributing factors to kinship care placement.

Characteristics of the families served were consistent with those identified in earlier research (Berrick, Barth, & Needell, 1994; Dubowitz, Feigelman, & Zuravin, 1993; Testa, 1992; Thornton, 1991). The ethnicity of kinship families was: 78 percent African American (90–95% in most of the urban areas), 11 percent Latino, and slightly less than 12 percent Caucasian. Relative caregivers were most often grandparents (63%) and aunts/uncles (15%), with siblings and cousins together constituting 17 percent. Income levels varied, but most families indicated a need for additional financial support.

Respondents reported a range of training available for staff providing kinship care services, from very extensive to none at all. Some agencies involved both professionals and kinship caregivers as trainers. Thirteen of the responding agencies offered specific formal training in kinship care services, and five did not. Some have incorporated casework with kinship families into their training about service delivery techniques, and some offer specialized kinship care training, or a combination of both.

This survey also asked narrative questions, including: What message or advice would you give an agency about instituting a kinship care program? Some of the responses can give insight to other family-serving agencies.

- Read the literature on kinship care; talk with local organizations to learn about community needs.
- Build a program that meets needs as they arise, one that is dynamic and able to change as needs change.
- Acknowledge that many families do not identify with foster care; be flexible and accommodating, making room for creativity.

- Develop a data base, and evaluate program outcomes.
- Encourage support groups and specialized training for kinship caregivers; make a commitment for outreach to and involvement with birth parents; arrange support groups for children in kinship care; provide for respite care.
- Engage and listen to the families served—their input is necessary to design a program
- Select staff who are dedicated to working with families with critical needs and who understand family dynamics.
- Examine agency mission and philosophy to see if they fit the goals of kinship care; institute programs that recognize and appreciate cultural differences.

Kinship Care in the Evolving Array of Services to Families

Kinship care as a formal family service program is relatively new in the field of social work. It is evolving along with changes in family needs, consumer requests, legislative and policy priorities, and the developing conventional wisdom on best practice.

Examining kinship care practice as a component of the evolving array of family services enables agencies to provide services shown to be effective, as well as to consider more flexible ways to design kinship care service programs.

Family-serving agencies have the opportunity to develop effective kinship care service programs at this relatively early stage in the programs' evolution. The social work field has already gained much knowledge from experience with family support and foster care programs. Kinship care provides an opportunity to retain the strengths of these programs, to avoid their weaknesses, and to build family-based programs that focus from the initial planning on desired outcomes for children and families.

Williams (1991) writes that the flexibility of successful programs is based on holistic, noncategorical approaches. Families receive services on the basis of need. A mixture of concrete and psychological services is provided in response to the specific needs of families. Workers are not hindered by categorical barriers to accessing resources. The focal unit of treatment is the family, rather than the child or any other identified patient.

Kinship care services can be regarded as a dynamic means of meeting the needs of children through the strengths of kin, rather than as a *category* of services. Kinship care does cut across several "types" of services, including but not limited to: family support, crisis intervention, family preservation, full-time care/placement, child day care, respite care, co-parenting, mentoring/parent education, group support, and advocacy. A strict categorical approach may be counterproductive in this instance.

In terms of developing effective kinship care service methods, it is important to pay attention to family-centered, strength-based approaches; cultural aspects of service delivery; and community involvement and advocacy.

Williams (1991) points to a disproportionate need for permanence in care among African American children. She states that this need is driven in part by the limited ability of the child welfare system to intervene early, prevent placement, and reunify families. A change in family service policy to seek kin as the first option for children who need placement can address the goal of keeping children with their families and also that of ensuring cultural continuity for children. Research has shown that the vast majority of children in kinship care are African American. This result is not necessarily "disproportionate," since it represents families coming forward to take care of their own. Still, the fact that child welfare and family service programs are so often required points to a need for more early intervention and prevention efforts and for a more ecological perspective in which outreach efforts to kin and community are routinely made. Kinship care practice, like social work in general, must recognize the resilient nature of African American families (Scannapieco & Jackson, 1996). This recognition will serve to reinforce the concept of partnership with the family with the goal of meeting the needs of the children, rather than having the agency view the family as "clients" only, or recipients of services.

Scannapieco and Hegar (1996) present an ecological approach to kinship care assessment that views families and their environments as intershaping systems that change over time and adapt to each other as the changes occur. This approach is strength and growth oriented. Services should encompass families and their communities in a holistic way to ensure a nurturing environment for the children. Recent literature also allies kinship care services with family preservation and support (CWLA, 1994; Hegar & Scannapieco, 1995; Ingram, 1996; Scannapieco & Jackson,1996). Kinship care does enable children to stay connected to their families, their culture, and often their communities. It can enrich children's sense of identity, belonging, family connection, and self-esteem (CWLA, 1994).

Cole and Duva (1990) state that the job description of a family preservation service contains four principal categories of tasks:

1. Dealing with intrapersonal & interpersonal problems
2. Teaching skills and knowledge
3. Linking clients with community resources and services
4. Advocating for broader societal reforms that will benefit families

Cole and Duva conclude that most agencies and staff members struggle to provide the first three categories of help. The fourth is almost universally neglected or at best underdeveloped. When it comes time to collect the energy needed for social action, most feel that they expended their energy and served a useful purpose in giving direct services (1990). Family-serving agencies would do well to advance advocacy on behalf of families as well as family interventions as legitimate roles of staff and governing boards.

At this time, when many legislative changes and proposals are meant to reform society in ways that would make it more difficult for families served by child welfare and family support, advocacy becomes all the more important to ensure that adequate services are available. In addition, advocacy could result in improved community relations and neighborhood support.

Danzy (1996) states that the multidimensional nature of the kinship care population requires the creation of strong collaborative networks. "In the arena of public policy for the kinship care population, it is critical that the human services community work with their political officers and their constituents in any efforts to create policy initiatives" (p. 658). She also concludes that child welfare and supportive services call for a collaborative process, since the kinship family, like any family, depends upon a number of systems for its basic needs. Service agencies are challenged to forge effective partnerships among the political, private, and public sectors and to establish working collaborative relationships.

According to Everett, Chipungu, and Leashore (1991), key characteristics of successful programs serving families are: flexibility in service delivery and design, commitment and caring on the part of the staff, provision of basic necessities in addition to services, and innovation in service delivery. Innovation requires coordination, which can be attained by crossing the professional and programmatic lines of authority or boundaries of service delivery. Everett, Chipungu, and Leashore (1991) believe that this innovation is based on the belief that change is possible, that the necessary steps to make change can and will be taken, and that the components of the system that are working well, albeit imperfectly, should be continued.

CONCLUSION

Although kinship care services are still relatively new, practice experience and research over the past several years are available to guide family-serving agencies as they develop a practical approach to kinship care services. While the growth in kinship care caught family-serving agencies unaware and unprepared a few years ago, the challenge was met, and keeping track of what is working in kinship care will continue to help in program development. It is important to seek the input of the relative caregiver community as programs are developed, because this will keep us grounded in the practical issues confronting the families we serve. At the Child Welfare League of America National Conference in 1993, a kinship care institute was held, in which kinship caregivers constituted a panel of presenters. At the end, when the panel was asked for advice on the future direction of family-serving agencies, the response was, "When there are problems with the program, change the policies to fit the families, instead of trying to change the families to fit the policies." This is the challenge that family-serving agencies must accept.

References

Barbell, K. (1995). *Foster care today: A briefing paper.* (unpublished). Washington, D.C.: Child Welfare League of America.

Berrick, J. D., Barth, R. P., & Needell, B. (1994). A comparison of kinship foster homes and foster family homes: Implications for kinship foster care as family preservation. *Children and Youth Services Review, 16* (1/2), 33–64.

Child Welfare League of America. (1994). *Kinship care: A natural bridge.* Washington, D.C.: Author.

Cole, E., & Duva, J. (1990). *Family preservation: An orientation for administrators & practitioners.* Washington, D.C.: Child Welfare League of America.

Danzy, J. (1996). Philadelphia's collaborative process for building a responsive agenda for kinship care. *Child Welfare, 75* (5), 651–660.

Dubowitz, H., Feigelman, S., & Zuravin, S. (1993). *A profile of kinship care. Child Welfare, 72,* 153–169.

Everett, J., Chipungu, S., & Leashore, B. (1991). Conclusion: Within our power. In J. Everett, S. Chipungu, & B. Leashore (Eds.), *Child welfare: An Afrocentric perspective* (p. 309). New Brunswick, N.J.: Rutgers University Press.

Gleeson, J., & Craig, S. (1994). Kinship care in child welfare: An analysis of states' policies. *Children and Youth Services Review, 16* (1/2), 7–31.

Hegar, R., & Scannapieco, M. (1995). From family duty to family policy: The evolution of kinship care. *Child Welfare, 74,* (1), 200–216.

Ingram, C. (1996). Kinship care: From last resort to first choice. *Child Welfare, 75* (5), 550–565.

Scannapieco, M., & Hegar, R. L. (1996). A nontraditional assessment framework for formal kinship homes. *Child Welfare, 75* (5), 567–579

Scannapieco, M., & Jackson, S. (1996). Kinship care: The African American response to family preservation. *Social Work, 41* (2), 190–196

Testa, M. F. (1992). Conditions of risk for substitute care. *Children and Youth Services Review, 14,* 27–36.

Thornton, J. L. (1991). Permanency planning for children in kinship foster homes. *Child Welfare, 70* (5), 593–601.

Williams, C. (1991). Expanding the Options in the Quest For Permanence. In J. Everett, S. Chipungu, & B. Leashore (Eds.), *Child welfare: An Africentric perspective* (p. 283). New Brunswick, N.J.: Rutgers University Press.

CHAPTER 7

Paradigm Shift

Training Staff to Provide Services
to the Kinship Triad

SONDRA M. JACKSON, M.S.W.

Although kinship care is a traditional system of child care, it is the most recent service delivery program in the continuum of child welfare services. The development of kinship care programs followed a tremendous increase in the use of relatives as a placement option for children who could not live with their parents. A large part of the reason for the increased use of relatives as caregivers was the decline in the number of available foster parents. As more social workers were assigned to this population, it became evident that the traditional foster care training did not meet the training needs of staff working in kinship programs. Development of effective curricula for kinship care staff demands a shift in training paradigm from services to the dyad to services to the triad.

The debate over whether there are unique differences between kinship care and traditional foster care placements has not been resolved for some administrators and practitioners. Those who understand traditional foster care theory and practice with children in out-of-home placements are likely to find more similarities than differences between the two placement alternatives. Foster care training focuses on topics such as "helping children adjust to a new environment," "assessing parents' histories and capacity to parent," "encouraging foster parent role modeling," and "helping workers to make permanency planning decisions." However, practitioners who view kinship placements as a means of preventing traditional foster care placement interventions take a family preservation approach to services, and training for them focuses on "assessing extended family relationships, structure, and function," "empowering extended family members to make permanency planning decisions," and "providing services to the triad of child, parent, and caregivers."

Training will not resolve the debate, but, by helping workers make a shift in the child placement paradigm, it can prepare them to address the needs of the triad. Child welfare trainers are beginning to recognize that foster care training is not adequate to meet the needs of kinship care practitioners and are seeking appropriate curricula.

This chapter presents the issues related to the need for a paradigm shift; the unique training needs of workers in kinship care; the important components of a training curriculum, and child welfare workers' response to kinship care training.

THE PARADIGM SHIFT

In-service training is a necessary part of any child welfare system that depends on its staff to achieve program goals. Trainers in child welfare share the responsibility for helping practitioners acquire specialized knowledge and skills to provide high-quality, comprehensive, and culturally competent services to families and children. Therefore, it is important for trainers who are charged with this complex and difficult task to be aware of the paradigm shifts in the child welfare service delivery system. In the past decade, kinship care has challenged the child welfare system to make a paradigm shift. The term "paradigm" was popularized in behavioral sciences by Dorfman (1988). A student of the history of science, Kuhn uses the term in several ways in his work. However, for the purpose of this chapter, a paradigm is defined as "a conceptual-interpretive framework—an interlocking network of presuppositions, assumptions, attitudes, beliefs, premises, expectations, and values" (Dorfman, 1988).

Kinship care presents a new way of conceptualizing out-of-home placement when children are with their relatives. It is, therefore forcing us to shift our network of assumptions, attitudes, beliefs, and premises about children in placement from the regular foster care paradigm to a paradigm more appropriate for kinship care.

To contrast the shift from the old to the new or from the traditional to the modern, trainers should examine the paradigms that existed before the advent of kinship care in order to understand where we are headed in the new child welfare continuum of services (see Figure 7.1). As we prepare to make a paradigm shift from the traditional child placement model to a new service delivery model, we might consider the following shifts.

In highlighting some of the changes pointed out by Lawrence-Webb (1993), an assumption is made that there is common understanding among child welfare professionals of the transitions illustrated in Figure 7.1. Therefore, we discuss those that are the core concepts related to kinship.

Prior to home-based family preservation programs, the field of child welfare was *child centered*. Very little attention was given to working with parents who allegedly had abused or neglected their children. Child welfare training defined the areas of social services centered around the needs of children who were at risk of being or who had been removed from their families. Child protection and child placement were the primary focus of the training for child welfare practitioners.

Traditional Paradigm		New Paradigm
child centered	→	family centered
nuclear family focus	→	extended family and community
fathers uninvolved	→	outreach to fathers
foster care maintenance	→	custody and guardianship
AFDC/no payment	→	foster care payment
Counseling/Case Management	→	Therapeutic Approach
Cultural Blindness	→	Cultural Competence
Court-based adversarial	→	Court-based Mediation
Individual Client Meetings	→	Extended Family Meetings
Dyad Assessments	→	Triad Assessments

Figure 7.1 Comparison of Paradigms. Adapted from work by Lawrence-Webb, 1993.

An emphasis on *family-centered* social work practice began with the development of family preservation programs. Training was developed as a part of the new home-based models of practice. Homebuilders and Maryland's Intensive Family Services were two of the earlier family preservation models (National Commission on Family Foster Care, 1991). For the first time, child welfare training that emphasized working with families and involving parents was developed. Family strengths, cultural sensitivity, and the ecological approach were themes that ran through all of the child welfare training.

The challenge has been to utilize family preservation principles even when the child is temporarily placed outside of his or her own home (Pecora, Whittaker, Maluccio, Barth, & Plotnick, 1992). Achieving permanence for the child by focusing on the *nuclear family* was the new thrust. Permanency planning centers around the biological parents' capacity and ability to parent. In traditional training in the hierarchy of permanency, options include maintaining in their own homes children who are at risk of placement; reunification of children in placement with their biological parents or relatives; adoption; and permanent or long-term foster care. In the new system of care, the focus must shift to include the *extended family* on the front end of placement. The task for the practitioner in the traditional system of care is to determine the biological parents' capacity and willingness to provide care for the child. If the parents are unable or unwilling to provide a safe home for the child, foster parents are selected from a pool of approved or licensed people, and the child is presented for their consideration. This is very different from placing children with relatives who are not often selected from an approved or licensed group of people. Relatives do not apply for the job of caregiver, which creates a very different dynamic in the role of the caregiver and the extended family.

Another paradigm shift forced by kinship care has to do with the inclusion of cultural considerations as a part of the training. *Cultural blindness* must be replaced by *cultural competence*. Because most of the kinship placements involve minority families, a culturally based perspective is needed to grasp the nuances and intricacies of this system of care (Scannapieco & Hegar, 1995).

The shift from the *nuclear family meeting* to *extended family meetings* (EFMs) for decision making is a new concept for trainers. Further elaboration of these elements are in a later section of this chapter.

KINSHIP CARE TRAINING PRINCIPLES AND PHILOSOPHY

Difference from Foster Care

Specialized training should be designed to increase the competence, knowledge, and skills of family and child welfare professionals and to familiarize them with a system of social work practice that is unique to the kinship triad—child, parent, and caregiver. The training focuses on the child welfare system of care that places children with relatives when their biological parents are unable to provide them with a safe and secure environment. The goal is to teach practitioners to empower families and extended families, when appropriate, to create a permanent living arrangement for the child. Workers will acknowledge that there are different dynamics in service provision to the triad, and they should demand training to identify the differences.

The initial question for most kinship care workers is "how does this training differ from regular foster care training?" When children are placed with extended family, the system may effectively prevent foster care or achieve reunification. Kinship care is best conceptualized as an important component of family preservation services (Danzy & Jackson,1997). Placements with relatives may help families with stresses and provide a safe environment as well as be a resource for the family in crisis (Child Welfare League of America, 1994). Kinship care should, therefore, be understood in keeping with the principles and guidelines of family preservation services (Danzy & Jackson, 1997). Effective family preservation services involve family and community supports in the resolution of the problems related to placement prevention and rehabilitation (Children's Defense Fund, 1990).

Family structures vary in America, and not all families are based on the nuclear family structure. The extended family, for example, has traditionally been the primary family unit for many African Americans (Billingsley, 1992). This tradition is evident in the overwhelming number of kin placements among African American families in the child welfare system. It can be intimidating to the worker that the caregiver usually has more information about the family history and the issues that led to the placement of a child. However, when workers become familiar with the strengths within the extended family network, they are able to build a framework for service delivery. Working through generation issues and understanding the role of the extended family are often identified among the training needs of practitioners.

Achieving Permanence

Achieving permanency for children placed with relatives is the primary issue for practitioners as they plan intervention strategies with the triad. All children need permanent homes, and the preferred home is with parents or relatives.

The training ought to consistently focus on the hierarchy of permanency planning, which is discussed in this chapter. Child welfare administrators are concerned that permanent plans are not being achieved within a desirable time frame in kinship care cases and want to be assured that staff understand permanency planning. Practitioners should understand that the hierarchy of placement should guide service delivery efforts. In developing permanency planning goals, workers need to be trained to make decisions that reflect the use of kinship placements on the front end of the system as a means of preventing foster care or on the back end of the system, to reunify the family as a means of achieving permanence for children.

Cultural Considerations

While kinship families span all racial and economic groups, most of the children placed with kin in the child welfare system are people of color (Berrick, Barth, & Needell, 1994). Practitioners must be familiar with cultural differences and cultural strengths (for further discussion see Scannapieco & Jackson, 1996). They need to understand that the kinship network within African American families, for example, is "an effective mechanism for providing extra emotional and economic support in the lives of thousands of children. These are black family strengths that are clearly in need of support through imaginative adoption policy" (Hill, 1972, p. 8). When children are placed with extended family, they are more likely to have their emotional, social, spiritual, and nurturance needs met (CWLA, 1994). Practitioners should learn to use the natural helping process of the extended family network in African American families to provide services (Everett, Chipunga, & Leashore, 1991). Consideration ought to be given in program development, policy, and practice to the accommodation of cultural strengths within this group. Adequate assessment and treatment cannot be effective without knowledge of the cultural nuances and traditions that affect service delivery to the triad.

It is important that this training component recognize the practitioners' need to be aware of the impact of cultural and ethnic differences on clients' readiness and capacity for utilizing kinship care services. The training content should provide an overview of issues related to the delivery of kinship care services from a culturally competent perspective. Through the training, the worker should be able to define the concept of diversity and cultural awareness; describe his or her own experience with informal kinship care; describe the importance of cultural awareness in providing kinship care services; and employ culturally appropriate intervention strategies consistent with cultural values.

Extended Family Meeting

In extended family services training, practitioners should be taught to use the extended family meeting as a primary component of the decision-making process in kinship care. The EFM involves the convening of all "significant" adult family members to participate in developing a plan for addressing the needs of the family members in crisis. The training curriculum should emphasize comprehensive services to the triad and provide encouragement to caregivers who care for their relatives as a permanent plan or until a permanent plan is achieved. Respect and concern for the caregivers, as well as provision of adequate services to meet the needs of the child in their care, is stressed. It is important to recognize that some caregivers are devastated by the family crisis; some have experienced episodic crises leading up to the placement; and others have cared for the children for periods of time in the past and must now get accustomed to agency intervention. Most of all, caregivers need agency support initially and should be viewed as full partners in service decisions.

Consideration for the rights of the child's parents are very important in convening the EFM. Depending on the parents' relationship with the caregiver, the child, and other family members, it may well be necessary to include them in the preparation of the EFM. The practitioner should understand that as a facilitator for the EFM, there may be issues of confidentiality on the part of the parent that may not be shared by the extended family. Parents are more willing to participate in the family meeting when the worker assures them that information that they may not want to share about their situation will remain confidential.

Families reject the intrusiveness of the social services agency over long periods of time. Therefore, the practitioner ought to be taught to empower the family and to limit the number of decisions made without family involvement. Practitioners should also learn to quickly determine the permanent plan, engage other family members, make accurate service needs assessments, clarify treatment strategies for parents and children, and determine the termination process.

Resource Provision

Another training need concerns resources available to the triad. For effective service delivery, training should address appropriate and available resources. The rights and responsibilities of children, parents, and caregivers need to be understood from the beginning and clarified if necessary. Some kinship providers are more resourceful than others, and the worker should assess the availability of resources and the family's willingness to share them with the children in care. Relative caregivers' households are likely to need financial support to help defray the considerable expenses of raising unplanned for children. Similarly, parents may need resources and treatment if reunification is the plan. Funding to meet the immediate concrete needs of the triad such as special food, clothing, and furniture should be made available. Also, health care, day care, therapy, school placements, and housing are of vital concern for the caregiver and important to the well-being of the child. Workers need to be trained in clear policy direction to accommodate these issues.

Strengths Perspective

The strengths perspective must be emphasized to practitioners as they work with extended families. Understanding the importance of identifying, observing, and utilizing the strengths of the family system is extremely important and requires training for the practitioner. The use of systems theory is effective in working with the triad because of the level of interactions necessary to understand the dynamics of the triad in relation to environmental systems (Scannapieco & Hegar, 1996; Scannapieco & Jackson, 1996).

Specialized training programs for kinship care staff are essential for effective service delivery. Competency-based pre-service and in-service training, as well as good supervision and administrative leadership, should also be available to supplement the training curriculum. However, before a training program is selected, administrators and practitioners should understand that service to the kinship triad is not an adaptation of regular foster care services but requires the development of a unique system of services.

DEVELOPING A KINSHIP CARE TRAINING CURRICULUM

To be effective, training should address staff needs in the areas of knowledge, skills, and abilities to carry out their responsibilities to clients. Training directed toward improving and upgrading the staff to work with assigned populations is important. A sound training program will provide administrative support, supervisory support, and an organizational climate that accommodates the need to look at problems and resolutions.

Unlike other areas of child welfare, kinship care does not have a long history of training activity. Over the past ten years, the child welfare field has held some conference workshops and only a few practice seminars on kinship care. The child welfare system is still trying to decide whether children living with relatives is a viable placement option; those within the field who have accepted kin placements as an option apply regular foster care principles.

Child welfare agencies should invest in training staff to provide services to the triad of child, parent, and caregiver. This intrusive service system should recognize that the triad is desperate to stabilize its situation, and practitioners should be trained to be sensitive to the needs of the triad (Jackson, 1998). In developing any training, trainers should include a variety of experiential exercises as well as discussion, brainstorming, role play, and other appropriate training methodologies. This chapter emphasizes training content, rather than techniques.

Kinship Definition

The first step in developing the training is to have a clear definition of the kinship population served by the child welfare agency. Most child welfare systems define "kin" to include any relative by blood or marriage or any person with close family ties to the child (Takas, 1993). Distinctions are also made between formal and informal care by some professionals. When children who have been abused or neglected by their biological parents are placed with relatives by the social services agency, they fall within the formal child welfare system. However, some children who are living with relatives were placed there by the parents in an informal arrangement. Because of the legal and fiscal issues in the formal system, it is important to make this distinction in the training definition.

History of Kinship Care

Staff are usually assigned to agency programs without much information about the history of the program. Child welfare workers are generally more concerned about service delivery than with the origin of the service program. However, the service has more meaning when workers learn how this particular system of services fits into the continuum of services. The fact that formal kinship care had its beginnings in the early 1980s, almost fifty years after the public foster care system, explains that practice with this population is evolving. Child welfare agencies have been reluctant to accept relatives as viable placement alternatives for children because of the theory of generational abuse; the publication *Beyond the Best Interest of the Child* suggested that parents who abused their children had themselves been abused (Goldstein, Freud, & Solnit, 1972), and for this reason relative placements were not encouraged or considered viable. However, given the difficult social and economic conditions that exist in the 1990s and the effects that drug use has had on families, child welfare professionals are taking a new look at relatives who are willing to care for children. In an effort to comply with P.L. 96-272, some states have used relatives to reduce the number of foster care placements. It is also important to point out that the Supreme Court decision (*Miller v. Youakim*, 1979) giving relatives the right to the same payment as nonrelatives for providing care opened the doors to relative placements in the 1980s. Each state has its own unique history of the use of kin placements, and this should be shared with the trainees, as well.

The Child Welfare League of America convened the first national committee to develop guidelines for kinship care policy and practice in 1992. It is not yet clear what the effects will be of the Family Preservation and Support Services Act (1996), which was passed by Congress and signed by President Bill Clinton as part of the Omnibus Reconciliation Act. As part of this legislation, states are offered the opportunity to include kinship care among the elements that make up the continuum of care. Federal and state welfare reform legislation passed in 1996 will have an impact on kinship care, particularly on relatives who are dependent on government subsidies to provide care. The chronology of events outlined in Figure 7.2 may be presented in the training to help trainees understand the evolution of kin placements in child welfare.

Specialized Competencies for Kinship Care

Competency-based training is the prescribed design used by child welfare curriculum developers today (Child Welfare Institute, 1996). This method begins with a statement of the general outcomes to be achieved through service provision to a particular population. Curriculum designers then specify casework practice outcomes to be achieved. These practice outcome statements become the core competencies that agencies or programs expect caseworkers to achieve with the targeted population. Most trainers agree that competency-

1972	Impact of Child Abuse Theory, *Beyond the Best Interest of the Child* by Goldstein and Solnit
1979	*Miller v. Youakim*, Supreme Court Decision
1980	P.L. 96-272
1980s	Lawsuits on behalf of children in placement *Lipscomb v. Simmons* (Oregon); *King v. Mahan* (California); *Eugene v. Gross* (New York); *LJ v. Massinga* (Maryland)
1992	CWLA Convened the North American Kinship Care Policy and Practice Committee
1993	Family Preservation and Support Services Act
1995	*Anderson v. Edwards*, Supreme Court Decision
1996	Welfare Reform

Figure 7.2 History of Kinship Care Placements.

based training is the best way of developing areas of knowledge, skills, and attitudes in professional practice. However, the debate continues over the "right" competency statements for services to special populations. A kinship care competency-based curriculum model would include hierarchically organized statements framed in terms of service outcomes to the family triad. Examples of worker competency statements are these:

- Is able to describe the importance of kinship care from the philosophical base of family preservation
- Is able to identify implications of P.L. 96-272 for service delivery to families in distress
- Understands how the values inherent in permanency planning are reflected in the process of engaging the kinship triad
- Is able to assess the appropriateness of placement with the triad, including initial placement, as well as monitor changing needs and developing progress
- Is able to identify and assess the child's emotional, cultural, educational, and safety needs in extended-family cases
- Is able to list the rights and responsibilities of parents of children placed in care
- Is able, with other staff, to develop a family service agreement between the kinship triad and the service provider
- Is able to identify how a relative care provider may be affected by the placement of a family member's child
- Understands the importance to the child of supporting the continuity of relationship between biological parents and extended family members
- Is able to demonstrate techniques for conducting an Extended Family Meeting

- Knows how to apply specific techniques for intervening with the extended family system
- Understands the relationship between the need of the kinship triad for support and the effective use of the court process in securing such support
- Is able to identify barriers to a child's return home that are unique to extended-family service cases
- Is able to identify techniques for worker and kinship triad empowerment
- Is able to explain his or her role relative to a framework for service delivery to kinship triads

Value Statements

When presenting training to employees working in the area of kinship care, it is important for the trainer to emphasize the value to children of appropriate kin placements. A paradigm shift is taking place as child placement agencies have come to realize that kinship care provides important continuity of relationships within the family and culture. The kinship bond is the most important relationship in ensuring healthy identity, self-esteem, and security when children are unable to live with their parents. According to the Child Welfare League of America, kinship care is valuable because it:

- Enables children to live with people they know and trust
- Reduces the trauma of living with persons who initially are unknown
- Supports the transmission of a child's family identity, culture, and ethnicity
- Helps children stay connected to siblings
- Encourages families to rely on their own family members and resources
- Increases opportunities for children to stay connected to their own communities and encourages community responsibility for children and families
- Promotes the ability of children to receive support and services in their own families (including extended families)
- Eliminates the unfortunate stigma that children may experience from being labeled "foster children" (CWLA, 1994)

As these values are discussed with participants, the trainer must be able to unequivocally accept and explain these value statements to encourage practitioners to support kin in their efforts to care for children.

Legal Foundation for Kinship Placements

Although state statutes relating to kinship care vary (Gleeson & Craig, 1994), practitioners need to be aware of the legal foundations for providing services to this population. The trainer should begin this component by explaining the impact of P.L. 96-272, the Adoption Assistance and Child Welfare Act of 1980, on child welfare and kinship care. P.L. 96-272, which is a landmark piece of legislation, serves as the foundation for state child welfare policies and regulations regarding children in placement. Therefore, the trainer should introduce the philosophy of permanency planning as well as relate the impact of the protections for children as mandated under P.L. 96-272. It is the intent of the federal legislation that is important to child welfare workers as they attempt to understand kinship placements. It is also important to present state laws that affect placements with relatives and the regulatory and statutory references that apply.

It is necessary also to provide workers with information about the role of the court in making decisions in kinship care placements. The predilections of juvenile court judges vary from state to state regarding kin placements. In some areas of the country the courts favor kinship placements more than they do in others. In providing training for workers, it is a good idea to bring in legal experts to explain the position of the courts on kinship placements and what the courts expect of the workers in these cases.

Permanency Planning Hierarchy

Even though the impetus for permanency planning came from the passage of P.L. 96-272, practitioners should understand that good child welfare practice should focus on permanent living arrangements for children. Therefore, child welfare workers need to be trained in the hierarchy of permanent planning, especially when relatives are involved.

Workers should be trained first to explore the interest of relatives before they place children in nonrelated foster homes. Training can help workers shift paradigms from the traditional foster care hierarchy of permanent plans to a new hierarchy that includes kinship placements.

Differences among permanency options and their meaning in terms of creating a permanent living arrangement for the child need to be understood when the child is placed with kin. One of the problems in placing children with relatives is that the workers sometimes get comfortable with the placement and fail to make permanency decisions as quickly as they should. When children are placed with relatives, workers should be encouraged to begin by trying to achieve reunification with the parents.

Relative adoption is second in the hierarchy of planning options. In a kinship care training session, workers are often quick to share their lack of success with this plan and the reasons given by grandparents, in particular, for not accepting adoption as an option. Much of the decision by relatives is rooted in the concept of extended family care as a cultural norm that gives families the right to care for children without legal authority. There may be other factors as well that contribute to relative caregivers' reluctance to adopt, but training should still cover this as an option once reunification with birth parents has been ruled out.

Custody and guardianship of the child by the relative appears to be somewhat easier to achieve once the service needs have been met in kinship care.

This permanency option is often decided on the basis of the state's funding policies for children who are living with relatives and the financial needs of the caregiver. Workers need to be taught to explore the feasibility of this option by collecting information in the assessment and intervention phase of the case.

For adolescents, where independent living programs are available, permanency may mean helping the child to achieve some life skills to prepare for emancipation. This child may live with a relative or in a semi-independent living situation with relative support.

It is important for the trainer to note the difference in the hierarchy of permanency planning in regular foster care and kinship care (see Figure 7.3).

Permanency planning should be the focus of assessment and intervention strategies. Workers should learn to make a decision regarding permanency after the initial assessment has been completed. As the plan is implemented, the worker needs to understand the importance of changing the plan as situations and conditions change in a timely manner.

ASSESSMENT OF THE KINSHIP CARE FAMILY SYSTEM

The assessment process is unique when children are placed with relatives, and practitioners should consider making the paradigm shift from assessing the dyad to assessing the triad. A major component of curriculum development, therefore, is techniques for assessing the kinship triad.

The practitioner's choice of service goals and intervention strategies with the triad will depend on his or her assessment skills and knowledge about the nuances of the kinship triad. To develop accurate assessments that advance permanent plans for children, the worker must understand the extended family system and the problems and issues the triad brings to the helping process.

Assessment provides the basis for decision making. In developing this training component, a clear framework for assessing the triad is critical. Practitioners are usually not clear about how to assess the triad. Participants in training should learn to use an assessment framework in the context of the child, the parents, and the caregiver. An intergenerational perspective on the triad members, an understanding of a multidimensional assessment of intrapersonal family and environmental systems, and the acknowledgment of cul-

Regular Foster Care	Kinship Care
• Return home	• Return home
• Place with relatives	• Relative Adoption
• Adoption	• Relative Custody/Guardian
• Permanent Foster Care	• Independent Living (age 16)
• Long-Term Foster Care	

Figure 7.3 Hierarchy of Permanent Plans.

tural realities within extended families form the basis for the development of an assessment framework in kinship care training.

The following assessment skills or competencies are important in curriculum development. Training participants should learn to:

- Organize descriptive information about the triad, including family relationships, family strengths/problems, family structure, family function, and cultural considerations
- Come to tentative agreements with the triad regarding the elements, subsystems, factors, and forces within the extended family system that affect and maintain the precipitating problems
- Begin to identify with the triad potential targets for change
- Predict and describe probable consequences to the child if things do not change
- Assess risk and determine the urgency with which the intervention must be undertaken
- Identify potential resources and avenues for change, as well as potential barriers
- Identify with the family and the case supervisor intervention strategies that might be applicable to resolve the problems
- Identify other interested extended family members
- Use the technique of mapping such as genograms
- Develop a means for case planning and evaluation and set a time frame for work with the triad

A comprehensive guide to assessing the triad is helpful to practitioners and may serve as a training tool. This guide should include three levels of assessment—individual, triad family, and extended family.

Individual Assessment

Trainers should always emphasize the importance of first assessing the child's safety in the caregiver's home. It is also necessary to assess the child's behavior and emotional adjustment in the caregiver's home, the child's history with the caregiver, and the child's environmental, health, and educational needs.

Assessment of the parent's physical and mental health and behavior toward the child and the caregiver is ongoing as workers attempt to make decisions about permanency for the child. It is important that the child's parents be actively involved in the planning process. Workers often avoid working with the parents, particularly when the child is safe and happy with the relative caregiver. Therefore, the trainer ought to stress parental involvement in achieving permanence for the child.

The caregiver is a part of the individual needs assessment process. Some of the issues to be assessed are the caregiver's willingness to provide for the child and his or her financial situation, health and emotional needs and supports, and other responsibilities.

Triad Assessment

Level two of the assessment process involves assessing the triad family. This includes: (1) triad relationships, (2) strengths and problem identification within the triad, (3) triad structure, and (4) triad functioning. A framework is helpful in understanding the triad to make an informed decision about the child's future (see Figure 7.4). Workers are very receptive to presentation of a clear framework for assessing extended families. Case examples may be discussed in groups to give participants an opportunity to use the suggested framework to practice assessing the triad.

Other Extended Family Assessment

Level three involves assessing the capacity of other extended family members to assist the triad. Convening an Extended Family Meeting (EFM) of interested family members helps in the assessment process and therefore should be done in the assessment phase. Trainers should remind trainees that families usually come to the aid of family members in times of crisis. Historically, when a crisis situation has come to the attention of government agencies and required government intervention, the extended family has been left out. The EFM provides an opportunity to explore with the extended family what addi-

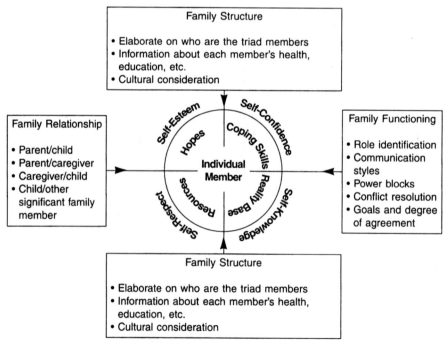

Figure 7.4 Family Dynamics/Extended Systems Framework.

tional resources are available. Strategies for facilitating and utilizing the EFM in case decision making can be taught through the use of role play as an exercise. Skills in mediation and group facilitation ought to be learned by staff before using this case strategy.

As the assessment phase progresses, there should be a consensus within the triad on issues for intervention and follow-up activity. In preparation for intervention, a service agreement or contract involving members of the triad, EFM participants (if appropriate), and the practitioner should be signed by all parties involved. Trainers should present contracting and service agreement information.

Service Intervention with the Kinship Triad

Training in basic intervention skills in the process of working toward the goals jointly agreed on by the triad should follow the assessment component of the curriculum. Workers should understand how to make the transition from gathering information, formulating a permanent plan, and negotiating a service agreement to resolving problems and promoting change.

Intervention strategies should ensure a comprehensive array of services to the triad, which may include mental and physical health, educational, developmental, social, addiction, protection, and/or financial services. It is usually helpful to give workers some ways to begin this phase of work with the triad, such as clarifying with the triad members the reason for placement and agency involvement, the current permanent plan, and the triad and agency expectations.

Training should focus on teaching workers to determine their roles with the triad, utilize appropriate therapeutic techniques, build trust, encourage family interaction, build on family strengths, clarify issues of abuse and neglect, and make referrals for appropriate treatment. Basic family therapy terminology should be introduced such as joining, reframing, processing re-enactment, feedback, aligning, boundary setting, rehearsing, advising, confronting, evaluating, and pointing out endings. These techniques can be used as the worker intervenes with individual members of the triad and works with the triad family. When the worker is able to work with the triad together to resolve problem areas, interventions are more successful and less time consuming.

Working with the triad relationship is quite different for the kinship care practitioner. As workers engage the triad in the therapeutic process, they would benefit from understanding that: (1) it is important to recognize the views of each person involved, (2) each member has a part in supporting the case outcome, and (3) the family can do more to increase the quality of relationships and support each member.

Family strengths as well as problem areas should be understood in kinship care. It is important to teach practitioners to use the strengths of the kin family in designing the treatment. For example, grandparents are often dependent on their faith and religion to solve problems. As the worker realizes the value of religion to the caregiver and/or the family, he or she might inquire about the grandparents' expectations in treatment by referring to their faith or religious beliefs. From the use of an assessment tool such as the eco-map, trainees should be able to focus on the triad's interaction with different systems, such as church, school, community, health care facilities, and employers. Case studies are very effective in helping trainees learn to choose effective intervention strategies that empower the triad in these interactions.

In linking the assessment with the intervention, the training must emphasize the child's treatment needs as they result from prior neglect or abuse. The research suggests that children placed with relatives have the same physical and emotional treatment needs at the time of placement as do children placed with nonrelatives. Therefore, the treatment needs of the child may include help with emotional problems due to separation, severe abuse and/or neglect, substance abuse, family tragedy, handicapping conditions, or loss of parents through death or abandonment. Workers should be made aware of treatment resources to meet the needs of the children in their area. As part of training, resource people should discuss special-needs children as well as the availability of programs to meet these children's physical and mental health needs.

In order to make a decision about the future ability of parents to assume responsibility for children living with kin, workers should provide services to the parents and develop treatment plans that meet the needs of the parents. Workers should always be reminded to be sure to include fathers in service provision. In the assessment phase, workers are trained to review with the triad the parents' capacity, willingness, and ability to make the necessary changes to care for the child. It is important to acknowledge that it can be difficult to work with parents, because of their inaccessibility or their lack of cooperation or because of a lack of available treatment resources or, sometimes, the agency's or the court's lack of responsiveness to the needs of the parents.

Caregiver support, as noted, is very important in kinship care. The training should stress the rights, needs, and expectations of relative caregivers. Unlike other child welfare placements, in kinship placements it is relatives who come to the aid of family members in crisis. Depending on the circumstances and the reasons for agency intervention and removal of the child from his or her parents, the caregiver may experience feelings of emotional trauma, disappointment, helplessness, uncertainty, grief, loss, guilt, obligation, pride, or anxiety. Brainstorming with participants is an excellent way to sensitize them to the problems of the caregiver. Training should emphasize appropriate interventions to help the caregiver with the problems associated with the new responsibility of caring for kin. Exercises that relate to stages of the family life cycle and to theories of adult development may be helpful in generating appropriate interventions with the caregiver.

The majority of caregivers in kinship care are grandparents who are between forty-five and sixty years of age (Link, 1996). Interventions with persons within this age range may include providing access to health-related services, community supports, employment/career guidance, and financial planning.

Workers need to understand the importance of sharing with the caregivers the agency's expectations, such as being available for mandated court appearances, health care appointments, parent visitation, and sessions with the worker. Agency monitoring of the child's progress in the relatives' home may be stressful to the caregivers if the worker is not trained to be sensitive to the need to respect "family business," including family history, traditions, secrets, taboos, and life experiences. Workers should be trained to work with caregivers in resolving problem areas and in determining permanent living arrangement for the child. The worker should listen to the desires of the caregiver and must have the skills to partialize the caregivers' concerns, understand the obstacles, and negotiate action steps. It is important to note that most caregivers are concerned primarily about the progress of the child's parents toward reunification. Even though they recognize the possibility of long-term care of the child, they are hoping that the worker's interventions with the parent will be successful. In rare instances, caregivers have given up hope that the child will be reunited with the parent. There are also a few cases in which the relative sabotages parents' efforts to have the child returned. The worker should be trained to recognize the power of the caregiver to control the service outcomes in kinship care situations.

Ending and Transition in Kinship Care

The final component of the training should focus on the unique dynamics and skills associated with ending the services to the triad and helping members to make the appropriate transition. In the ending and transition phase of kinship care, the worker should understand that the most important goal in working with the triad is to achieve a permanent living arrangement for the child. Because of the feelings involved in possible shifts in relationships among the triad, the worker's skills in this phase are important. Specific worker skills include helping the caregivers redefine their role in the child's life if the child is returned to the parents. The worker ought to examine with the triad areas of conflict resolution such as understanding the power base, unresolved conflicts, use of corporal punishment, the child's need for additional services, parent/child conflict, and the role of other intervening family members. It is crucial that the worker and/or the caregivers face their own ambivalence about reunification and move to support the process. The worker then should make a recommendation to the court regarding reunification, and the court should accept the plan and rescind the agency's involvement.

If the final decision is adoption or the transfer of custody and guardianship to the relative, the worker should have the skills to work on the ending, identify the process of arriving at the ending decision, clarify the parent's and the child's feelings related to the ending, summarize the work with the triad, and address the transition issues. It would be helpful for the worker to learn the legal steps to finalizing adoption by the relative or the legal aspects of rescinding custody and guardianship by the state in favor or the relative.

In spite of endings and transitions in kinship care, most relationships are changed but not severed. The worker should understand that each triad will make the transition in its own way, on the basis of the family's values and strengths.

CONCLUSION

This chapter has focused on the training needs of kinship care workers. Particular emphasis has been placed on the implications of a shift in philosophy and practice away from the traditional foster care paradigm. Although the core elements of the training curriculum are the same—the components of the service delivery, the importance of permanency planning, the necessary assessment, intervention, ending and transition skills, and so on—there are significant differences when using these elements in providing services to the kinship triad and to individual members of that triad. Specific training for kinship care workers has not been given priority among child welfare professionals. However, as the numbers continue to increase and the field learns more about kin placements, there will be more recognition of the need for training designed to increase the competence, knowledge, and skills of child welfare practitioners who work in kinship care programs. An investment must be made in training staff to work with the triad if we are going to continue to use kinship care effectively as an alternate to the traditional placement options (Jackson, 1996). The triad is desperate to stabilize it's situation, and practitioners should be trained to approach service delivery with the same urgency.

References

Berrick, J. D., Barth, R. P., & Needell, B. (1994). A comparison of kinship foster homes and foster family homes: Implications for kinship care as family preservation. *Children and Youth Services Review, 16* (1/2), 33–63.

Billingsley, A. (1992). *Climbing jacob's ladder: The enduring legacy of African-American families.* New York: Simon & Schuster.

Child Welfare League of America. (1994). *Kinship care: A natural bridge.* Washington, D.C.: Author.

Child Welfare Institute. (1996). *Putting ideas into action.* Atlanta, Ga.: Author.

Children's Defense Fund. (1990). *A report card briefing book and action primer.* Washington, D.C.: Author.

Danzy, J., & Jackson, S. (1997). Family preservation and support services: A missed opportunity for kinship care. *Child Welfare, 76,* 1.

Dorfman, R. A. (1988). *Paradigms of clinical social work practice.* New York: Brunner/Mazel.

Everett, J. E., Chipunga, S. S., & Leashore, B. R. (1991). *Child welfare: An Afrocentric approach.* New Brunswick, N.J.: Rutgers University Press.

Gleeson, J. P., & Craig, L. C. (1994). Kinship care in child welfare: An analysis of states policies. *Children and Youth Services Review, 16* (1/2), 7–32.

Goldstein, J., Freud, A., & Solnit, A. (1979). *Beyond the best interest of the child.* (2nd ed.). New York: Free Press.

Hill, R. B. (1972). *The strengths of black families.* New York: Emerson Hall.

Jackson, S. M. (1996). The kinship triad: A service delivery model. *Child Welfare, 75* (5), 583–599.

Jackson, S. M. (1998). *Kinship care services to the triad: A training manual of child welfare practitioners.* Washington, D.C.: Child Welfare League of America.

Lawrence-Webb, C. (1993). *Relative placement: Training curriculum.* Baltimore, Md.: University of Maryland School of Social Work.

Link, M. K. (1996). Permanency outcomes in kinship care: A study of children placed in kinship care in Erie County, NY. *Child Welfare, 75* (5), 509–528.

Miller v. Youakim, 440 U.S. 125 (1979).

National Commission on Family Foster Care. (1991). The significance of kinship care. In *A blueprint for fostering infants, children and youth in the 1990s.* Washington, D.C.: Child Welfare League of America.

Pecora, P. J., Whittaker, J. K., & Maluccio, A. N., with Barth, R. P., & Plotnick, R. D. (1992). *The child welfare challenge.* New York: Aldine de Gruyter.

Scannapieco, M., & Hegar, R. L. (1996). A nontraditional assessment framework for kinship foster homes. *Child Welfare, 75* (5), 567–582.

Scannapieco, M., & Hegar, R. L. (1995). Kinship care: Two case management models. *Children & Adolescent Social Work, 12,* 147–156.

Scannapieco, M., & Jackson, S. (1996). Kinship care: The African American response to family preservation. *Social Work, 41* (2), 190–196.

Takas, M. (1993). *Kinship care and family preservation: A guide for states in legal and policy development.* Washington, D.C.: American Bar Association Center on Children and the Law.

CHAPTER 8

Whanau Knows Best
Kinship Care in New Zealand

JOY SWANSON ERNST, M.S.W.

In 1989, New Zealand broke new ground in child care and protection by passing the Children, Young Persons, and Their Families Act of 1989 (the 1989 Act). Although the term "kinship" care never appears in the Act, a philosophy of kinship care pervades the Act's objects and principles. Innovations in the Act include the practice of family decision making through Family Group Conferences, placement of children within the extended family network whenever possible, recognition of the cultural needs of children, and an expanded role for community-based agencies. New Zealand's model offers a way of practice that strives to empower families, rather than to view them as dysfunctional and unable to cope (Connolly, 1994).

The 1989 Act sparked international interest in child welfare practice in New Zealand, an island nation of 3.6 million people in the South Pacific. New Zealand, originally inhabited and settled by the Maori, is a Westernized, largely English-speaking parliamentary democracy. The majority (about four-fifths) of its population is of European, primarily British, descent. Maori make up about 13 percent of the population, and Pacific Islanders (e.g., Samoans, Tongans, Cook Islanders, Fijians) make up about 5 percent of the population.

Much of the attention given to child welfare reform in New Zealand has focused on Family Group Conferences (Ban, 1993; Connolly, 1994; Hardin, 1996; Hudson, Morris, Maxwell, & Galaway, 1996; Ryburn, 1993). The Act's emphasis on kinship care has received less attention. The concerns addressed by the 1989 Act correspond to concerns raised about foster care and the practice of child welfare in the United States and elsewhere. These include alienation of children from their ethnic, racial, or tribal heritage (see, e.g., Miller, Hoffman, & Turner, 1980), instability of placements (Rittner, 1995), the failure to include family members' perspectives in decisions about placement (Petr &

Entriken, 1995; Rittner, 1995), and the many minority children in the care and custody of the state (Everett, 1991; Stehno, 1982).

New Zealand's experiences offer a unique perspective on two issues that arise in kinship care policy and practice in the United States and perhaps elsewhere. The first is the 1989 Act's extraordinary recognition of the importance of cultural identity in child protection policy. The Act incorporates Maori understandings of kinship, and the Family Group Conference (FGC) is modeled on Maori methods of problem resolution. The second issue is the ethos of family responsibility. New Zealand's ideal is that child welfare is a private, rather than a state-supported, venture. The 1989 Act obligates a child's extended family to decide if a care and protection matter exists and to formulate a plan to address it, children should remain within their family network, if possible, and stay out of the formal care of the Department of Social Welfare.

Thus, kinship care in New Zealand is a response to efforts to alter the focus and purpose of government and an effort to redress past practices that harmed and alienated Maori children and families. These two goals sometimes reinforce each other and sometimes conflict. Tensions emerge that are familiar to practitioners in the field of child welfare—the importance of culture and family versus a child's needs for safety and stability, and the balance between empowerment and dependency.

This chapter describes what happens when children enter the care and protection system in New Zealand and discusses the points at which the extended family becomes involved.[1] It draws upon published and unpublished sources, from interviews with New Zealand Children and Young Persons and Their Families Service (NZCYPFS) staff at five different offices, and from conversations with professionals involved in child care and protection. Although the policies and reports provided by the NZCYPFS give valuable information, the implementation of the 1989 Act relies upon the skill and discretion of NZCYPFS staff (Drew, 1996; Mason, 1992a). Practice varies by office (Robertson & Maxwell, 1996) and is subject to fiscal constraints (Cockburn, 1994; Jefferson & Laven, 1995). Research on the outcomes of the Act is limited (Maxwell, Robertson, Thom, & Walker, 1995); a few studies examine families' experiences with practice under the Act (Gilling, Patterson, & Walker, 1995; Human Rights Commission, 1992; Rimene, 1993) and two unpublished studies examine aspects of kinship care (J. Walker, 1990; Worrall, 1996). Although this chapter draws upon the best information available, the extent to which kinship care addresses the needs of abused and neglected children in New Zealand requires further study.

This chapter commences with a discussion of the historical background of the 1989 Act. It then describes the elements of the 1989 Act relevant to kinship care and discusses early review of and reaction to the 1989 Act. This section also describes the organization and structure of the NZCYPFS, provides

---

1. This chapter focuses on kinship care used in care and protection. Family decision making and placement within the extended family also are outcomes of youth justice interventions that take place under the 1989 Act (Maxwell & Morris, 1993).

statistical information, and discusses the role of community agencies. The chapter then delineates processes used by NZCYPFS following a report of child abuse or neglect and discusses four themes—availability of family, assessment of caregivers, financial help, and support and monitoring—that arise in kinship care practice. This discussion touches upon the tensions and contradictions that emanate from New Zealand's concurrent attempts to care for abused and neglected children, to recognize the importance of culture, and to empower families to take responsibility for their own.

Throughout the chapter, the term "extended family" means a kinship network larger than a unit of parent or parents and children or even grandparents and children. New Zealand law distinguishes among children, persons less than fourteen years old, and young persons who are between the ages of fourteen and seventeen. In this chapter, the term "children" encompasses all three age groups.

HISTORICAL BACKGROUND

This section describes the historical influences on the 1989 Act: the relationship between the Maori and *Pakeha* (the Maori word for New Zealanders of European descent) and resulting Maori activism, the changing role of the state, and the context of child and social welfare services. The events that immediately preceded the passage of the legislation influenced its outcome, and early experience of practice under the Act shaped the nature of kinship care today.

Maori and Pakeha

Maori are the *tangata whenua* (the people of the land) and the indigenous people of New Zealand. British colonists began settling in New Zealand during the nineteenth century, more than one thousand years after the first Maori arrived from other South Pacific islands (Metge, 1995). In 1840, representatives of many Maori tribes and the British Crown signed the Treaty of Waitangi (Orange, 1987). The treaty appeared to safeguard Maori control over their interests, practices, possessions (including land), and customs in exchange for the rights attached to British citizenship and for yielding their sovereignty to the Crown (Spoonley, 1993).

Today, the exact meaning of the rights and responsibilities accorded to the parties of the treaty is the subject of considerable debate, in part due to variations in the English and the Maori language versions and to the incompatible expectations of the original parties (Orange, 1987; Spoonley, 1993). The Treaty has always occupied a central role in Maori society (Ministerial Advisory Committee, 1988). Because the Maori derived their strength and their worldview from their relationship with the land, alienation from their land meant alienation from their culture and traditional social structures (discussed further later) centered on *whanau* (extended family, pronounced FAH-now), *hapu* (subtribe), and *iwi* (tribe).

As increasing numbers of British settlers arrived and demanded land, the Treaty was largely ignored, and the Maori were separated from their land.

British laws, customs, and social structures dominated New Zealand society. Laws regarding marriage, adoption, and the guardianship of children outlawed some practices of the *whanau*, the basic social unit of Maori society (Durie-Hall & Metge, 1992). Public policy was based on the assumption that assimilation of the Maori into Pakeha society was desirable (Spoonley, 1993).

After World War II, opportunities for employment in urban areas and the government's relocation policies encouraged many Maori to migrate from rural areas (Spoonley, 1993). While migration improved the material well-being of Maori, it further weakened rural social structures (Metge, 1995). During the 1960s, New Zealand experienced an influx of immigrants and guest workers from the Pacific Islands (Spoonley, 1993). These immigrants were also separated from traditional family structures that provided support, identity, and social control (Foliaki, 1994).

Today, the population of New Zealand is highly urbanized. The proportion of Maori in the population varies by region. Some areas of the North Island have a high population of Maori, while very few Maori live in the South Island. Most of the Pacific Island Polynesian population lives in the two largest cities, Auckland and Wellington (Statistics New Zealand, 1994).

Maori in urban areas had to adapt to a materialistic culture and cope with monocultural institutions of the government. The proportion of Maori who left school and appeared in the juvenile courts or criminal justice system exceeded their proportion in the general population. Schools, social welfare agencies, and criminal justice institutions that dealt with these problems were not sensitive to cultural differences and often compounded rather than alleviated problems (R. Walker, 1992). Today, Maori account for a large percentage of the indicators of poor health, high infant mortality, single parenthood, low rates of school completion, unemployment, and criminal activity. These problems are linked with urbanization (Spoonley, 1993).

Urbanization also spurred Maori activism (R. Walker, 1992; Spoonley, 1993). Over the past twenty years, many Maori have shown interest in recapturing their culture. They have made efforts to receive fair compensation for their tribal lands and recognition as partners in a bicultural society. The activism and renewed ethnic pride of the Maori have characterized their relationship with the dominant *Pakeha* society (Spoonley, 1993; Vasil, 1990; R. Walker, 1992).

Maori activism has included efforts to improve the policies and practices of the Department of Social Welfare (Ministerial Advisory Committee, 1988). Today, the Treaty of Waitangi has a central role in New Zealand's social welfare policy, and the Department of Social Welfare has a commitment to its principles (Department of Social Welfare, 1994).

It is important to note that there is no single definition of who is Maori. According to Pool, the popular usage of the word Maori implies someone who feels he or she is Maori and who is recognized as such by other people (1993, p. 11). Legal and statistical definitions have varied over time. Because of high rates of intermarriage of Maori and Pakeha, many New Zealanders have mixed ancestry. The census identifies people who classify themselves as Maori (ethnic identity) and those who have Maori ancestry. The latter group is larger.

During the past ten to fifteen years, more Maori have begun to identify with their *iwi* (tribes) rather than simply as Maori (Bradley, 1994). Seventy-two percent of the people with Maori ancestry named an *iwi* affiliation on the 1991 census (Wereta, 1994). Viewpoints among Maori are diverse regarding matters such as identifying oneself as a member of an *iwi* (the tribal view) or simply as Maori (the pan-Maori view).

Pakeha[2] are New Zealanders who are European immigrants or who are descended from immigrants of European origin (Metge, 1995). Since 1840, patterns of immigration have shifted depending upon economic conditions, world wars, and government-sponsored initiatives to encourage or restrict settlement. Immigration from the British Isles and subsequently from other European nations such as The Netherlands and Germany increased in the years following World War II.

New Zealand's ethnic diversity today extends beyond the *Pakeha*, Maori, and Pacific Islanders. Recent changes in immigration law have altered the nation's ethnic mix by increasing the numbers of Asian immigrants. Immigration has presented political and social challenges for contemporary New Zealand. The country must learn how to adapt to a more diverse population against the historical background of Maori and *Pakeha* relations.

The Welfare State and Afterwards

The New Zealand government, whether led by the conservative National Party or by the more liberal Labour Party, has a history of support for a strong welfare state. Before the 1970s, New Zealanders enjoyed a protected economy characterized by low unemployment (Kelsey, 1995). The state provided or funded most social welfare services, while voluntary agencies played a complementary role (Barretta-Herman, 1994).

The role of the state shifted dramatically during the 1980s (Rice, 1992). In 1984, the Fourth Labour Government initiated free-market reforms in response to the rising unemployment and low growth of the 1970s and early 1980s. This structural readjustment program greatly affected the underlying philosophy of and the structure, funding, and delivery of the services of the state (Kelsey, 1995). Privatization led to increased reliance on informal care and community agencies.

The government responded to calls by voluntary agencies, community groups, and the Maori community to increase their role in the delivery of social welfare services (Barretta-Herman, 1994). In the child welfare arena, however, many advocates wanted New Zealand to adopt a comprehensive approach to dealing with child abuse and neglect. This approach relied on research and standards developed abroad and stressed involvement of multidisciplinary child protection teams of professionals (Tapp, Geddis, & Taylor, 1992).

---

2. Some New Zealanders dislike or reject the label of *Pakeha*. For discussion of the term and its usage, see Spoonley (1993, pp. 57–61), Metge (1995, pp. 19–20).

Child and Family Welfare

In response to the economic and social distress of the nineteenth century, the New Zealand government passed laws that provided support for widows, the elderly, and neglected and dependent children (Koopman-Boyden & Scott, 1984). In 1867, the Neglected and Criminal Children Act authorized the creation of industrial schools. In 1882, the Industrial Schools Act allowed for boarding out of their residents in foster homes (Worrall, 1983). The Child Welfare Act of 1925 widened the state's responsibility for the country's orphans and delinquent and neglected children. It established the Child Welfare Branch (later Division) and the Children's Courts (Koopman-Boyden & Scott, 1984). Children in care were placed with foster parents, and little contact was maintained with their families of origin. No written policies emphasized keeping children within their wider family networks (J. Walker, 1990). The child welfare system displayed little regard for the extended kin networks of Maori children.

In 1972, a merger of the Child Welfare Division and the Department of Social Security (Statistics New Zealand, 1994) created the Department of Social Welfare (DSW). New Zealand made its first systematic attempt to deal explicitly with the issues of child abuse and neglect and juvenile delinquency with the Children and Young Person's Act of 1974. This law required that interests of the child be treated as paramount (Tapp, Geddis, & Taylor, 1992). It did not contain references to care of children by their kin group (J. Walker, 1990).

Concern about the plight of children in state care grew in the 1970s and early 1980s. The New Zealand Foster Care Federation (now the New Zealand Family and Foster Care Federation) was formed in 1976 to provide support for foster parents and to advocate for children in foster care (Worrall, 1983). Reports of inquiries (Auckland Committee on Racism and Discrimination, 1978; Johnston, 1982) and research (Mackay, 1981) revealed that: high numbers of Maori children were in state care; there was a high rate of placement breakdown and instability; Maori children frequently were placed with non-Maori families; and DSW institutions were abusive and were not meeting the cultural needs of children in care.

The *Maatua Whangai* program, a cooperative effort of the Department of Social Welfare, the Department of Justice, and the Department of Maori Affairs, attempted to divert the numbers of children and young persons from institutions and place them within whanau networks. For several reasons, *Maatua Whangai* failed to meet expectations (Bradley, 1994).

A report released in 1986, *Puao-Te-Ata-Tu (Day break)*, recommended that the Department of Social Welfare change to meet the needs of Maori (Ministerial Advisory Committee, 1988). The report raised concern about monocultural practices, such as foster care placement of Maori children with *Pakeha* families. These practices alienated Maori children from their kin and contributed to the breakdown of Maori families. It noted that the centrality of the child in the 1974 legislation was not in keeping with Maori traditions. *Puao-Te-Ata-Tu* and a subsequent report (Working Party on the Children and Young Person's Bill, 1987) recommended that revised legislation recognize that a

Maori child's interests cannot be set apart from those of that child's *whanau* and *hapu*. Two of *Puao-Te-Ata-Tu*'s recommendations influenced the 1989 Act and kinship care practice. One is the ideal that children who need foster care should live with members of the extended family. A second is the requirement that social workers and the Courts research a child's family and tribal links.

Some groups, predominantly groups of professionals who worked with abused children, thought the 1974 law did not adequately deal with child abuse and neglect. They endorsed changes incorporated into a bill introduced in 1986. Their recommendations included mandatory reporting, which had never been a part of New Zealand's child protection law, and a coordinated multi-disciplinary approach to child abuse cases. The concerns raised in *Puao-Te-Ata-Tu* and the estimated costs of carrying out the legislation thwarted this bill (Cockburn, 1994; Tapp, Geddis, & Taylor, 1992). DSW social workers[3] supported the changes introduced by the 1989 Act; the legislation codified practices, such as inclusion of family in decision making, that had been initiated by some DSW offices (Wilcox et al., 1991).

THE CHILDREN, YOUNG PERSONS, AND THEIR FAMILIES ACT 1989

This section describes key elements of the 1989 Act and discusses how the 1989 Act combines recognition of cultural identity with privatization of child welfare. The section includes discussion of reaction to the 1989 Act, early assessments of practice, and a description of the New Zealand Children, Young Persons, and Their Families Service.

Description of the 1989 Act

The overall object of the 1989 Act is to promote the well-being of children, young persons, and their families and family groups through several means, one of which is to help parents, families, *whanau, hapu, iwi,* and family groups to discharge their responsibilities to prevent their children and young persons suffering harm, ill treatment, abuse, neglect, or deprivation (Children, Young Persons, and Their Families Act, 1989, from now on cited as CYPF 1989, Sec. 4[c]). Three of the general principles of the Act are pertinent to kinship care: (a) participation of the extended family in decisions affecting the child, (b) maintenance and strengthening of the relationship between a child or young person and his or her family, *whanau, hapu, iwi,* and family group, and (c) consideration not only for the welfare of the child, but also the stability of the child's family group (CYPF 1989, Sec. 5 [a–c]).

The Director General must ensure that the policies and services of the Department of Social Welfare recognize social, economic, and cultural values

---

3. Both the DSW and NZCYPSFS use the term "social worker" for direct service workers although they may not have university-level qualifications. This chapter follows the same usage. For discussions of the social work profession and social work education in New Zealand, see Barretta-Herman (1994), Nash (1994).

of all groups and have particular regard for the values, culture, and beliefs of the Maori people (CYPF 1989, Sec. 7 [c] [i and ii]). These policies and services must also support the role of families, *whanau, hapu, iwi*, and family groups and avoid the alienation of children and young persons from their family, *whanau, hapu, iwi*, and family group (Sec. 7 [c] [iii and iv]).

The Care and Protection Principles of the Act stress the maintenance of a child's links with family and cultural identity. According to these principles, intervention should be the minimum necessary to ensure a child's safety. The family should receive necessary assistance and support to enable the child to receive care within his or her own family, *whanau, hapu, iwi*, or family group (Sec. 13[d]). Removal of a child should occur only in cases of serious risk or harm. The first choice of placement is within the family group.

The Family Group Conference (FGC) is the statutory process for making decisions about children in need of care and protection (CYPF 1989, Sec. 20–38). Members of a child's *whanau, hapu, iwi*, and/or family group have a right to attend the FGC. NZCYPFS staff and other professionals provide information on care and protection issues. Only members of the family group may be present during the discussions and deliberations (CYPF 1989, Sec. 22). The family group is responsible for coming up with a plan to address the issue presented. When possible, the plan involves the wider family network (Atkin, 1991). The FGC has the power to make binding decisions. An FGC must take place before the family court will take any action or make any court orders, except the emergency removal of a child who is at immediate risk. The FGC is discussed in detail later.

The 1989 Act and Cultural Identity

The Maori terms *whanau, hapu*, and *iwi* appear throughout the legislation. The 1989 Act does not define these terms. It leaves the definition of family open for each child (Durie-Hall & Metge, 1992). Understanding of Maori kinship terms helps the outsider appreciate that the term kinship care has unique meanings in New Zealand. Maori understanding of kinship and family responsibility varies from Western notions based in European traditions where the nuclear family has become the basic familial unit.

The term most commonly used as the English translation for *whanau* is "extended family." This definition does not capture the many historical and contemporary meanings of the word *whanau* (for discussion, see Bradley, 1994; Metge, 1995). Extended family fails to uncover the importance of descent in forming and shaping the *whanau* and giving identity to its members (Metge, 1995).

The *hapu*, or sub-tribe, is a collection of *whanau*. The *iwi*, a collection of *hapu*, is a tribe, linked by kinship ties and descent from a common ancestor. The importance of keeping tribal lands also holds *iwi* together (Bradley, 1994).

The purposes or functions of *whanau* may include: support of individual *whanau* members and parent child families, the shared upbringing of members' children, management of group property, organization of *hui* (meetings and large-scale gatherings), and dealing with their own problems and conflicts through family meetings, or *whanau hui*. Individual *whanau* carry out these functions with varying degrees of organization and formality (Metge, 1995). The functions of support and shared child rearing dovetail with the kinship care philosophy of the 1989 Act. The *whanau hui* provides the model for the family group conference (H. Walker, 1996).

The extent to which today's *whanau* can effectively carry out these functions depends on how much they have been damaged by social problems that have disproportionately affected the Maori over the past few decades. Maori in rural areas belong to active *whanau* in more cases than do those living in urban areas (Statistics New Zealand, 1994). Many Maori children who come to the attention of the NZCYPFS do not have a connection to a functioning *whanau*.

In the Maori world view, children, are *taonga*, or treasures. They belong to the *whanau* and not exclusively to their parents (Selby, 1994). In Maori society, relatives other than their birth parents sometimes raise children. The parties involved make these arrangements openly but do not legally formalize them (see Metge, 1995, pp. 210–257; also Cairns, 1990). Placement of children with relatives is one way of strengthening *whanau* structures. Children are kept apprised of their kinship links through recitation of *whakapapa*, or genealogy (Ministerial Advisory Committee, 1988). Such informal adoption, or *whangai*, was once little understood or appreciated by the Department of Social Welfare and the practice clashed with New Zealand's Western-style adoption laws. This practice continues today.

The 1989 Act and Privatization

The value underlying the family decision making model is that families, broadly defined, have the knowledge, expertise, and ability to be responsible for the safety and well-being of their children (Ryburn, 1993). FGCs often result in or confirm a change in care for child. Since the intention of the 1989 Act is to reduce state intervention and to keep children out of formal care, many children placed with kin as the result of a Family Group Conference are not placed in the formal care, custody, or guardianship of the Director General of Social Welfare.

The 1989 Act broadened the role of community-based agencies. Four categories of agencies may provide services under the 1989 Act—Community and Family Support Services, *Iwi* Social Services, Cultural Social Services, and Community Services. The first three can serve as custodians or guardians of children in need of care and protection. All approved organizations must provide culturally appropriate services and uphold the Act's Objects and Principles (Bradley, 1995).

Iwi Social Services blur the distinction between family and institutional care. If a child is in the custody of his or her *iwi*, the objects and principles of the Act are met. The DSW envisions a much bigger role for *Iwi* Social Services in future provision of care and protection services (Department of Social Welfare, 1995b). To meet their strategic goals, the DSW will have to shift significant funding to *iwi* to provide their own social services.

While many Maori social and community service organizations provide services under contract with the New Zealand Community Funding Agency,[4] few are approved as *Iwi* Social Services. Development of approval standards for *Iwi* Social Services has involved many consultations with *iwi* and pan-Maori groups on matters, not easily resolved, of financing, accountability, and power sharing. If the DSW is committed to the principles of the Treaty of Waitangi, *Iwi* Social Services must be structured so that decision making and control of resources are shared equitably between *iwi* and the Crown (Bradley, 1994, 1995).

Elements identified by the DSW's Social Policy Agency that set an *Iwi* Social Services apart from other community services are that the social service uses *whakapapa* (genealogy) to establish *hapu* and *iwi* links for children and that the service is *marae*-based.[5] An *Iwi* Social Service must also have the mandate of the governing body of its own *iwi* (Denny, 1995). Under these guidelines, not all Maori social service organizations qualify as *Iwi* Social Services.

Reaction to 1989 Act

Social work practice under the 1989 Act generated public interest and the scrutiny of professionals and child advocates. Many (e.g., Tapp, Geddis, & Taylor, 1992) raised concerns that the Act did not include enough safeguards for children. Others praised the Act's indigenous approaches. Durie-Hall and Metge noted that the Act is unique among family statutes in New Zealand in that it recognizes the diversity of family forms in New Zealand in general and among the Maori in particular (1992, p. 74).

Early review of the organization and operation of the Act by the DSW (Paterson & Harvey, 1991; Renouf, Robb, & Wells, 1990) did not address kinship care in any detail. Statistics from the first year did not readily reveal whether children were placed with kin when there was a change in care as the result of an FGC (Maxwell & Robertson, 1991).

Eighteen months after the 1989 Act became law, the Minister of Social Welfare established a Ministerial Review Team to examine the operations of the Act in detail. This report, known as the Mason Report (Mason, 1992a) endorsed the basic philosophy of the 1989 Act. It criticized, among other things, funding constraints, poorly handled organizational changes in the Department of Social Welfare, scarcity of community agencies, and poorly trained staff. The report warned that the needs of children were sometimes lost amid the focus on family. Criticism about kinship care included inadequate training and support of kin caregivers. One Maori commentator complained that, in effect,

---

4. The New Zealand Community Funding Agency (NZCFA), a unit within the Department of Social Welfare, is the key provider of funds to voluntary social welfare agencies and to agencies providing service under the 1989 Act.

5. A *marae* is a Maori meeting house and the focal point for Maori life. Traditionally, *marae* were linked to *whanau* or *hapu*; today, *marae* in urban areas may serve a pan-Maori group. For more information see R. Walker (1992).

whanau had been abandoned rather than empowered to care for their own (pp. 80–81).

The Mason Report recommended a stronger emphasis on the primacy of children's needs. While the 1989 Act had a provision making the welfare and interests of the child or young person to be the deciding factor, the 1994 amendments to the Act state that "The welfare and interests of the child will have first and paramount consideration" regarding the general principles and care and protection principles of the Act (Children Young Persons and Their Families Amendment, 1994, Sec. 3). Some see these changes as a retreat from the 1989 Act's focus on family well-being and autonomy; others see this as an appropriate reassertion of the child's interests apart from those of his or her family.

The New Zealand Children and Young Persons Service

The themes of cultural recognition and privatization affect the manner in which the New Zealand Children and Young Persons Service (NZCYPFS) administers the 1989 Act. This section describes the organizational context of NZCYPFS and provides recent statistics on children in formal care.

Organizational context. NZCYPFS, created in 1992, is a business unit of the Department of Social Welfare. An area manager oversees the services of several offices in each of fifteen regional areas (NZCYPFS, 1995). Differences in structure and delivery of services in local offices result from many factors including the geographic area served, the diversity of the population, budget constraints, and the experience, ability, and morale of staff.

A survey of 362 professionals working in the area of child care and protection revealed that the general view of NZCYPFS is "of an understaffed, underfunded, generally underresourced, and unevenly skilled organization" (Child Protection Trust Advocacy Committee, 1994, p. 30). Some offices have high staff turnover rates, leaving inexperienced staff to work with troubled families (Corbett, 1995). Frequent organizational changes have affected staff morale and delivery of services (Fulcher & Ainsworth, 1994).

The 1989 Act required social services staff to alter their role from decision maker to facilitator of other people's decisions (Hardin, 1996). Some workers have been reluctant to give up their decision-making authority and have not fully involved the whole possible range of a child's extended family. The level of commitment to family decision making and family empowerment varies. Workers differ in their ability to deal flexibly and effectively with clients of differing cultural backgrounds (Human Rights Commission, 1992; Rimene, 1993). NZCYPFS does not currently require its social services staff to have formal social work qualifications. It has addressed the issue of staff training through its Competency Programme (NZCYPS, 1993) and other strategies to recruit and retain staff with degrees in social work.

Out-of-family placement. Nationwide, NZCYPFS has a bed capacity of one hundred for residential services. Twenty beds are allocated to care and protection and eighty to youth justice. The limited availability of care and protection beds in NZCYPFS residences, a sharp reduction from pre-1989 levels (Maxwell & Morris, 1992), results from the emphasis on placement within family/*whanau* or home community. Besides family/*whanau* caregivers, the NZ-CYPFS uses family homes (i.e., group homes), foster homes sponsored by private agencies, and foster parents recruited by NZCYPFS.

As of January 1996, a total of 2,595 children was in the care of the Director General. Of these, 729, or 28 percent, were placed with family or *whanau*. Most of the remaining children were in NZCYPFS foster homes (personal communication, S. Johnson, July 4, 1996). The percentage of children in care of the family or *whanau* varied greatly; one area (with only ten children in care) had no children in family/*whanau* care, whereas in another area, more than 50 percent of children were placed within the family. These figures do not reveal whether the children are with their usual caregivers (e.g., parent or parents) or placed with other relatives.

THE CHILD PLACEMENT PROCESS

This section describes how intervention by NZCYPFS involves a child's extended family. It discusses intake, investigation, temporary care agreements, family/*whanau* agreements, family group conferences, decisions about placement with kin, the use of court orders, and follow-up. The themes of cultural recognition and privatization influence all phases of the process.

Intake and Investigation

Following a report of abuse or neglect, an NZCYPFS social worker either makes an immediate referral to another agency or investigates the case to decide if the concerns raised warrant further action. If the child is at serious risk of harm, the court may issue an emergency court order. The order allows NZCYPFS to remove the child from his or her usual caregiver and to place the child with a relative or in out-of-family care.

The investigation includes locating the members of a child's *whanau* or extended family. Workers are expected to identify a Maori child's *iwi* affiliation(s).

Although finding members of the child's extended family can be difficult and time consuming, involving as many relatives as possible expands placement options and increases the possibility that the child will not come into formal care (Department of Social Welfare, 1990). One social worker said that, if he foresees a change in care as necessary, he asks the family to consider relatives with whom the child might live. During some investigations, a child's relatives decide independently that the child should move, and the involvement of the NZCYPFS ceases.

Temporary care agreements, entered voluntarily by the parents and NZCYPFS, allow a child to come into departmental care for twenty-eight days, renewable once for a total of fifty-six days. Private, nonprofit agencies provide much of this short-term care (bed nights) under contract with the NZCFA. If the child must remain in care longer, an FGC must be held.

In fiscal year 1995 the NZCYPFS received more than 24,000 care and protection notifications (Department of Social Welfare, 1995a).[6] A study of 918 notifications to NZCYPFS's twelve largest offices in 1993 revealed that approximately 20 percent of the notifications lead to either the use of a family/*whanau* agreement or to an FGC (Robertson & Maxwell, 1996).

Family/Whanau Agreements

Family/*whanau* agreements are time-limited agreements between families and social workers that center on well-defined tasks (e.g., enrolling in school, obtaining counseling)(NZCYPS, 1995). NZCYPFS tries to resolve problems through this process before referral to an FGC (Robertson & Maxwell, 1996). If the family does not fulfill its obligations under the agreement, referral to a Family Group Conference may be necessary. For the year ending June 30, 1995, NZCYPFS reported 3,015 family/*whanau* agreements (Department of Social Welfare, 1995a).

Some family/*whanau* agreements involve placement with kin for respite care (Drew, 1996). NZCYPFS policy says that the social worker should assess the placement if there is reason for concern about the proposed caregiver or caregiving situation (Department of Social Welfare, 1992). Social workers interviewed reported that they generally do not object to a family's choice of caregiver.

With family/*whanau* agreements, the Act's emphasis on cultural identity may conflict with its philosophy of privatization. Family/*whanau* agreements may meet the criteria of minimum necessary intervention and are seen as cost-effective (Drew, 1996). From a cultural standpoint, the child remains at risk of alienation from culture and extended family because the process frequently involves fewer family members than a full FGC. Family/*whanau* agreements made in isolation of the child's wider *whanau, hapu,* and *iwi* leave more power to make decisions affecting the child with the NZCYPFS workers (Rimene, 1993). Family/*whanau* agreements are also riskier, because the NZCYPFS must rely on a voluntary agreement (Hardin, 1996).

Family Group Conferences

The function of the FGC is to ensure that the family group has the first right and responsibility to resolve care and protection issues in relation to its children (Fraser & Norton, 1996, p. 40). A successful FGC depends on three major factors: (a) the preparation and skill of the NZCYPFS staff involved, (b) whether the extended family is able and willing to attend and to assume responsibility, and (c) the resources available to address care concerns.

---

6. Statistics exist for notifications, family/*whanau* agreements, FGCs, plans and court workers requiring ongoing NZCYPFS service, and number of beds provided through NZCYPFS's Residential and Caregivers Services. These "outputs" do not provide clear details on the extent to which children are placed within the extended family as the result of intervention by NZCYPFS.

Resources include care within the family network, help from community agencies, and financial support.

During the year ending June 30, 1995, almost 5,000 FGCs were held. More than half of the care and protection FGCs resulted in ongoing service by NZ-CYPFS (Department of Social Welfare, 1995a). Some FGCs are reconvened FGCs held to review or reformulate plans made by an earlier FGC. Although FGCs often result in a change in care for a child, national statistics do not reveal how many outcomes entailed kinship care. Sometimes interim custody or guardianship orders are used to secure a child's care while NZCYPFS workers arrange to place the child within his or her extended family. An FGC may also result in a kinship care placement with no court orders.

Family Group Conference preparation. The Care and Protection Coordinator (Coordinator) is the member of the NZCYPFS staff responsible for overseeing FGCs. A social worker makes a referral to a Coordinator if he or she has decided, upon investigation and consultation with the supervisor and the Care and Protection Resource Panel,[7] that significant care and protection (e.g., abuse or neglect) concerns exist. Under S. 19 of the 1989 Act, other community organizations may initiate an FGC.

The Coordinator invites as many members of the child's extended family as possible. Other entitled members of the FGC are the child, the referring social worker (from the NZCYPFS or other community agency), counsel for the child, and any other persons approved by the family. NZCYPFS's guidelines for coordinators say that "The key strength of family decision making is the involvement of all those who know and are committed to the child or young person concerned" (NZCYPS, 1992, p. 24). These guidelines recommend extensive consultation with the family group to increase the amount of information and available options for the child.

In keeping with the 1989 Act's recognition of family and cultural identity, Coordinators sometimes ignore the wishes of the child's immediate family and contact as many members of the extended family as they can identify. Ideally, the referring social worker locates many family members in advance. One social worker reported making many phone calls, being referred from one person to the next, to find family members to attend an FGC for an adolescent girl. The women who eventually came to the conference agreed to become the young woman's caregivers (personal communication, M. Calversberg, June 11, 1996).

Contacting family members presents challenges. For example, a single mother may decline to identify the father of her child. Thus, she prevents communication with the father's side of the family, a potential source of support and cultural identity. Some families, especially families who are recent immigrants, have few relatives in New Zealand. Coordinators will contact family

---

7. The Care and Protection Resource Panel is a group of community members who have knowledge of issues relating to child protection. Some members may be representatives of the area's *iwi*, Pacific Islanders, or other cultural groups.

members who live abroad, but the NZCYPFS has limited funds to reimburse a family's expenses if its members decide to attend the FGC.

The Coordinator consults with the Care and Protection Resource Panels for advice and information, especially when dealing with a family from a culture different from his or her own (NZCYPS, 1992). *Pakeha* coordinators reported that the Panels are helpful when they are working with Maori and Pacific Island families. For example, members of the Panel may provide assistance in detecting a Maori child's family links or in deciding what the most appropriate venue for the conference might be.

Coordinators find it helpful to brief family members on the procedures of the FGC and the issues to be presented. Social workers at Raukawa Social Service, an *iwi*-based organization, hold pre-FGC *hui* (meetings) with their clients to make sure everyone involved has a thorough understanding of the process (personal communication, S. Taylor, May 16, 1996).

During the Family Group Conference. The FGC has three phases. The conference may begin with a prayer or other culturally appropriate ritual (Fraser & Norton, 1996). The Coordinator then explains the purpose of the FGC, and the social worker and other professionals make a presentation of care and protection concerns. In cases involving physical or sexual abuse, families must receive thorough, accurate, and accessible information and education about the dynamics of abuse within families. Family members may have difficulty listening to the information if it elicits anger and shame (Fraser & Norton, 1996) or if the presentation is delivered insensitively (Gilling et al., 1995).

Second, the family meets alone to discuss and consider the issues presented and to devise a plan for the child's care and protection. Outsiders may be present during this phase only if every family member present agrees. Many social workers and coordinators discuss in advance potential decisions, including exploring options for placement within the family. However, social workers and coordinators must not take away the family's power and ability to make its own decisions. Some family members have complained that they were brought together to approve a decision already made, making family time a nonevent (Gilling et al., 1995, p. 81).

Third, the family meets with the Coordinator and the referring social worker to secure agreement with its plan and to negotiate how the plan will be carried out. If there is no agreement, the Coordinator refers the matter to the Family Court for decision by a judge.

Decisions and plans. Decisions made by a family group conference must balance the family's expectations and the requirements of the legislation. Since the purpose of the FGC is to shift responsibility back on the family, the weighting given to the wishes of the family group in the matter is significant (Fraser & Norton, 1996, p. 39). The Coordinators interviewed were positive about the ability of families to take responsibility and to make good decisions when provided with the opportunity.

FGC plans must state where the child will live and who will support the caregiver. Protection elements of the plan include arrangements for assessment of the caregiver, monitoring, controlling access by the perpetrator or other threatening person(s), and ensuring the child's future safety. Care elements include decisions on changes in legal responsibility, guardianship, or custody. The plan must consider how the family will make the placement work, what needs to be supported and strengthened, and what needs to change. The plan must address how the child will maintain his family links. The plan should build services and resources for all elements of the plan and provide for unforeseen contingencies and a regular review (NZCYPS, 1992, pp. 46–50).

Wide family participation in the FGC and prior discussion ensures that a family caregiver proposed by the FGC is suitable. The proposed caregiver's links with the *whanau* and willingness to be monitored are other factors (NZCYPS, 1992, p. 56).

A Coordinator's duty in the third phase of the FGC is to initiate discussion of financial support for kinship caregivers. NZCYPFS policy says that where a child is placed in kinship care, but not in the custody of the Director General, "The ability of the family, family group, or whanau to finance the reasonable needs of the child will need to be explored and included in the recommended plan" (NZCYPS, 1993, p. 2). Upon encouragement, the family group often comes up with resources such as furniture, bedding, clothing, respite care, and money for outings and extracurricular activities.

Family members and NZCYPFS often share the initial costs of a kinship care placement. The amount of financial support provided to kin caregivers varies by office. The manager of each NZCYPFS office, at his or her discretion and subject to budgetary constraints, can reimburse family or *whanau* for reasonable care costs as part of the FGC plan (personal communication, J. Worfolk, June 26, 1996). Frequently, NZCYPFS provides for such items as furniture and bedding and recommends that the caregivers apply for the Unsupported Child Benefit (UCB), which is available from the New Zealand Income Support Service if the child is to be in their care for more than a year.

The decision may be that the child comes into the care of the Director General (i.e., formal care) and live with kin. The social worker will conduct a more thorough assessment of the proposed caregiver in these instances. If the child is in formal care, the caregiver will receive the same board payments as NZCYPFS pays its out-of-family foster parents. These payments are higher than the UCB the family would otherwise receive.

On the rare occasions when the FGC cannot reach agreement, the Family Court sets the terms of the plan through custody orders, guardianship orders, and service orders. Court orders may be part of the FGC plan. Sometimes, kinship caregivers request orders to clarify matters such as custody and access and to ensure stability for the child. If there are court orders, the plan is subject to periodic review by the court and more oversight by NZCYPFS (Hardin, 1996).

Examples of Kinship Care

When children enter kinship care, they may move locally to a relative's home, or they may move from their urban home to a rural area or vice versa. Siblings may live with different members of the extended family or *whanau*. Occasionally, children of Pacific Island descent leave New Zealand to live with relatives in Samoa or the Cook Islands (see, e.g., Fraser & Norton, 1996), although the Coordinator's Guidelines suggest that this should be a rare occurrence (NZCYPS, 1992).

NZCYPFS workers in one office described the situation of an infant whose parents were unable to care for it due to their severe psychiatric disorders. The FGC plan was for the infant to live with a family member, with NZCYPFS paying for some child care costs. The caretaker became overwhelmed by her dual commitment to the child and to completing her education. The infant was placed in out-of-family foster care while the social worker made a wider search of the infant's extended family to find him a permanent home. The eventual goal was to find a family member to assume permanent guardianship for the child.

A social worker described an incident that illustrates the deference accorded to the wishes of the extended family. He placed a child in temporary out-of-family foster care so that she could remain near her mother while her mother tried to work out the problem that had initiated the involvement of the NZCYPFS. The social worker located members of the child's *whanau*, from whom the child's mother had been estranged. The *whanau* met and approved the caregiver. When the child's mother was unable to work out her problems, the child moved from her hometown to live among her *whanau* in the northern part of New Zealand's North Island. The mother eventually moved there also, to live near her *whanau* and to be near her child.

KINSHIP FOSTER CARE ISSUES

The existing literature and conversations with staff from NZCYPFS community agencies revealed four major issues that confront the practice of kinship care in New Zealand: (a) availability of family, (b) assessment of kinship caregivers, (c) financial concerns, and (d) support and monitoring. Disagreement about the balance of responsibility between the state and the extended family contributes to the problems identified in this section, as does the tension between the value placed on family and culture and the need to address the child's immediate needs for care and protection.

Availability of Family

Members of a child's extended family or *whanau* are available if the NZCYPFS finds them and if they attend the FGC or provide some support for the plan. Families are unavailable if they are not notified, if they refuse to get involved, or if they are unable to attend the FGC.

Social workers may not find extended family for several reasons. Searching for family can be time-consuming and discouraging, especially if the immediate family members are reluctant to identify relatives or if those contacted show reluctance or hostility. Limited time prevents staff from doing background work, such as searching electoral roles, calling a range of community agencies, or calling people in the phone book who share the child's surname. Some social workers either lack or overlook connections to Maori or Pacific Island communities, such as the Care and Protection Resource Panel, *iwi*-based social service organizations, or churches. Some FGCs have been poorly arranged, with few *whanau* members invited (Human Rights Commission, 1992; Rimene, 1993).

Some children do not have large extended families in New Zealand or do not have the *whanau, hapu,* and *iwi* affiliations of Maori that open a range of connections. Some families (of all cultures) do not respond to efforts to get them to attend the conference. How people are approached affects whether they will be willing or feel an obligation to attend a family/*whanau* meeting or FGC.

In the Act's early days, the philosophy of family involvement and the importance of cultural identity prompted willingness, now restricted, to reimburse family members' expenses for travel and accommodation. Today, travel expenditures are considered the family's responsibility. The tension is that short-term cost savings of not bringing family together means the potential exclusion of caretakers and sources of support. There are instances where children have had multiple family group conferences. One well-attended, expensive FGC may result in a more stable, less costly outcome for the child than several FGCs where few family members are involved. Studies that examine expenditures with the reasons for and outcomes of the FGCs would shed some light on this issue.

Assessment of Kinship Caregivers

The 1989 Act reflects enormous faith in the ability of families to care for their own. In the early days of the Act, some NZCYPFS workers were reluctant to question or challenge decisions made by families at FGCs. The Mason Report noted that some DSW staff rejected any placements that were not within the extended family (Mason, 1992a). Some commentators have raised concern that families do not make sound decisions for children (see, e.g., Tapp, Geddis, & Taylor, 1992).

Practice regarding assessment of kinship caregivers reveals this belief. Past standards for foster homes excluded culturally appropriate caregivers and served to remove children from familiar surroundings and to sever their cultural ties. Reaction to this legacy has created a hands-off approach that may leave a child in an unsafe situation that will remain hidden. One FGC participant noted that his teenage stepdaughter could move to her father's house, although the father was not particularly stable. The terms of the legislation would have allowed her to move without much review or assessment (Gilling et al., 1995, p. 89). Sometimes, assessment of kinship caregivers has been limited or nonexistent (Gilling et al., 1995; Worrall, 1996).

NZCYPFS is responsible for assessing a caregiver proposed by a plan or decision of an FGC. The extent of the assessment depends on the specific needs of the situation (Department of Social Welfare, 1992). Some NZCYPFS workers interviewed reported that they do not object to the family's choice of caregiver unless that person has previous involvement with NZCYPFS or the Department of Social Welfare. One worker expressed quite strongly that it was really none of his business. The ideal of keeping children within the family or *whanau* and the reality of limited resources (e.g., staff time, money) combine to create a climate where workers rarely question a family's decision about a caretaker.

A group of social workers who pioneered the family decision-making model during the 1980s acknowledged the possibility of flawed decisions. They said that social workers had made mistakes in judgment and reached decisions harmful to children: "The luxury we (the social workers) had, of making subsequent decisions following a mistake, had to be extended to them (the extended family)" (Wilcox et al., 1990, p. 8). The first FGC is frequently not the last one for families; initial solutions often require revision.

Financial Support

The issue of financial support for kinship caregivers represents the tensions between NZCYPFS goal of privatization and the needs of the children and families who make up the bulk of the Service's clientele. The views of NZCYPFS staff interviewed varied. Some said that financial support increases the likelihood that the placement will be stable, while others said that it undermines family responsibility.

The Mason Report recommended that extended family members who provide care and protection for children and young persons according to a plan formulated by an FGC be paid the same as unrelated caregivers (Mason, 1992a, p. 47). The government did not agree because of philosophical issues "in respect of the obligations that families have to provide for their own members; obligations that are underpinned by the objects and principles of the Act" (Mason, 1992b, p. 16).

Many kinship caregivers receive the Unsupported Child Benefit (UCB) from the New Zealand Income Support Service. Family members (excluding parents or usual caregivers) who care for children in the care of the Director General receive weekly board rates higher than the UCB from NZCYPFS. NZCYPFS policy says that families should seek court orders to ensure a competent guardian, to secure stable care and custody, or to secure necessary support. The policy says that staff should challenge families who seek orders solely for a higher weekly payment (NZCYPS, 1993, p. 7).

The Act's goals of family empowerment, family responsibility, and minimum necessary intervention lead to short-term involvement by NZCYPFS and the expectation that families will take on full financial responsibility. To be sure, families do take on these responsibilities. But, many kinship caregivers are poor and have experienced the consequences of the government's economic and fiscal reforms: lower wages, reduced social welfare benefits, and less secure employment (e.g., see Worrall, 1996). Thus, the likelihood of self-sufficiency seems doubtful.

Many workers emphasize that families must take on financial responsibility so that they will not become dependent on NZCYPFS. Some workers spoke of the family's obligation to care for its children in cultural terms. However, they recognize that an additional child (or often, children), especially one who has experienced severe maltreatment, will create emotional and financial stress in a household. Kinship caregivers interviewed by Worrall (1996) experienced significant problems with the children in their care. One must ask whether kinship care in fact empowers families or simply reinforces families' sense of being powerless by placing them in situations where they are bound to fail. For relatives caring for children with multiple problems, is dependency on the state for resources that will help them in providing care necessarily negative?

Sometimes, fiscal constraints, rather than cultural concerns, are the impetus for encouraging families to provide their own financial support. Families report feeling pressured to come up with solutions at moments when they feel they have exhausted their options (Gilling et al., 1995). Sometimes, families have not received information about the UCB, other available financial support, or the option to have the child come into formal care (Gilling et al., 1995; Rimene, 1993; Worrall, 1996). The Nelson office of the NZCYPFS has made a deliberate effort during the past year to ensure that during FGCs, family members who will assume caretaking duties are fully briefed on options available for financial and other support (personal communication, S. Bird, May 17, 1996).

Support and Monitoring

The current system cannot always draw together resources and services that would help kinship caregivers. The consequence is a failed or unstable placement. A submission to the Mason Report noted: "We have grave concerns for members of the extended family who take on a problem child. It is obvious that no supports are set in place for family and ultimately not only the child will suffer but also the extended family" (Mason, 1992a, p. 53).

In the early days of the Act, families were left alone to care for difficult and disturbed children because of the belief in the efficacy of family. This belief, combined with the crisis-oriented, short-term nature of much of the NZCYPFS's work, has led to a noninterventionist approach to kinship caregivers. NZCYPFS focuses its formal training efforts on out-of-family caregivers (personal communication, J. Worfolk, June 26, 1996). Research and published anecdotal information suggest that follow up by NZCYPFS is limited. Families interviewed by Rimene (1993) and Worrall (1996) reported little or no contact with social workers.

Growing awareness of struggling kinship caregivers has led to altered practice in some offices. The extent of coordinated, systematic follow-up of children in kinship care is unknown. Kinship caregivers on their own initiative have approached the New Zealand Family and Foster Care Federation for support and advice, but NZCYPFS has not made a coordinated effort to ensure that kinship caregivers are aware of available community support.

Community-based services, tribal networks, and informal caregivers that work in cooperation with NZCYPFS help children and families as they deal with the effects of child abuse and neglect. The Commissioner of Children's submission to the Mason Report noted that few districts have an adequate range of suitable, approved services to which it can refer families and their children (Mason, 1992a, p. 103). Staff at an NZCYPFS office serving a small town north of Wellington confirmed this concern. They noted that, with few local community services available, reliance on the extended family was the only feasible alternative.

The Act's emphasis on cultural identity and the demographics of the NZCYPFS's clientele make social services sponsored by *iwi* and cultural groups serving Pacific Island communities desirable places for some families to receive ongoing services. However, these agencies are more likely than established *Pakeha* agencies to lack the resources and managerial skills to obtain funding. The NZCFA has approved some *iwi*-based services, pan-Maori organizations, and Pacific Island cultural groups as Community and Family Support Services. Because the services provided must fit into output categories decided by the New Zealand Community Funding Agency, these agencies do not always have the flexibility to provide services as they see fit (Foliaki, 1994).

Raukawa Social Services, an *iwi*-based group funded as a Child and Family Support Service, receives funding to provide direct services. It cannot obtain grants for capital expenditures such as improving its facilities, and it does not have a base of donors as the church-supported private agencies do. While it would like to emphasize preventive services to try to break cycles of problems, it receives funding to provide for the caregivers of children who are at risk. It uses this money in creative ways to provide respite care, such as summer camps and money for weekend outings. Members of the *iwi* who provide care to children receive financial support. This agency has a good working relationship with the local office of the Children and Young Persons and Their Families Service. The NZCYPFS social workers notify them when a member of their *iwi* comes to notice. However, they have less money, fewer workers, and fewer resources than NZCYPFS (interview, Raukawa Social Services, May 16, 1996; see also Jacob, 1995).

The lack of community supports compounds problems presented by some children in kinship care, who require more help than loving and willing kinship caregivers can provide. Some caregivers take on children due to pressure from NZCYPFS staff or on the basis of an emotional impulse, rather than after a realistic assessment of what they can do (Mason, 1992a, p. 46). Decisions made under these circumstances may lead to breakdown, not stability, of a placement.

Concern about foster care drift contributed to the 1989 Act. Seven years later, some children have experienced many placements within their extended family. The impact on children of movement from household to household depends on culture and context (Hardin, 1996). The concern is that practice influenced by the need to respect culture and family autonomy may prevent workers from closely examining the situations of children who have had frequent moves. Now that the 1989 Act has been in force for seven years, some extended families and *whanau* have become exhausted by caregiving. For instance, a family will come to the FGC and state that it can no longer handle the children, now teenagers, in its care. Possibly, the needs of these children were not adequately addressed when they first entered kinship care.

Staff in all the NZCYPFS offices visited voiced concerns about severely troubled adolescents. Options for care of children with difficulties such as psychiatric disturbances, out-of-control behavior, and suicidal tendencies are limited. Residential facilities have been closed; community agencies cannot always provide the needed care. The philosophy of family autonomy and privatization has not served these troubled adolescents well.

Linked with support of kinship caregivers is the monitoring of children in kinship care. Someone must ensure that the plans formed at the FGC are being carried out and that the child is safe. Practice under the Act places monitoring in the realm of family responsibility. Because the extended family has a vested interest in the child, it holds the most potential for building a supportive safety net (Hardin, 1996). Early reviews of the Act suggested that monitoring and follow-up of FGC decisions was lacking (Mason, 1992a; Paterson & Harvey, 1991). Families interviewed by Gilling et al. (1995) and Rimene (1993) voiced dissatisfaction that social workers did not contact them after they assumed a caregiving role.

The 1989 Act mandates periodic review of the situations of children in care or custody of the Director General. Children in kinship care as the result of FGCs must rely on reviews initiated by members of the Family Group Conference. As with other issues, the level and extent of monitoring raises the balance of state and family responsibility in the ensuring of care and protection for children.

CONCLUSION

In the United States, the growth in the use of kinship care originates as much from an overloaded child welfare system as from a belief that family knows best (Gleeson, 1995). Does kinship care practice in New Zealand embrace a *whanau*-knows best philosophy, or is it an excuse to spend fewer government resources on children at risk? Are children adequately protected under the current system? This chapter suggests that the dual forces of cultural recognition and privatization influence the form and practice of kinship care. New Zealand gives families the opportunity to participate in decisions that professionals used to make alone, often with little knowledge of the particular family or culture. The process helps families restore and maintain links. Families decide what to do when their members are having difficulties. The greater role for family, the greater emphasis on culture, and the importance of extended family provides a focus that has the potential to maintain a child's sense of family and identity over a long time.

One should look at New Zealand's experiment with child care and protection and ask what differences there would be if resources were greater. Almost no one in New Zealand wants to return to the days when a child who went into care was lost to his or her family and cultural ties. There is widespread support for the objects and principles that underlie the Act and for the greater emphasis on family involvement and culturally appropriate social work practice.

Most dissatisfaction is with the practice, not the principles, of kinship care. Sources of dissatisfaction vary. Many spoke of the need for more resources for families, but the nature and form those resources differ. A *Pakeha* family may need better access to mental health services or respite care for the weekend. Resources for Maori may imply the return of or compensation for tribal lands, which they can turn into economic development, jobs, and better opportunities for their *whanau*. More research is necessary to see if New Zealand has realized the ideals of the legislation. The need for research on the experiences of Maori and Pacific Island families is especially critical.

Clarity on several issues would enhance the understanding of kinship care in New Zealand. Who provides kinship foster care? If it is grandparents, New Zealand must examine the implications of having aging caregivers of young children. If women provide the bulk of the care, gender issues must be examined. The social work profession must contemplate where the work of supporting, empowering, and advocating for children and their caregivers needs to take place.

New Zealand's experiences raise several issues that apply to kinship foster care in the United States. Child welfare professionals must address concerns about involving the extended family in permanency planning, financial support of caregivers, instability of placements, and the increased difficulties experienced by children and young people. While the position of the Maori in New Zealand differs in some ways from that of ethnic minorities who are overrepresented in the child welfare systems of the United States and some other countries, the world can learn from New Zealand's extraordinary efforts to account for the child's cultural identity and to expand the role of the family in child care and protection.

References

Atkin, B. (1991). New Zealand: Families, children and ethnicity. *Journal of Family Law, 30*, 357–366.

Auckland Committee on Racism and Discrimination (ACORD). (1978). *Social welfare children's homes: Report on an inquiry held June 11, 1978.* Auckland: Author.

Ban, P. (1993). Family decision-making—The model as practiced in New Zealand and its relevance in Australia. *Australian Social Work, 46*, 23–30.

Barretta-Herman, A. (1994). *Welfare state to welfare society: Restructuring New Zealand's social services.* New York: Garland Publishing.

Bradley, J. (1994). Iwi and the Maatua Whangai programme. In R. Munford & M. Nash (Eds.), *Social work in action* (pp. 178–198). Palmerston North, New Zealand: Dunmore Press.

Bradley, J. (1995). The resolve to devolve: Maori and social services. *Social Work Now: The Practice Journal of the Children and Young Persons Service, 1*, 29–35.

Cairns, T. (1990). Whangai—Caring for a child. In I. Hassall, G. Maxwell, & J. Robertson (Eds.), *Toward a child and family policy for New Zealand: Proceedings of the seminar "Toward a Child and Family Policy for New Zealand," 15–17 November 1990,*

Wellington (pp. 100–102). Wellington, New Zealand: Office of the Commissioner for Children.

Child Protection Trust Advocacy Committee. (1994). *The New Zealand Children and Young Persons Service: An evaluation by professionals working in the field of child and adolescent care and welfare.* Auckland: Author.

Children, Young Persons, and Their Families Act. (1989). No. 24.

Children, Young Persons, and Their Families Amendment. (1994). No. 121.

Cockburn, G. (1994). The Children, Young Persons, and Their Families Act 1989: Past, present, and future. In R. Munford & M. Nash (Eds.), *Social work in action* (pp. 85–104). Palmerston North, New Zealand: Dunmore Press.

Connolly, M. (1994). An act of empowerment: The Children, Young Persons and Their Families Act (1989). *British Journal of Social Work, 24,* 87–100.

Corbett, L. (1995, July). Service not included. *Metro,* 60–65.

Denny, F. (1995, November). Iwi SS policy statements. Wellington, New Zealand: Department of Social Welfare, Social Policy Agency.

Department of Social Welfare. (1990, July). *Circular memorandum 1990/147: Resource paper: Children and young persons in the care of the Director General: Placement with caregivers.*

Department of Social Welfare. (1992, January). *Circular memorandum 1992/6: Reiteration of departmental policy and procedures on the assessment and approval of caregivers.*

Department of Social Welfare. (1994). *Te Punga: Our bicultural strategy for the nineties.* Wellington, New Zealand: Author.

Department of Social Welfare. (1995a). *Fiscal 1995 statistical information report.* Wellington, New Zealand: Author.

Department of Social Welfare. (1995b). *Social services strategy 1995–2005.* Wellington, New Zealand: Author.

Drew, J. (1996). Best practice and financial management: Bringing children into care. *Social Work Now: The Practice Journal of the Children and Young Persons Service, 3,* 38–40.

Durie-Hall, D., & Metge, J. (1992). Kua tutu te puehu, kia mau: Maori aspirations and family law. In M. Henaghan & B. Atkin (Eds.), *Family law policy in New Zealand* (pp. 54–82). Auckland: Oxford University Press.

Everett, J. E. (1991). Introduction: Children in crisis. In J. E. Everett, S. Chinpungu, & B. R. Leashore (Eds.), *Child welfare: An Africentric perspective* (pp. 1–14). New Brunswick, N.J.: Rutgers University Press.

Foliaki, L. (1994). Social work and the Pacific Island community. In R. Munford & M. Nash (Eds.), *Social work in action* (pp. 152–177). Palmerston North, New Zealand: Dunmore Press.

Fraser, S., & Norton, J. (1996). Family group conferencing in New Zealand child protection work. In J. Hudson, A. Morris, G. Maxwell, & B. Galaway (Eds.), *Family Group Conferences: Perspectives on policy and practice* (pp. 37–48). Leichhardt, NSW, Australia: Federation Press; Monsey, N.Y.: Willow Tree Press.

Fulcher, L., & Ainsworth, F. (1994). Child welfare abandoned? The ideology and economics of contemporary service reform in New Zealand. *Social Work Review, 6*(5/6), 2–13.

Gilling, M., Patterson, L., & Walker, B. (1995). *Family members' experiences of the care and protection Family Group Conference process.* Research Report Series No. 18. Wellington, New Zealand: Social Policy Agency.

Gleeson, J. (1995). Kinship care and public child welfare: Challenges and opportunities for social work education. *Journal of Social Work Education, 31,* 182–193.

Hardin, M. (1996). *Family group conferences in child abuse and neglect cases: Learning from the experience of New Zealand.* Chicago: American Bar Association.

Hudson, J., Morris, A., Maxwell, G., & Galaway, B. (Eds.). (1996). *Family group conferences: Perspectives on policy and practice.* Leichhardt, NSW, Australia: Federation Press.

Human Rights Commission. (1992). *Who cares for the kids? A study of children and young people in out of family care.* Wellington, New Zealand: Author.

Jacob, E. (1995). Ngati Raukawa iwi social service profile. *Social Work Review, 7*(1), 36.

Jefferson, S., & Laven, R. (1995). *The care & protection provisions of the Children, Young Persons, & Their Families Act 1989 revisited.* Wellington, New Zealand: New Zealand Law Society.

Johnston, A. H. (1982). *Report of committee to report to the Minister of Social Welfare on the current practices and procedures followed in institutions of the Department of Social Welfare in Auckland.* Wellington, New Zealand: Government Printer.

Kelsey, J. (1995). *The New Zealand experiment: A world model for structural readjustment?* Auckland: Auckland University Press.

Koopman-Boyden, P., & Scott, C. (1984). *The family and government policy in New Zealand.* Sydney: Allen & Unwin.

Mackay, R. A. (1981). *Children in foster care: An examination of the case histories of a sample of children in care, with particular emphasis on placements of children in foster homes.* Wellington, New Zealand: Research Section, Department of Social Welfare.

Mason, K. (1992a). *Review of the Children, Young Persons, and Their Families Act 1989. Vol. 1: Report of the ministerial review team to the Minister of Social Welfare Hon. Jenny Shipley: Children & Young Persons Act 1989.* Wellington, New Zealand: Government Printer.

Mason, K. (1992b). *Review of the Children, Young Persons, and Their Families Act 1989. Vol. 2: Government's response to the report of the ministerial review team to the Minister of Social Welfare: Children & Young Persons Act 1989.* Wellington, New Zealand: Government Printer.

Maxwell, G. M., & Morris, A. (1992). The Family Group Conference: A new paradigm for making decisions about children and young people. *Children Australia, 17* (4) 11–15.

Maxwell, G. M., & Morris, A. (1993). *Family, victims, and culture: Youth justice in New Zealand.* Wellington, New Zealand: Social Policy Agency, Department of Social Welfare.

Maxwell, G. M., & Robertson, J. P. (1991). Statistics on the first year of the Children, Young Persons, and Their Families Act. In Office of the Commissioner for Children, *An appraisal of the first year of the Children, Young Persons and Their Families Act 1989. A collection of 3 papers* (pp. 14–23). Wellington, New Zealand: Office of the Commissioner for Children.

Maxwell, G., Robertson, J., Thom, A., & Walker, B. (1995). *Researching care and protection: A proposal for study of the outcome of interventions under the Children, Young Persons, and Their Families Act 1989.* Wellington, New Zealand: Office of the Commissioner for Children and Social Policy Agency.

Metge, J. (1995). *New growth from old: The whanau in the modern world.* Wellington: Victoria University Press.

Miller, D. L., Hoffman, F., & Turner, D. (1980). A perspective on the Indian Child Welfare Act. *Social Casework, 61,* 468–471.

Ministerial Advisory Committee on a Maori Perspective for the Department of Social Welfare. (1988). *Puao-Te-Ata-Tu (day break): The report of the Ministerial Advisory*

Committee on a Maori Perspective for the Department of Social Welfare. Wellington, New Zealand: Department of Social Welfare.

Nash, M. (1994). Social work education in Aotearoa/New Zealand. In R. Munford & M. Nash (Eds.), *Social work in action* (pp. 37–57). Palmerston North, New Zealand: Dunmore Press.

New Zealand Children & Young Persons Service. (1992, December). *Coordinator's guidelines: The legal and policy guidelines for the care and protection coordinators along with a comprehensive guide to practice*. Wellington, New Zealand: NZCYPS National Operations Unit, National Office.

New Zealand Children & Young Persons Service. (1993). *NZCYPS competency programme workbook*. Wellington, New Zealand: Author.

New Zealand Children & Young Persons Service. (1993, December). Operations Information 1993/17. *Payments to caregivers: Director General's obligations.*

New Zealand Children & Young Persons Service. (1995). *Breaking the cycle: An interagency guide to child abuse*. Wellington, New Zealand: Author.

Orange, C. (1987). *The Treaty of Waitangi*. Wellington, New Zealand: Allan & Unwin.

Paterson, K., & Harvey, M. (1991). *An evaluation of the organisation and operation of care and protection family group conferences*. Wellington, New Zealand: Evaluation Unit, Department of Social Welfare.

Petr, C. G., & Entriken, C. (1995). Service system barriers to reunification. *Families in Society, 76* (9), 523–532.

Pool, I. (1993). *Te iwi Maori: A New Zealand population past present & projected*. Auckland: Auckland University Press.

Renouf, J., Robb, G., & Wells, P. (1990). *The Children, Young Persons and Their Families Act: A report on its first year of operation*. Wellington: Department of Social Welfare.

Rice, G. (1992). A revolution in social policy, 1981–1991. In G. Rice (Ed.), *The Oxford History of New Zealand* (2nd ed., pp. 482–497). Auckland: Oxford University Press.

Rimene, S. (1993). *The Children, Young Persons, and Their Families Act, 1989 from a Maori perspective*. Unpublished master's thesis, Victoria University of Wellington, New Zealand.

Rittner, B. (1995). Children on the move: Placement patterns in children's protective services. *Families in Society, 76* (8), 469–477.

Robertson, J., & Maxwell, G. (1996). *A study of notifications for care and protection to the Children and Young Persons Service*. Office of the Commissioner for Children Occasional Paper No. 5. Wellington: Office for the Commissioner for Children.

Ryburn, M. (1993). A new model for family decision making in child care and protection. *Early Child Development and Care, 86*, 1–10.

Selby, R. (1994). My whanau. In R. Munford & M. Nash (Eds.), *Social work in action* (pp. 144–151). Palmerston North, New Zealand: Dunmore Press.

Spoonley, P. (1993). *Racism & ethnicity* (2nd ed.) Auckland: Oxford University Press.

Statistics New Zealand. (1994). *New Zealand Official Yearbook 94*. Wellington, New Zealand: Author.

Stehno, S. M. (1982). Differential treatment of minority children in service systems. *Social Work, 27*, 39–45.

Tapp, P., Geddis, D., & Taylor, N. (1992). Protecting the family. In M. Henaghan & B. Atkin (Eds.), *Family law policy in New Zealand* (pp. 168–208). Auckland: Oxford University Press.

Vasil, R. (1990). *What do the Maori want? New Maori political perspectives*. Auckland: Random Century New Zealand.

Walker, H. (1996). Whanau hui, family decision making, and the family group conference: An indigenous Maori view. *Protecting Children, 12* (3), 8–10.

Walker, J. (1990). *Kinship care in the Department of Social Welfare.* Unpublished master's thesis, Victoria University of Wellington, Wellington, New Zealand.

Walker, R. (1992). The Maori since 1950. In G. Rice (Ed.), *The Oxford history of New Zealand* 2d ed. (pp. 498–519). Auckland: Oxford University Press.

Wereta, W. (1994). Maori demographic trends. *Social Policy Journal of New Zealand, 3,* 52–62.

Wilcox, R., Smith, D., Moore, J., Hewitt, A., Allan, G., Walker, H., Ropata, M., Monu, L., & Fetherstone, T. (1991). *Family decision making: Family group conferences: Practitioners' views.* Lower Hutt, New Zealand: Practitioners' Publishing.

Working Party on the Children and Young Person's Bill. (1987). *Report of the working party on the children and young person's bill: Review of the children and young persons bill, December 1987.* Wellington, New Zealand: Department of Social Welfare.

Worrall, J. (Ed). (1983). *100 years of foster care.* Auckland: New Zealand Foster Care Federation.

Worrall, J. (1996). *Because we're family: A study of kinship care of children in New Zealand.* Unpublished master's thesis, Massey University, Palmerston North, New Zealand.

PART III

Kinship Care Research

Kinship Care in the Public Child Welfare System

A Systematic Review of the Research

MARIA SCANNAPIECO, PH.D.

Kinship care, or care provided to children by extended families, has had a long tradition among families in the United States, particularly among African American families. It emerged as a child welfare issue in the late 1980s, but it was not until recently that it became a part of the formalized system of out-of-home care (Hegar & Scannapieco, 1995). Today, kinship care is the fastest-growing funded service provided within the child welfare system (Gleeson & Craig, 1994), and it is becoming the predominant form of out-of-home care, particularly in urban areas (Berrick, Barth, & Needell, 1994a; Takas, 1993; Thornton, 1991; Wulczyn & Goerge, 1992). Kinship care has been most utilized in minority populations, particularly among African Americans (Scannapieco & Jackson, 1995). Social work research has begun to embrace this new trend and is striving to catch up with child placement practice. This chapter presents an exhaustive systematic review (SR) of kinship care research.

RESEARCH REVIEW METHOD

The SR method decreases the problems identified with less scientifically rigorous literature review methodologies by using quantitative research methods that lead to objective results (Larson, Pastro, Lyons, & Anthony, 1992). The SR method is appropriate when reviewing understudied areas of research and, unlike meta-analytic reviews, does not require experimental or quasi-experimental designs. SRs examine the frequency with which a particular research question, variable, or measure was assessed, the method by which it was assessed, and the quality of the studies that include the variables of concern (Larson et al., 1992). In addition, the SR methodology allows for strict, objective criteria for the selection and analysis of the research reports. Standardization of the review process decreases the likelihood of bias and makes replication possible.

The objectives of this SR of the kinship care research literature are twofold: (1) the kinship care research methodologies are described and critiqued, conclusions are drawn regarding their impact on interpretation of findings, and recommendations are given for improving methodological strategies, and (2) a synthesis of the findings of the research studies is presented. The chapter concludes with a discussion of future directions for kinship care research.

Kinship Care Defined

For the purposes of this review, kinship care is defined as out-of-home placement with licensed or approved kin of children in the custody of a public child welfare agency. Kin are legally recognized to include any family member one step removed from the birth parent who is related to the child by blood, marriage, or adoption. The term "kin" often includes any person with close family ties to another (Takas, 1993). Billingsley refers to this type of kinship as relationships of appropriation, meaning "unions without blood ties or marital ties. People can become part of a family unit or, indeed, form a family unit simply by deciding to live and act toward each other as family" (1992, p. 31). Children may be placed formally in these homes only if the fictive kin become licensed foster parents. While it is acknowledged that there are many kinship networks involved in other service systems, the focus of this chapter is on families involved in the child welfare system.

An exhaustive SR requires the identification of all possible peer-reviewed studies from each relevant field of study that includes information on the factor of interest. Multiple bibliographic databases from related disciplines were searched from 1980 through 1997. Manual searches also were conducted of the more recent (1995 to 1997) pertinent journals. The search identified twelve relevant articles for review (see Table 9.1). Items were included from the review cohort if they: (1) reported on kinship care programs in the public child welfare sector, (2) were reports of research, and (3) presented findings relevant to direct practice.

Description of Review Cohort

Studies in the review cohort (listed in Table 9.1) were categorized by purpose, research method, sample method, response rate and/or sample size, existence of a comparison group, and the type of analysis conducted. All of the studies, with the exception of the Dubowitz studies (Dubowitz et al., 1992, 1993a, 1993b, 1994), defined kinship care as the care of children in homes of relatives who were licensed foster parents (see chapter 5 for further details on differences between programs). The Dubowitz studies examined children in the care of relatives and children in the care and custody of the state, but the relative caregivers received Aid to Families with Dependent Children (AFDC), not foster

TABLE 9.1
Comparison of Study Purpose, Research Method, Sample Method, Sample Size, and Analysis

Study	Purpose	Research Method	Sample Method	Response Rate, Sample Size	Comparison Group	Statistical Analysis
Benedict, Zuravin, Stallings (1996)	Comparison of adult outcomes	Survey	Nonprobability	sample = 214 40% kin	Yes	Bivariate Multivariate
Berrick, Barth, Needell (1994)	Comparison of characteristics	Mailed survey and follow-up survey	Two-tiered sampling plan Random start	sample = 4,234 14% response rate 600 (41%) kin	Yes	Bivariate
*Dubowitz, Feigelman, Zuravin, Tepper, Davidson, Lichenstein (1992)	Health status and adequacy of health care	Medical record abstraction Surveys to caseworkers, caregivers, parents, and primary health care provider Physical and mental health assessment	I Population II Population	Case Abstraction population = 524 sample = 431 (82%) I Survey response rates: caseworker 100% caretakers 91% parents 33% health care 55% II—407 completed clinical assessment = (78%)	No	Bivariate Multivariate
Dubowitz, Feigelman, & Zuravin (1993)	Demographics	Mailed surveys completed by caseworkers and caregivers	Population	I—Population = 524 Survey response rates: caseworker 100% caregivers 78%	No	Bivariate
Dubowitz, Zuravin, Starr, Feigelman, & Harrington (1993)	Behavioral assessment of children in kinship care	Child Behavior Checklist (CBCL) completed by caregiver	Nonprobability Assessed all children who had a completed CBCL of the original sample (524)	CBCL completed on 346 children (66% of original sample)	No	Bivariate Multivariate

(continued)

TABLE 9.1 (*continued*)
Comparison of Study Purpose, Research Method, Sample Method, Sample Size, and Analysis

Study	Purpose	Research Method	Sample Method	Response Rate, Sample Size	Comparison Group	Statistical Analysis
Dubowitz, Feigelman, Harrington, Starr, Zuravin, & Sawyer, (1994)	Assessment of physical, mental health, and educational status of children in kinship care	Two Phases: I. Surveys to caseworkers, caregivers, parents, teachers, and current primary health care provider II. Physical & mental health assessment	I. Population II. Population	Survey response rates: caseworker 100% caregivers 78% parents 38% health care 45% teachers 75% Clinical assessment = 407 (78%)	No	Bivariate Multivariate
Gebel (1996)	Description of characteristics, perceptions, and attitudes	Mail survey	Random sample	Nonkin response rate = 79% (111) Kin response rate = 59% (82)	Yes	Bivariate multivariate
Iglehart (1994)	Comparison of characteristics of adolescents	Survey of caseworkers	Nonprobability	Nonkin response rate = 64% (638) Kin response rate = 36% (352)	Yes	Bivariate Multivariate
Le Prohn (1994)	Comparison of characteristics, role perceptions	Mail survey Social worker Interviews	Disproportion stratified random sampling	Nonkin response rate = 56% (98) Kin response rate = 64% (82)	Yes	Bivariate
Scannapieco, Hegar, & McAlpine (1997)	Comparison of characteristics and outcomes	Two-tiered case abstraction Foster home records Children in placement records	Population and random sample	Nonkin response rate = 40% (56) Kin response rate = 100% (33) 100% response rate = (106) 56% = (59) nonkin 44% = (47) kin	Yes	Bivariate

(continued)

TABLE 9.1 (*continued*)
Comparison of Study Purpose, Research Method, Sample Method, Sample Size, and Analysis

Study	Purpose	Research Method	Sample Method	Response Rate, Sample Size	Comparison Group	Statistical Analysis
Thorton (1991)	Permanency planning goals for children in kinship care	Social worker questionnaire Semistructured interview with kinship caregivers Case abstraction	Population and random sample	Social worker response rate = 81% (86) 20 kinship caregivers 100% (95) records	No	Bivariate
Wulczyn & Goerge (1992)	Placement history of children in Illinois and New York	Secondary analysis of administrative data	Population	9064	No	Bivariate

See Dubowitz (1990) for complete study description.

care payments. These relatives did not go through the more rigorous foster care licensing procedure.

The purpose of most of the studies was the description of the demographics for caregivers, children in kinship care or foster care, and parents, as well as descriptions of service delivery and outcomes (Benedict et al., 1996; Berrick et al., 1994; Dubowitz et al., 1993a; Dubowitz et al., 1994; Gebel, 1996; Iglehart, 1994; Le Prohn, 1994; Link, 1996; Scannapieco et al., 1997; Thornton, 1991; Wulczyn & Goerge, 1992). Dubowitz and colleagues (1992; 1993b) also examined the health status and performed a behavioral assessment of children in kinship care. Le Prohn (1994) compared kin and nonkin caregivers' perceptions of their roles in the foster care system. Benedict, Zuravin, and Stallings (1996) conducted one of the first adult follow-up comparisons of children placed in kinship care versus children placed in foster care.

Surveys were the predominant means of data collection (Benedict et al., 1996; Berrick et al., 1994; Dubowitz et al., 1992, Dubowitz et al., 1993a; Dubowitz et al., 1993b; Dubowitz et al., 1994; Gebel, 1996; Iglehart, 1994; Le Prohn, 1994; Link, 1996; Scannapieco et al., 1997; Thornton, 1991). Depending on the source of information, parent or caseworker, the response rates varied from 14 percent to 100 percent. Random sampling or the entire population was used most often (Berrick et al., 1994; Dubowitz et al., 1992, Dubowitz et al., 1993b; Dubowitz et al., 1994; Gebel, 1996; Iglehart, 1994; Le Prohn, 1994; Link, 1996; Scannapieco et al., 1997; Wulczyn & Goerge, 1992).

The sample source for all but the Le Prohn (1994) study was public child welfare agencies. Le Prohn (1994) used an agency data source that contracts with a public child welfare agency to deliver kinship care services. Kinship care characteristics were compared to foster care characteristics in the majority of the studies (Benedict et al., 1996; Berrick et al., 1994; Gebel, 1996; Iglehart, 1994; Le Prohn, 1994; Link, 1996; Scannapieco et al., 1997; Thornton, 1991; Wulczyn & Goerge, 1992). Multivariate analyses were conducted in all but five (Berrick et al., 1994; Le Prohn, 1994; Link, 1996; Scannapieco et al., 1997; Thornton, 1991) of the studies.

Methodologic Concerns

An examination of study methodologies reveals substantial similarities, as described in the preceding section, but also some differences. As discussed, the definition of kinship care is different in four of the ten studies (Dubowitz et al., 1992, Dubowitz et al., 1993a; Dubowitz et al., 1993b; Dubowitz et al., 1994). These four studies also do not have a comparison group, and although all four come from the same data source, they nonetheless make up much of the research literature to date. The Iglehart study (1994) focuses exclusively on the adolescent population, unlike the other studies, which examined all age groups.

Clearly, kinship care research is in its infancy. The methodology reported in this chapter is consistent with that used in most new areas of inquiry; sample sizes are small and may not be highly representative of the study population. Although most of the studies rely heavily on surveys, most also employ case record abstraction as a secondary source of data. Standardized measurements concerning caregivers and children are not available. For example, an array of operational definitions is used for behavioral problems of children in out-of-home care. Many of the studies did use comparison groups, but the equivalency of the groups is not ensured.

Each of these factors may serve to impede the integration of findings across studies and impair the generalizability of results. However, the many similarities in measurement used among the studies promote integration and knowledge development concerning kinship care. As is demonstrated in the next section, the majority of the studies examined similar variables across demographics, process variables, and outcomes.

FINDINGS

The findings of the systematic research review are presented in three broad categories: (1) characteristics of children, birth parents, and caregivers; (2) provision of child welfare services while in care; and (3) goals and outcomes of placement.

Characteristics of Caregivers, Children, and Parents

Characteristics of caregivers. Women are the most frequent kinship caregivers (Benedict et al., 1996; Berrick et al., 1994; Dubowitz et al., 1992, 1993a,b; 1994; Gebel, 1996; Le Prohn, 1994; Scannapieco et al., 1997; Thornton, 1991). The relatives who most frequently provide kinship care are maternal grandmothers (more than 50% of the time), followed by aunts (up to 33% of the time) (Dubowitz et al., 1994; Le Prohn, 1994; Scannapieco et al., 1996; Thornton, 1991).

Relative caregivers tended to be older than nonrelative caregivers (Berrick et al., 1994; Dubowitz et al., 1993a; Gebel, 1996; Le Prohn, 1994). The majority of caregivers completed high school (Berrick et al., 1994; Dubowitz et al., 1993a; Gebel, 1996; Scannapieco et al., 1996), although nonrelative caregivers completed higher levels of education (Berrick et al., 1994; Gebel, 1996; Le Prohn, 1994; Scannapieco et al., 1996). Relative caregivers were more likely to be single parents than were nonrelative caregivers (Berrick et al., 1994; Dubowitz et al., 1993a; Le Prohn, 1994; Scannapieco et al., 1997), although Gebel (1996) found no significant difference on this variable.

Up to 48 percent of kinship caregivers are employed outside the home (Berrick et al., 1994; Dubowitz et al., 1993a; Gebel, 1996; Le Prohn, 1994), but nonrelative caregivers have higher levels of income (Berrick et al., 1994; Gebel, 1996; Le Prohn, 1994). Many relative caregivers (53% to 59%) own their own homes (Berrick et al., 1994; Le Prohn, 1994), but nonrelative caregivers are even more likely to do so (Berrick et al., 1994; Le Prohn, 1994).

The percentage of caregivers assessing their own health as poor ranges from 6 percent (Dubowitz et al., 1994) to 20 percent (Berrick et al., 1994). Traditional foster parents rate themselves as having significantly better health than do kinship caregivers (Berrick et al., 1994).

Kinship caregivers differed from nonrelative caregivers in their perceptions of their role, as well as in their attitude towards the children they were caring for in their homes (Gebel, 1996; Le Prohn, 1994). Le Prohn (1994) found that relative caregivers scored higher (meaning they felt more responsible) on four out of five subscales on role perception. The four roles about which relatives expressed stronger feelings of responsibility were: facilitating child's relationship with birth family, assisting with social/emotional development, parenting, and partnering with the agency. There was no significant difference between relative caregivers and nonrelative caregivers on the spirituality role perception subscale score. After multiple regression analysis, relative status alone helps predict how the caregiver might view his or her role on only two of the subscales: facilitating child's relationship with birth family and parenting.

Gebel (1996) concluded that there was no difference in the willingness of relative and nonrelative caregivers to continue to care for the children in their homes. This study did find that relative caregivers were more likely to have a favorable attitude toward physical discipline and a lower level of empathy for children's needs than were nonrelative caregivers (Gebel, 1996).

Characteristics of children.   Children in kinship care average seven or eight years of age in most studies (Berrick et al., 1994; Dubowitz et al., 1993a; Scannapieco et al., 1996), and there are differences in age between children in the care of relative caregivers and those placed with nonrelative caregivers. Berrick and colleagues (1994) found no significant difference in age of children in care, while Scannapieco and colleagues (1997) found that children placed in nonrelative homes were significantly younger. The children in out-of-home care are predominately African American (Benedict et al., 1996; Berrick et al., 1994; Dubowitz et al., 1993a; Iglehart, 1994; Scannapieco et al., 1997), and African American children make up a larger proportion of children in kinship care than of those in traditional foster care (Berrick et al., 1994; Iglehart, 1994; Scannapieco et al., 1997). The gender of children in kinship care is fairly evenly split between male and female (Berrick et al., 1994; Dubowitz et al., 1993a; Le Prohn, 1994; Scannapieco et al., 1997).

The reason for placement in out-of-home care is most often either parental neglect or substance use, often including prenatal drug exposure (Berrick et al., 1994; Scannapieco et al., 1997; Thornton, 1991). Dubowitz and colleagues (1993a) indicate that neglect is the most common reason for placement, as does Iglehart (1994). Iglehart's study of adolescents, however, reports significant differences in reasons for placement between kinship and traditional foster care. Youth in kinship care were more likely to be placed because of neglect (43%) than were adolescents in foster care (29%). Benedict and colleagues (1996) indicate that a significantly higher proportion of children placed in relative care were placed because of maltreatment (50.6%) compared to children placed in nonrelative care (22%).

The range of findings concerning groups of brothers and sisters in kinship placement may be due to differences in the way family groups of children in care were defined and counted. Dubowitz and colleagues (1993a) report that 68 percent of children with brothers and sisters have at least one sibling placed together with them, while Scannapieco and colleagues (1994) found that 45 percent of children in kinship care were placed with one or more sibling. That figure was not significantly different than the percentage for children placed in nonrelative care. Berrick and colleagues (1994) report that for those kinship homes with more than one child in placement, at least two of the children were siblings in 95 percent of the homes.

Reports on the physical health of children in kinship care appear to vary with the source of assessment. On the basis of medical evaluations, Dubowitz and colleagues (1992) found that only 10 percent of the children in kinship care were free of any medical problems. In contrast, Berrick and colleagues (1994) found that most children were assessed by the care provider to be in excellent or good health, despite the fact that 40 percent of the children had been exposed prenatally to drugs. Of the children in that study, 15 percent required medical regimens, and 15 percent had other known medical needs (Berrick et al., 1994).

Children in kinship care were judged to be behaving satisfactorily in school in approximately 60 percent of the cases (Berrick et al., 1994; Dubowitz et al., 1994; Iglehart, 1994). However, with regard to scholastic performance, 36 percent (Iglehart, 1994) to 50 percent (Dubowitz et al., 1994) of the kinship care children were performing below grade level.

When the children in kinship care were assessed using standardized instruments, many were revealed to have behavior problems. Berrick and colleagues (1994) found that children of all ages in kinship care scored at least one standard deviation above the norm on the Behavior Problem Index (BPI), and Dubowitz and colleagues (1994) found that 35 percent of the children had an overall Child Behavior Checklist score in the clinical range. However, it is noteworthy that Berrick et al. (1994) reports that kinship care children between the ages of four and fifteen had fewer behavioral problems than children in the same age group in traditional foster care. In the same vein, Iglehart (1994) reports that, while 33 percent of children in kinship care had behavioral problems serious enough to be noted in the case record, children in traditional foster care were even more likely to have adjustment problems. Benedict and colleagues (1996) also report that children in relative care were less likely to have developmental or behavioral problems than children in nonrelative care. Gebel (1996) found that kinship caregivers rated more children as good natured and fewer children as being difficult to handle than did nonrelative caregivers.

Characteristics of parents. While most of the studies reviewed reported characteristics of kinship caregivers and children, only the Benedict (Benedict et al., 1996) and Scannapieco (Scannapieco et al., 1997) studies reported data on parents. Maternal characteristics of age, income, and type of housing were comparable for relative and nonrelative placements. There were, however, significant differences in marital status, race, and number of children in the family (Scannapieco et al., 1996). Mothers with children in kinship care were predominantly African American, were more likely to be married, and had fewer children than mothers of children in nonrelative care (Scannapieco et al., 1996). Benedict and colleagues (1996) found that the only significant difference in the characteristics of the mothers of children placed with kin and those whose children were in nonkin placements was that maternal drug use was reported to be higher (25% versus 13%). Conversely, health problems were reported for 30 percent of birth mothers of children placed with nonkin, compared to 16.5 percent for birth mothers of children placed with kin (Benedict et al., 1996).

Provision of Child Welfare Services

Most of the studies include information about agency services provided while the children are in out-of-home care, and all that do so identify deficiencies in this area (Berrick et al., 1994; Dubowitz et al., 1993a; Gebel, 1996; Iglehart, 1994; Scannapieco et al., 1996; Thornton, 1991). For example, 91 percent of kinship caregivers had not received any formal training during the previous year (Berrick et al., 1994). Participants in foster care were more likely to be offered services than were participants in kinship care, and levels of agency monitoring of children in kinship care were below those for children in traditional foster care (Berrick et al., 1994; Gebel, 1996; Iglehart, 1994). However, Berrick and colleagues (1994) note that kinship caregivers are very satisfied with their social workers.

Goals and Outcomes of Kinship Care Placement

Outcome research on kinship care is limited, making it difficult to reach conclusions about the strengths and challenges of kinship care for families and children. Moreover, many kinship placements have not yet ended, limiting the pool of cases where placement outcomes can be thoroughly assessed. This section examines such issues as the duration and stability of placement, permanency planning goals for children in kinship care, and the kin caregivers' intentions about continued care.

Kinship care placements last longer than traditional foster parent placements, and reunification rates are lower (Berrick et al., 1994; Dubowitz et al., 1993a; Thornton, 1991; Scannapieco et al., 1996; Wulczyn & Goerge, 1992), but placements with relatives are very stable (Berrick et al., 1994; Dubowitz et al., 1993a; Iglehart, 1994; Scannapieco et al., 1997). However, in the only follow-up study of foster care to examine the differences between outcomes for children in relative and nonrelative care, Benedict and colleagues (1996) found no difference in length of stay in care. They found the median length of stay for both groups to be twelve years. The sample for this study was unique in that it was a long-term foster-care group.

The kinship caregivers expressed commitment to the children in their care and indicated their willingness to care for them as long as needed (Berrick et al., 1994; Dubowitz et al., 1993a; Gebel, 1996; Thornton, 1991). The majority, however, were not willing to adopt children who were already related to them (Berrick et al., 1994; Thornton, 1991), nor were they likely to assume legal guardianship of the children (Iglehart, 1994). Gebel (1996) found no difference between relative and nonrelative caregivers in the length of time they would care for the children or in their willingness to consider adoption of a child placed with them.

Studies vary widely concerning permanency planning goals for children in kinship care. For example, the proportion with the goal of independent living upon discharge ranges from 15 percent (Scannapieco et al., 1996) to 88 percent (Thornton, 1991). Return to parental custody is the reported goal in 33 percent (Dubowitz et al., 1994) to 43 percent (Scannapieco et al., 1996). However, Scannapieco and colleagues (1996) found that children in kinship and traditional foster care do not differ in agency permanency planning goals.

As already mentioned, only one study has compared the adult functioning of children in relative and nonrelative care (Benedict et al., 1996). In this study, no difference was found in later education, employment, income, or housing. Social support and experiences of life stress were reported at similar levels for both groups. Differences were found, however, in the area of physical health: young people in nonrelative care reported higher levels of hypertension than young people in kinship care. In addition, although the usage of cocaine and marijuana was similar for the groups, a greater number of young people placed with kin reported heroin usage at sometime in their lives, and a significantly higher number of youth in kinship care reported trading sex for drugs.

DISCUSSION OF THE SYSTEMATIC REVIEW OF FINDINGS

In spite of the previously discussed shortcomings of the research methodologies and the relatively small number of studies conducted, certain trends emerge from the review, suggesting direction for future studies. The integration of descriptive findings for caregivers, children, and birth parents gives a good picture of the differences and similarities among the groups.

A disproportionate share of African American children reside in kinship care. This pattern may be due in part to a tradition of family caregiving among African Americans that is discussed in the literature (Gray & Nybell, 1990; Hegar & Scannapieco, 1995; Martin & Martin, 1985; Scannapieco & Jackson, 1996). It may also reflect a successful recruitment strategy by Department of Social Service agencies that is congruent with that cultural tradition. A less agreeable interpretation, one the coeditors explore in the final chapter of this book, is that African American children continue to be undeserved by traditional child welfare services such as foster care and group home care, leaving kinship care as one of the few placement options available.

Kinship caregivers are single parents and are likely to be older, poorer, and less educated than foster caregivers. These differences do not seem to impact on the well-being of children during care (Berrick et al., 1994; Iglehart, 1994) or, as far as studies to date have shown, in adult functioning (Benedict et al., 1996).

A pattern of fewer services successfully delivered to parents, caregivers, and children seems to emerge from the review. This trend, together with the markedly longer average stay in kinship homes compared with traditional foster homes, does suggest that efforts to work with parents toward the goal of returning children to parental custody may be less successful when children are in kinship care. This conclusion is highly consistent with findings of the major studies (Berrick et al., 1994; Dubowitz, 1990; Scannapieco et al., 1997; Thornton, 1991; Wulczyn & Goerge, 1992). The critical unanswered questions are: (1) why is this so? and (2) should it change?

It may be that many parents are comparatively content to have children raised in the homes of relatives and decline to engage with agencies in working for their return. It may be that agencies put less energy into permanency planning efforts when children are in kinship care, or it may be that they select cases for kinship placement when there is a poorer prognosis for the return of the children. At present, permanency planning mandates apply equally to children in kinship homes and to those in traditional foster homes, but it would certainly be possible to think of long-term placement with close relatives as meeting the goals of permanency planning, particularly when that plan has the explicit or implicit agreement of the children's parents. The issue of permanency planning for children in kinship care is among the next major policy and practice challenges to face the child welfare system.

Implications for Policy and Practice

As discussed in other sections of this book, policy has to address whether kinship care is a permanency planning option or a temporary plan for out-of-home care. Ideologically, if kinship care is an extension of family preservation programs, then identification of client and program characteristics that are associated with success or failure (however they are defined) are necessary beginning steps. Caregivers' perceptions of their roles must continue to be examined in this context, since they seem to differ for the two groups (Le Prohn, 1994). The idea that kinship caregivers see themselves not in the role of foster parents but rather as parents is worthy of further investigation. Within this same discussion, clarification of what constitutes an appropriate level of stable supervision of kinship homes is necessary, with safety issues a key area of concern. The explication of program descriptions and service characteristics is required as an integral part of any research study.

The effects of paying kin the higher foster care rate for caring for relative children, rather than the AFDC rate, needs to be systematically examined. Within this framework, questions of incentives and their impact on permanency planning need to be addressed, as well as the impact of the 1996 federal welfare reforms. Kinship care has not been a part of the welfare reform discussions, but the impact of the funding changes on kinship care is an important new avenue of study. For example, the more restrictive policies on welfare payments may force more kin into the foster care system as more caregivers seek to collect the higher foster care payments.

Future Directions for Research

Kinship care research is in its infancy. Many questions remain about the impact of kinship care on caregivers, children, birth parents, families, and the child welfare system. Well-designed, controlled studies are essential to determining the efficacy of kinship care vis-à-vis other forms of out-of-home care. Within this context, operational definitions of behavior, child development, school performance, child and family functioning, and outcomes need to be standardized. Children's problems in kinship care may be hard to identify because of caregivers' perceived roles, differential reporting in social service records, and a lack of state supervision of these children, so new means of measuring these variables must be explored.

In the research section of this book some of the gaps in our information are identified. Pecora, Le Prohn, and Nasuti explore the role perceptions of kinship caregivers compared to those of other foster parents. They explore how the two groups differ in terms of demographics, values, attitudes toward childrearing, and other areas and consider the impact of these differences on programs. Berrick, Needell, and Barth examine child welfare workers' perspectives on the placement experience, differences between working with kinship caregivers and foster parents, and workers' perspectives on possible reforms. Starr, Dubowitz, Harrington, and Feigelman investigate behavior problems of teens in kinship care, using a cross-informant approach. According to the authors, this approach has been used only once before in foster care research, and they believe it advances the measurement of behavioral problems. Last, Zuravin, Benedict, and Stallings address the adult functioning of former kinship and nonrelative foster care children. This is an expansion of their original work on this area (Benedict et al., 1996).

In one form or another, kinship care as a formal child welfare program has become a part of the continuum of social services. There are, however, many unanswered questions and gaps in our knowledge that must be further investigated. Researchers must now embrace kinship care as a meaningful area of study and work to advance the knowledge base in order to develop and promote best practice.

References

Benedict, M., Zuravin, S., & Stallings, R. (1996). Adult functioning of children who lived in kin versus nonrelative family foster homes. *Child Welfare, 75* (5), 529–549.

Berrick, J. D., Barth, R. P., & Needell, B. (1994a). A comparison of kinship foster homes and foster family homes: Implications for kinship foster care as family preservation. *Children and Youth Services Review, 16* (1/2), 33–64.

Billingsley, A. (1992). *Climbing Jacob's ladder: The enduring legacy of African-American families.* New York: Simon & Shuster.

Dubowitz, H. (1990, August). *The physical and mental health and educational status of children placed with relatives: Final report.* Unpublished manuscript, University of Maryland Medical School, Baltimore.

Dubowitz, H., Feigelman, S., Harrington, D., Starr, R., Zuravin, S., & Sawyer, R. (1994). Children in kinship care: How do they fare? *Children & Youth Services Review, 16,* 1–2, 85–106.

Dubowitz, H., Feigelman, S., & Zuravin, S. (1993a). A profile of kinship care. *Child Welfare, 72* (3), 153–169.

Dubowitz, H., Feigelman, S., Zuravin, S., Tepper, V., Davidson, N., & Lichenstein, R. (1992) The physical health of children in kinship care. *American Journal of Diseases of Children, 146,* 603–610.

Dubowitz, H., Zuravin, S., Starr, R. Feigelman, S., & Harrington, D. (1993b). Behavior problems of children in kinship care. *Developmental and Behavioral Pediatrics, 14* (6), 386–396.

Gebel, T. J. (1996). Kinship care and non-relative family foster care: A comparison of caregiver attributes and attitudes. *Child Welfare, 75,* (1), 5–18.

Gleeson, J. P., & Craig, L. C. (1994). Kinship care in child welfare: An analysis of states' policies. *Children and Youth Services Review, 16* (1/2), 7–31.

Gray, S. S., & Nybell, L. M. (1990). Issues in African-American family preservation. *Child Welfare, 69,* 513–523.

Hegar, R. L., & Scannapieco, M. (1995). From family duty to family policy: The evolution of kinship care. *Child Welfare, 74* (1), 200–216.

Iglehart, A. P. (1994). Kinship foster care: Placement, service, and outcome issues. *Children and Youth Services Review, 16* (1/2), 107–122.

Larson, D., Pastro, L., Lyons, J., & Anthony, E. (1992). *The systematic review: An innovative approach to reviewing research.* Washington, D.C.: Department of Health and Human Services.

Le Prohn, N. (1994). The role of the kinship foster parent: A comparison of the role conceptions of relative and non-relative foster parents. *Children and Youth Services Review, 16* (1/2), 65–84.

Link, M. K. (1996). Permanency outcomes in kinship care: A study of children placed in kinship care in Erie County, New York. *Child Welfare, 75* (5), 509–528.

Martin, E. P., & Martin, J. M. (1978). *The black extended family.* Chicago: University of Chicago Press.

Martin, J. M., & Martin, E. P. (1985). *The helping tradition in the black family and community.* Silver Spring, Md.: National Association of Social Workers.

Scannapieco, M., & Hegar, R. L. (1995). Kinship care: A comparison of two case management models. *Child & Adolescent Social Work, 12* (2), 147–156.

Scannapieco, M., & Hegar, R. L., & McAlpine, C. (1997). Kinship care and foster care: A comparison of characteristics and outcomes. *Families and Society, 78* (5), 480–488.

Scannapieco, M., & Jackson, S. (1996). Kinship care: The African-American resilient response to family preservation. *Social Work, 41* (2), 190–196.

Takas, M. (1993). *Kinship care and family preservation: A guide for states in legal and policy development.* Unpublished manuscript. Washington, D.C.: American Bar Association Center on Children and the Law.

Thornton, J. L. (1991). Permanency planning for children in kinship foster homes. *Child Welfare, 70* (5), 593–601.

Wulczyn, F., & Goerge, R. M. (1992). Foster care in New York and Illinois: The challenge of rapid change. *Social Service Review, 66* (2), 278–294.

Role Perceptions of Kinship and Other Foster Parents in Family Foster Care

Peter J. Pecora, Ph.D.
Nicole S. Le Prohn, Ph.D.
John J. Nasuti, D.S.W.

State-sanctioned and reimbursed foster care has traditionally been provided by individuals unrelated to the child needing care, although a number of ethnic minority groups in the United States have maintained a tradition of informally caring for children using relatives.[1] Thus, we have had two basic systems of foster care—one using licensed placements and one consisting of family and unrelated "kin" who cared for children (see, for example, Stack, 1974). In addition, conflicting issues affect placement choices for children. Historically, child maltreatment has been seen as transmitted from one generation to the next, with some abused children growing up to become abusive adults (Belsky, 1980; Kadushin, 1980, p. 179). This view of the etiology of child abuse argues against the use of relatives as foster parents; if the parent was abused as a child, the agency would avoid placing the abused child with the grandparent.

Although intergenerational transmission of violence is a serious issue to be considered, there has also been movement toward a more ecological view of child maltreatment. This ecological approach suggests that a variety of factors contribute to the occurrence of child maltreatment. Although it is often the parent who is most directly responsible for the abusive or neglectful act, environmental factors such as stress, unemployment, or lack of housing enter into the equation. This broader view of the factors that contribute to child mal-

---

1. Literature review is adapted from Le Prohn & Pecora (1994).

treatment does not automatically exclude relatives from becoming foster parents to their related minor children (Garbarino, 1981).

In fact, kinship networks in many ethnic minority cultures have been able to balance successfully child-family contact and child safety. For example, the African American culture has a long history of caring for children through family-sanctioned kin (Billingsley & Giovannoni, 1972, pp. 45–46; Boyd-Franklin, 1989, pp. 42–63; Hill, 1972; Scannapieco & Jackson, 1996; Stack, 1974; Wilson, 1989). Because of the practice of slavery and institutional racism, African Americans especially have a strong sense of community, as exemplified by the following African proverb: "I am because we are. We are; therefore, I am" (Margaret Spearmon, personal communication, November 19, 1993). In many Latino families, "compadres" and "comadres" (godparents and coparents) play important roles in child rearing even though they often are not relatives by blood or marriage (Garcia-Preto, 1982, p. 172; Sena-Rivera, 1979; Sotomayor, 1991, pp. xiv–xix).[2] In Hawaiian families, a form of open adoption—"hanai"— has been practiced for many years in which children are given to other members of the community to be raised (Essoyan, 1992; Heighton, Jordan, & Gallimore, 1970; Chet Okayama, personal communication, April 12, 1993).

Many Native Americans are raised for periods of time with extended family or clan members, and tribal courts have officially sanctioned kinship care placements. And, in general, more relatives are being licensed as foster parents. The increased use of relative foster care in many states has brought with it questions about different perceptions of the foster parents and how best to work with them. Early chapters in this volume have discussed the historical background, policy influences, and current usage of kinship care across the United States. This chapter presents selected results from two related studies that examined the characteristics, role conceptions, agency involvement, and satisfaction of relative and nonrelative foster parents.[3]

RESEARCH QUESTIONS

Study Purpose

As described in the previous chapters, it is reasonable to assume that the use of relatives as caregivers will continue and perhaps increase. If this is true, several questions need answers. How do these groups of caregivers vary in terms of demographics, values, attitudes toward child rearing, and service needs? For example, are relative caregivers generally older than nonrelative foster parents? Does any age difference affect their care of the child? Are relatives in greater need of financial or supportive services when caring for their related foster child? Prior studies (e.g., Berrick, Barth, Needell, & Courtney,

---

2. In many Puerto Rican families, traditional values include family and extended family structure of very strong ties, along with use of the "compadrazgo" system of godparents and coparents (Inclan & Herron, 1989, p. 256).

3. In this study, the term "relative foster parents or caregivers" refers to foster parents related to the foster child by blood or marriage, and the term "nonrelative foster parents" refers to unrelated caregivers.

1993, pp. 110–111) have reported that relative caregivers receive less respite care, training, and contact with social workers and participate less in support groups.

Other questions include the following: Do relative caregivers have service needs that are different from those of traditional, unrelated foster care providers? Do they have different training needs? Is the relationship between agency social workers and relative caregivers different from that between agency social workers and nonrelative foster parents? Are relative caregivers satisfied with the services they receive from the foster care agency? Do relatives expect more or less from the agency than the agency can provide?

At least one study has found that relatives often say they felt "obligated" to become caretakers for a related child (Thornton, 1987, p. 108). Most relative caregivers, however, view this arrangement as a natural one. Does this sense of obligation and naturalness increase or decrease the child's well-being? How do social workers perceive the quality of child rearing provided by relative caregivers?

We do not yet know enough about relative caregivers to answer these questions. Because of the possibility that many of these children will reach maturity in relative homes, it is time to examine the needs of relative caregivers. These studies were designed, therefore, to examine the relationships between type of placement (relative or nonrelative) and foster parents' role conceptions, motivation, agency satisfaction, and foster children's contact with biological family members. With the increased placement of children in relative foster care—both by the Casey Family Program in Seattle, Washington, and by other public and private foster care agencies—finding out more about relative caregivers and how they are similar to or different from nonrelative foster parents will help social workers provide better services to all foster families.

This chapter summarizes the results of two linked studies regarding foster parent role perceptions and discusses some of the implications of the data for program design and practice. The terms "foster parent" and "caregiver" will be used interchangeably, as many relative foster parents and the children they care for perceive themselves more as extended family caregivers than as part of an agency-based foster care system.

Theoretical Framework

Role theory was one of the major theoretical frameworks that guided the design and implementation of the two studies.[4] Individuals have many roles in their lives, and each brings an accompanying set of expectations. Some of these expectations come from within, from the individual's perceptions and understanding of the role; other expectations come from others who interact with the individual in his or her role. These two different types of expectations are referred to in role theory as *role conceptions* and *role demands*.

While much has been written on the foster parent role (see, for example, Carbino, 1980; Eastman, 1982; Thornton, 1987), there is no clear consensus on the

---

4. For more information, see Le Prohn (1993).

definition of the foster parent role. Some studies have focused primarily on how agencies or social workers define the foster parent's role (e.g., Wasson & Hess, 1989). Studies that have focused on how foster parents themselves define their role have come up with almost as many role definitions as there are foster parents.

With so many definitions of the foster parent role, how the individual sees his or her role may be very different from how others see the individual's role, and role conflict may occur. Role conflict may also occur when an individual holds two roles that have incompatible expectations. For foster parents, role conflict occurs when the expectations or role demands of the agency are different from those of the foster parent based on his or her own conception of his or her role. The studies that have focused on the role of the foster parent have looked at primarily the role of the nonrelative caregiver. Little is known about if and how the role conception of the relative caregiver differs from that of nonrelative caregiver. If there are differences, role theory would predict that the role conflict between the agency staff and the relative foster parent about the caregiver's role would be different from the role conflict between the agency staff and the nonrelative foster parent. In addition, relative caregivers bring with them their role as a relative to the youth, in addition to their role as a foster parent, therefore, they may experience role conflict if their conceptions of these two roles—"relative" and "foster parent"—differ. This chapter examines role differences and a few other related areas.

Data Collection Approach

Instrument development.   Three instruments were developed for the original study conducted by the Casey Family Program (Casey): the *Foster Parent Mail Survey*, the *Foster Parent Interview Schedule*, and the *Social Worker Interview Schedule*. Items for each instrument were selected from a variety of preexisting instruments, as well as from the foster parent research and practice literature. Items were reviewed thoroughly for inclusion or exclusion by Casey staff, foster parents, and other experts. A variety of internal consistency and factor analysis procedures was applied to help verify the scale structure of each instrument (see Le Prohn, 1993).

The *Foster Parent Mail Survey* was the instrument used by both groups of collaborators (Casey, Louisiana State University) for the joint research effort. The next sections of this chapter summarize some of the major findings and practice implications of the study in the areas of role perceptions. Although mean averages, similarities, and differences between the two groups of foster parents in each study are highlighted, caution should be exercised to avoid stereotyping any particular type of foster parent. The demographic and other characteristics of these families vary—each family brings to fostering a unique constellation of abilities and characteristics that enables them to care for some of the most troubled and vulnerable children in our society.

Casey study sample.   Stratified random sampling without replacement was used to establish the sample of foster families from the Casey Family Program; the strata were relative and nonrelative foster families. As of

December 1993, 27.3 percent of the children in the Casey program were cared for by relatives (Casey Family Program, 1994). Relative placements were those where the child was related to one or more of the foster parents by blood or marriage. (For example, approximately eight placements that involved foster parents who were close friends of the birth parents but not related to the child were not included in the "relative foster care" group.) Of a potential 304 families in the initial sample (175 nonrelative and 129 relative), 234 families were eligible and invited to participate, and 230 families agreed to participate. Major reasons for being excluded from the sample included: there was no child in the home (thirty families), the family no longer was with Casey (thirteen families), or the family was a respite care provider at the time of this study (five families). Thirteen families were excluded for unknown reasons.

Survey design. Casey foster parents were asked to complete a mail survey and a telephone interview. Social workers were asked to complete a telephone interview. This two-stage data collection approach allowed the collection of both qualitative and quantitative data.

Between March and October 1992, 373 surveys were mailed to the one or two primary caregivers in 230 foster families.[5] Two hundred and eighty-four surveys were completed and returned by 188 families. This represents a response rate of 76.1 percent of surveys mailed, or 81.7 percent of families.[6] Data from the social workers are available for all of the families interviewed.

Louisiana study sample. Data for the Louisiana study were collected as part of a foster parent training contract between the Office of Community Services of the Louisiana Department of Social Services and the Graduate School of Social Work at Louisiana State University. During June and July 1992, data were collected from 222 licensed foster parents who attended one of the foster parent training sessions. Training was provided in eight communities throughout two social service regions in southern Louisiana. To administer the survey, the questions were read aloud to groups of foster parents who were in the training. More than 90 percent of the parents participated.

CHARACTERISTICS OF FOSTER PARENTS

Casey Foster Parent Demographics

Table 10.1 presents data on the Casey foster families. The majority (63.9%) of foster families in the study were headed by a married couple. Nonrelative foster families were almost twice as likely (79.6%) as relative foster families (45.1%) to be headed by a married couple. A much larger proportion of nonrelative foster mothers were married (80.4%), compared with relative foster mothers (46.5%). Almost all foster fathers were married (95.8%). The average age of fos-

---

5. One family that received surveys later turned out to be ineligible for the sample because it no longer had a child placed in the home. This brought the sample to 229 families.

6. Families may have been sent two surveys if there were two foster parents, but each family returned only one.

TABLE 10.1
Casey Foster Family Demographic Information

	Relative Foster Families ($n = 82$)	Nonrelative Foster Families ($n = 98$)	All Foster Families ($N = 180$)
Household Composition***			
• % Married Couple	45.1	79.6[a]	63.9
• % Single Mother	51.2	19.4	33.9
• % Single Father	3.7	2.0	2.8
Family Income**			
• % Less than 10,000	33.8[c]	2.4[d]	17.1[e]
• % Greater than 30,000	24.3	56.0	41.1
Income Source (%)			
• Two Employed Adults	18.3	38.8***	29.4
• One Employed Adult	43.9	46.9***	45.6
% Owning Their Home	59.8	90.7***	76.5
% Living in Subsidized Housing	14.6	2.0**	7.8
Years of School Completed			
• Foster Mother	11.7 ($SD = 2.5$)[b] ($n = 80$)	14.0*** ($SD = 2.6$) ($n = 97$)	12.97 ($SD = 2.8$) ($N = 177$)
• Foster Father	12.3 ($SD = 2.5$) ($n = 40$)	13.7* ($SD = 2.8$) ($n = 80$)	13.3 ($SD = 2.8$) ($N = 120$)
Average Number of Adults in Home	1.9 ($SD = .9$)	2.3*** ($SD = 1.9$)	2.1 ($SD = .9$)
Average Number of Children in Home	2.3 ($SD = 1.2$)	2.3 ($SD = 1.1$)	2.3 ($SD = 1.2$)

a. The chi-square statistic was used to test for significant differences for the first five items; a *t* test was used to test for significant differences in mean scores for the last three items—years of school completed, average number of adults and children in the home.
b. Standard deviation scores are provided to present a picture of the average amount of variation of the scores for this variable.
c. The sample size for relative families varied between 74 and 82, with items marked having 5 or more missing cases.
d. The sample size for nonrelative families varied between 84 and 98, with items marked having 5 or more missing cases.
e. Total sample varied between 158 and 180 families, with items marked having 5 or more missing cases.
*$p \leq .05$
**$p \leq .01$
***$p \leq .001$

ter mothers was 48.0 years old; the foster fathers were slightly older (48.8 years). Relative foster parents were older than nonrelative foster parents, and, in fact, they represent a form of second-generation parenting. The average age of relative foster mothers was 50.2 ($SD = 10.9$), while nonrelative foster mothers had an average age of 46.3 ($SD = 9.2$). This difference was statistically significant ($p \leq .01$) when tested using the *t* test, which implies that there is a 1 percent likelihood that this difference would have occurred by chance alone. Relative foster fathers were also 50.3 years of age on average (*SD* = 12.3), and nonrelative foster fathers were slightly younger at an average of 48.1 (*SD* = 9.1) years of age. Years of education also varied between the two groups, with a larger difference found between foster mothers.

In terms of foster parenting experience, 43.1 percent of the foster parents had been foster parents before Casey; the foster parents had, on average, been with Casey for a little over 3.5 years. A significant percentage of these foster families (17.1%) are overcoming financial challenges to care for children, as they have family incomes of less than $10,000 per year. A much higher proportion of relative foster families (33.8%) than nonrelative families (2.4%) had incomes of less than $10,000 per year (see Figure 10.1).

The stresses created by low family income can be significant, even with familial and agency supports. Other studies have found that a substantial proportion of relative caregivers are raising children on low incomes (e.g., Berrick, Barth, & Needell, 1994; Thornton, 1991, p. 596). Therefore, the Casey foster payment constituted a sizable (or, for seven relative and one nonrelative families, the primary) source of income for these families.

Relative foster parents were significantly more likely to be people of color than were nonrelatives. Chi-square analysis revealed significant differences among the groups: X^2 = 41.5 [(df = 1), $p \leq$ .001]. Nearly three-quarters of nonrelative foster mothers (72.2%) and foster fathers (73.8%) were Caucasian, compared with 30.0 percent of relative foster mothers and 45.0 percent of relative foster fathers.

More specifically, social workers were asked to list up to four ethnic categories for each foster parent. Table 10.2 reports the primary ethnicity for foster mothers. Nonrelative foster mothers were most likely to be Caucasian (72.2%) or African American (12.4%); relative foster mothers were most likely to be African American (32.5%) or Caucasian (30.0%). If all non-Caucasian eth-

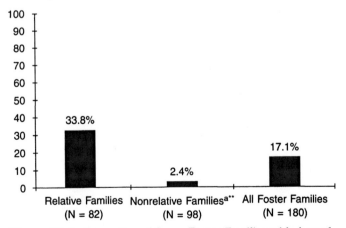

Figure 10.1 Proportion of Casey Foster Families with Annual Incomes of Less than $10,000

[a]The chi-square statistic was used to test for differences between the relative and nonrelative families.
**$p \leq$ .01

TABLE 10.2
Ethnicity of Casey Foster Mothers[a]

Ethnic Group	Relative Foster Mothers ($n = 80$)	Nonrelative Foster Mothers ($n = 97$)	All Foster Mothers ($N = 177$)
African American	26 (32.5%)	12 (12.4%)	38 (21.5%)
Asian	0 (0%)	1 (1.0%)	1 (0.6%)
Caucasian	24 (30.0%)	70 (72.2%)	94 (53.1%)
Hispanic or Latino	11 (13.8%)	8 (8.2%)	19 (10.7%)
Native American	19 (23.8%)	3 (3.1%)	22 (12.4%)
Pacific Islander	0 (0%)	1 (1.0%)	1 (0.6%)
Other	0 (0%)	2 (2.1%)	2 (1.1%)

a. Chi-square analysis revealed significant differences among the groups: $\chi2 = 41.5$ ($df = 6$), $p \le .001$.

nic groups are combined, 70.0 percent of relative foster mothers were persons of color, compared with 27.8 percent of nonrelative foster mothers.

Similar results were found for foster fathers. Less than half of the relative foster fathers (18 or 45.0%) were Caucasian, compared with 73.8 percent of the nonrelative foster fathers. Although the sample size of the relative foster fathers was small ($N = 40$), Native American (8), Latino (8), and African American (6) groups were represented.

Many of the relative caregivers had moved from a grandparent role to more of a full-time childrearing role. This required an adjustment in meeting child needs and called upon a slightly different set of skills and resources. In addition, some of the Native Americans and, possibly, other caretakers had moved from a tribal elder teaching role, with all the respect that is accorded that role in the tribe, to more of an ordinary parent role with the children and, possibly, others in the child's immediate circle.

Louisiana Foster Parent Demographics

Table 10.3 presents data on the foster parents[7] from Louisiana who participated in the study. The majority (70.3%) of foster families were headed by a married couple, with only slightly more married nonrelative foster parents (74.2%) than married relative foster parents (61.8%). Yet the majority of participants were foster mothers (73.4%), with foster fathers representing 24.8% of the sample and 1.8% identifying themselves as "other." Of the 222 respondents, 124 (55.9%) were African Americans, 65 (29.3%) were Caucasian, and fifteen (6.8%) were of other ethnic background (eighteen foster parents did not state their ethnicity). While the differences were not statistically significant, relative foster parents were more likely to be people of color than nonrelative foster parents (see Table 10.4).

The average age for relative and nonrelative foster parents was the same at 47.8 years. The average number of years as a foster parent was 6.8 for rel-

---

7. In contrast to the Casey sample, in which some of the demographic data were collected on families, demographic data in the Louisiana sample were collected on parents. Only one parent per family completed a form.

TABLE 10.3
Louisiana Foster Parent Demographic Information

	Relative Foster Parents ($n = 35$)[a]	Nonrelative Foster Parents ($n = 182$)[b]	All Foster Parents ($N = 222$)[c]
Household Composition			
• % Married Couple	61.8	74.2[d]	70.3[e]
Income Source (%)			
• Two Employed Adults	24.2	26.7[b]	24.8[c]
• One Employed Adult	51.5	49.4	46.8
% Owning Their Home	88.2	93.2[b]	89.6[c]
% Living in Subsidized Housing	2.9	2.2	2.3
Years of School Completed	12.2 ($SD = 2.5$)[e]	11.9[b] ($SD = 3.0$)	11.9[c] ($SD = 2.9$)
Average Number of Adults in Home	1.8 ($SD = .7$)	2.0 ($SD = .7$)	2.0 ($SD = .7$)
Average Number of Children in Home	1.9 ($SD = 1.3$)	1.6 ($SD = .9$)	1.7[c] ($SD = 1.0$)

a. The sample size for relative parents varied between 34 and 35.
b. The sample size for nonrelative parents varied between 172 and 182, with items marked having 5 or more missing cases.
c. Five foster parents did not indicate whether they were relative or nonrelative foster parents. Thus, they are included in the total column, but not in other columns. Total sample varied between 208 and 222 parents, with items marked having 5 or more missing cases.
d. The chi-square statistic was used to test for significant differences for the first six items; a *t* test was used to test for significant differences in mean scores for the last two items—average number of adults and children in the home.
e. Standard deviation scores are provided to present a picture of the average amount of variation of the scores for this variable.

TABLE 10.4
Ethnicity of Louisiana Foster Parents

Ethnic Group	Relative Foster Parents ($n = 35$)	Nonrelative Foster Parents ($n = 182$)	All Foster Parents ($N = 222$)[a]
African American	24 (72.7%)	100 (58.5%)	124 (55.9%)
Asian	1 (3.0%)	2 (1.2%)	3 (1.4%)
Caucasian	6 (18.2%)	59 (34.5%)	65 (29.3%)
Hispanic or Latino	0	0	0
Native American	2 (6.1%)	8 (4.7%)	10 (4.5%)
Pacific Islander	0	0	0
Other	0 (0%)	2 (1.2%)	2 (0.9%)

a. Eighteen foster parents did not answer this item.

ative foster parents, 8.7 for nonrelative foster parents, and 8.4 for all foster parents. The mean educational level for relative foster parents was slightly higher than that for nonrelative foster parents (12.2 years compared to 11.9 years).

How similar are both groups of relative foster parents to relative caregivers who participated in other studies? In comparing the Berrick et al. (1993) study of foster parents in California, the Casey and the Louisiana relative foster parents were similar to the California foster parents in a number of areas, including household composition, proportion of ethnic minority parents, and home ownership. In comparison to the Dubowitz et al. (1993, 1994) study of kinship providers in Baltimore, the Casey parents were again similar in terms of household composition, relationship of the child to the caretaker(s), and age of foster mother (Casey: $M = 50$; Louisiana: $M = 47.8$; Baltimore: $Mdn = 48$; California: $M = 48$). Differences on certain variables exist, however, so comparisons of the Casey and Louisiana samples with other studies should be made with caution.

Practice Implications of Foster Family Demographics

It is clear from this demographic information that relative and nonrelative foster families have some distinct differences. Relative foster families are more likely to be headed by older single women, have less family income, and are more likely to be African American, Native American, Hispanic/Latino, or members of another ethnic minority group.

Support from other family members may offset the greater need for support that many typical single foster parents experience. In some cases, however, other family members may not be available or may themselves be sources of stress. Thus, agency-provided supports such as respite care, tutoring, child therapy, foster care payments, and social support become critical. But what other services might help address the needs of the older, lower-income, ethnic minority relative and nonrelative foster families? Health insurance, for example, remains an important yet unmet need for some families. And should there be more flexibility in funding reasonable requests for the entire family for such items as food, entertainment, vacations, or clothes for the non-Casey youth in the household?

The fact that the agency foster care payment constitutes a large or primary source of income for some caregivers has implications for the nature of the relationship between these families and the agency. Are sensitive case decisions about removal of children more difficult to make because of the vulnerability of these families? Or because the children are with relatives? Are there situations where relative foster families are asked to carry out certain responsibilities that are not imposed on nonrelative foster families? Do some relative foster families fail to receive some benefits or services because they are not aware of them or feel that they can advocate for themselves? Conversely, do some child welfare staff feel more uncomfortable about speaking to relative foster families about the use of funds or their child care activities because of a different sense of relationship with certain relative caregivers?

FOSTER PARENT ROLE CONCEPTION OF THE CASEY SAMPLE

Casey Foster Parent Roles

The role conception of the Casey sample of foster parents was measured using the forty-item *Foster Parent's Role Perception Scale* developed for this study (see Table 10.5). Each item on the scale listed a task that the foster parent might do for the child or the agency. Foster parents were asked to rate each task on the level of responsibility foster parents should have for that task; ratings could range from 0 (no responsibility) to 100 (total responsibility), in ten-point increments.[8]

The task with the lowest mean score for the foster parents as a group was "Training new social workers to work with foster families," with a mean of 25.4, indicating that foster parents' viewed this task as only about 25 percent the foster parents' responsibility. This reflected agency practice in 1993, when few Casey Divisions formally involved foster parents in training new social work staff. The task with the highest mean score for the foster parents as a group was "Teaching teenage foster child housekeeping and home maintenance skills so she or he can maintain a home independently," with a mean of 94.9, indicating that foster parents felt that this task was 95 percent the foster parents' responsibility.

Within each of the subgroups, the highest and lowest ranked items differed slightly. Relative foster parents rated "Training new social workers" lowest, with a rating of 32 percent the foster parents' responsibility. They rated "teaching teenage child housekeeping" equal with "scheduling child's medical and dental appointments," at almost 97 percent the foster parents' responsibility. Although nonrelative foster parents also rated "teaching housekeeping" highest (95 percent foster parent's responsibility), they rated "supervising visits between foster child and birth parents" lowest, with a mean score of only 16 percent. This low score for nonrelatives contrasts sharply with the relative rating for the same item of 63 percent.

The majority of the items on the *Foster Parent's Role Perception Scale* (25 out of 40 items) showed significant differences between relative and nonrelative foster parents at the .05 level of significance. However, in terms of practical significance, there was considerable agreement between the two groups of caregivers with respect to degree of responsibility. The areas of greatest numerical difference that were also statistically significant follow, with the relative caregiver rating listed first:[9]

- Helping child with emotional problems (78.1, 68.2)
- Transporting child to visits with birth parents or other relatives (64.1, 37.3)

---

8. Ten-point increments were used to ensure comparability in the two sample analyses. Note that this analysis of the Casey data uses a different scaling approach from that reported in Le Prohn (1993) and Le Prohn & Pecora (1994), where five-point increments were used.

9. Although other role areas may have greater mean score differences, the large standard deviation scores lowered the statistical significance.

TABLE 10.5
Role Conception Scale Items

Item	Casey Relative Foster Parents ($n = 114$)	Casey Nonrelative Foster Parents ($n = 170$)	Louisiana Relative Foster Parents ($n = 35$)	Louisiana Nonrelative Foster Parents ($n = 182$)
	Level of Foster Parent Responsibility			
Providing the child with birthday or Christmas presents	92.21[a,b] (16.19)	87.57* (18.98)	75.14 (30.91)	78.85 (28.23)
Helping foster child with emotional problems	78.14 (18.64)	68.27*** (19.55)	72.00 (23.49)	77.64 (21.53)
Helping to build child's self-confidence	88.93 (13.12)	84.85* (13.37)	89.43 (13.49)	88.41 (14.57)
Promoting the child's spirituality	91.89 (14.62)	87.50* (16.87)	87.71 (18.00)	88.52 (18.16)
Recruiting new foster families	36.58 (29.28)	34.29 (24.04)	55.14 (32.48)	52.97 (33.77)
Helping foster child develop physical skills which need improvement	80.62 (17.34)	81.37 (14.96)	83.43 (18.62)	83.41 (18.79)
Preparing teenage foster child to handle sickness, loneliness, and other problems once the child is on his/her own	81.33 (16.45)	79.88 (17.44)	79.43 (23.00)	78.74 (25.73)
Transporting child to visits with birth parents or other relatives	64.12 (35.68)	37.26*** (31.39)	70.00 (32.08)	66.15 (33.03)
Assessing the child's level of development	70.36 (23.66)	60.24*** (22.42)	71.14 (25.76)	68.13 (27.97)
Training new social workers to work with foster families	31.61 (32.45)	21.30** (23.94)	35.43 (39.73)	37.03 (36.06)
Talking to birth parents about child's behavior	46.40 (36.22)	17.32*** (22.99)	44.57 (37.99)	43.52 (36.15)
Keeping a record of a child's foster placement history and progress notes	51.77 (38.13)	34.02*** (32.61)	58.29 (41.90)	63.02 (37.15)
Talking to child's birth family about child's adjustment to foster care	42.34 (36.20)	17.50*** (23.72)	42.86 (36.43)	47.36 (36.23)
Responding to medical emergencies at school	95.35 (9.33)	93.59* (12.03)	90.57 (21.69)	92.58* (13.68)
Supervising the child's recreation	88.14 (16.56)	89.65 (15.91)	87.14 (22.17)	87.97 (19.80)
Planning new foster care services for the agency	37.46 (32.28)	29.59* (25.03)	37.14 (37.30)	40.60 (36.67)
Selecting the child's counselor or therapist	63.60 (29.06)	52.88** (28.59)	56.86 (37.16)	57.58 (37.04)
Selecting the child's school	86.28 (17.43)	79.99* (20.98)	82.86 (28.55)	85.93 (26.49)
Helping teenage foster child to develop friends who can provide positive support and appropriate companionship	86.49 (17.85)	84.29 (17.94)	82.29 (19.26)	84.94 (20.58)
Seeking special funds for special activities for the foster child	55.23 (33.92)	48.41[d] (31.13)	57.43 (36.65)	63.74 (36.46)
Helping foster child deal with issues related to being separated from his/her birth parents	77.70 (21.51)	67.53*** (18.93)	72.86 (26.41)	79.40 (23.81)
Arranging visits with birth parents	55.05 (37.27)	23.81*** (26.74)	42.86 (40.99)	42.36 (38.13)

(continued)

166

TABLE 10.5 (*continued*)
Role Conception Scale Items

Item	Level of Foster Parent Responsibility			
	Casey Relative Foster Parents (*n* = 114)	Casey Nonrelative Foster Parents (*n* = 170)	Louisiana Relative Foster Parents (*n* = 35)	Louisiana Nonrelative Foster Parents (*n* = 182)
Keeping child's educational	81.50	71.00**	83.71	82.64
records	(25.04)	(29.91)	(21.84)	(24.94)
Scheduling the child's medical and	96.67	92.41**	90.86	91.81
dental appointments	(7.49)	(15.67)	(21.74)	(19.62)
Helping with public relations for the	45.66	39.87	42.86	50.60
foster care agency	(31.73)	(25.53)	(37.46)	(33.09)
Helping a child choose a religion	77.09	73.75	74.29	72.09
	(27.47)	(28.34)	(29.13)	(32.82)
Arranging visits with the foster	65.82	40.00***	40.86	54.73
child's brothers and sisters	(31.55)	(31.76)	(41.12)	(37.77)
Helping teenage foster child find	74.25	69.17	53.14	59.73
housing when she/he approaches	(24.52)	(24.11)	(37.16)	(35.58)
emancipation				
Investigating complaints against	37.59c	27.66*	32.00	43.35
social workers	(37.76)	(30.85)	(38.49)	(38.77)
Shopping for a child's clothes	95.27	90.71**	93.14	93.57
	(7.94)	(17.36)	(15.10)	(16.18)
Supervising visits between foster	63.06	15.68***	43.71	45.93
child and birth parents	(36.35)	(22.65)	(40.95)	(40.03)
Teaching foster child to deal with	74.47	59.53***	70.00	71.54
future relationships with member of	(24.75)	(22.63)	(30.20)	(29.52)
his/her birth family				
Keeping a child's medical records	83.30	70.29***	79.71	81.76
	(24.62)	(31.06)	(27.71)	(26.89)
Talking to child's counselor or	85.84	84.97	82.86	89.40*
therapist about the child's progress	(18.50)	(17.15)	(20.38)	(16.69)
Deciding the best way to discipline	80.62	80.65	75.14	84.45*
a foster child	(18.86)	(16.10)	(30.91)	(20.42)
Conducting in-service training for	38.84	35.71	40.29	42.91
other foster parents	(33.28)	(30.12)	(41.48)	(38.20)
Working with teachers to help the	89.12	88.24	87.71	93.30*
foster child to do better in school	(13.54)	(16.44)	(18.00)	(13.13)
Teaching teenage foster child	96.34	94.94*	91.43	92.53
housekeeping and home	(6.15)	(10.39)	(21.02)	(15.13)
maintenance skills so she/he can				
maintain a home independently				
Training new foster parents	32.48	28.45	30.00	37.75
	(32.94)	(27.47)	(37.73)	(39.40)
Transporting the child to medical or	90.09	89.53	85.71	88.46
dental appointments	(16.93)	(14.55)	(20.04)	(19.55)

a. Both the mean and the standard deviation (SD) statistics are provided. The T-test was used to test for significant differences.

b. For all items, the scale ranged from 0–100. Foster parents indicated the level of responsibility they had for a particular task as a percentage.

c. Sample for Casey relative foster parents varied between 108 and 114, with items marked having 5 or more missing cases.

d. Sample for Casey nonrelative foster parents varied between 164 and 170, with items marked having 5 or more missing cases.

*$p \leq .05$
**$p \leq .01$
***$p \leq .001$

- Assessing the child's level of development (70.4, 60.2)
- Talking to birth parents about a child's behavior (46.4, 17.3)
- Keeping a record of the child's foster placement history and progress notes (51.8, 34.0)
- Talking to child's birth family about child's adjustment to foster care (42.3, 17.5)
- Helping a foster child deal with issues related to being separated from his or her birth parents (77.7, 67.5)
- Arranging visits with birth parents (55.0, 23.8)
- Supervisory visits between foster child and birth parents (63.1, 15.7)
- Teaching foster child to deal with future relationships with member of his or her birth family (74.5, 59.5)
- Keeping a child's medical records (83.3, 70.3)
- Arranging visits with the foster child's brothers and sisters (65.8, 40.0)

A variety of reasons was found for the differences in role perception. Relative caregivers, by virtue of their blood or other relationship to the child, tend to have a different type of relationship with, and investment in, the children in their home. In some cases, birth family members may not be nearby, especially for nonrelative foster parents, inhibiting contact and lessening nonrelative foster parent recognition of these role areas. The variation across caregivers may reflect different individual orientations to each child's situation and differences in social workers' approaches. In effect, parent ratings reflected what they saw as appropriate for the particular child in their home at that time.

Finally, depending upon their life experiences and the agency training provided, certain foster parents may bring a different perspective and/or a lower level of comfort to working with birth families. So, although some of the differences in role perception may be situational, there may be differences in attitudes across subgroups of foster parents that affect their perceptions of role.

Note that for some task areas, there was wide variation in foster parent ratings, as indicated by large standard deviation scores. For example, both groups of foster parents had similar scores of 35–37 percent for the task "recruiting new foster families," but the standard deviation scores (between 24 and 29) for both groups indicate there was a large amount of variation in opinion within each group (see Table 10.5). Some of the responsibility areas with the largest standard deviation scores for *both* groups of parents included:

- Supervising visits between foster child and birth parents ($SD = 37.0$)
- Keeping a record of a child's foster placement history and progress notes ($SD = 35.9$)
- Transporting child to visits with birth parents or other relatives ($SD = 35.6$)
- Arranging visits with birth parents ($SD = 34.8$)
- Arranging visits with the foster child's brothers and sisters ($SD = 34.1$)

As with the role responsibility variations between the two groups of caregivers, the wide variation within each group in certain role areas may be situational. With respect to work with birth family members, it is likely that foster parents in both Casey groups may differ in the proximity and ability of birth family members to see the children and in the foster families' degree of comfort with facilitating this contact.

For other areas, moderate-to-large standard deviation scores may reflect the individual variations relating to matching the talents and interest of a particular foster family with a particular child. Some foster families have excellent skills at working with school resources and might assume more responsibility in that area. The differences found, therefore, may reflect the individualized case plan and the variety of responsibilities that are negotiated by the social worker and the foster parent (Annette Sandberg, personal communication, September 10, 1993).

From this perspective, role clarification and general boundary setting are necessary, but strictly limiting role performance to particular persons is not beneficial. The amount of role variation, however, does indicate the need for additional efforts to build some consensus in these areas through orientation, training, and ongoing consultation.

Casey Foster Parent Role Scales

Factor analysis was used to combine individual items into scales measuring different aspects of the foster parent role using the Casey data only and based on ten-point scale increments. On the basis of the factor analysis, five role subscales were developed.[10] The first subscale, labeled *Birth Family Facilitator*, incorporated items that relate to maintaining the foster child's relationship with his or her biological family, such as transporting the child to a visit or arranging visits. Relative foster parents scored significantly higher (56.8) on this subscale than did nonrelative foster parents (30.5) (see Table 10.6).

The second subscale was labeled *Assist with Social and Emotional Development*. It incorporated items that relate to helping the foster child develop skills necessary for adult living, such as building self-confidence and teaching housekeeping skills. In addition, this subscale included tasks the foster parent may perform that relate generally to the child's well-being, such as responding to medical emergencies or helping the child with emotional problems. For the entire sample, the mean average score (M) on this subscale was 81.8, with statistically significant (but numerically small) differences between the two groups (M for relatives = 83.8, M for nonrelatives = 80.4).

Nevertheless, when various "control" variables such as foster parent age, years of education, income, and ethnicity were used in a multiple regression analysis to control statistically for these variables, ethnicity was a more powerful predictor of higher scores on this scale. In other words, being a person of color was more strongly correlated with *Assist with Social and Emotional*

---

10. For more information about the factor analysis method and results see Le Prohn (1993), ch. 3 and 4.

TABLE 10.6
Role Scale Scores of the Casey Foster Parents

Subscale	Relative Foster Parents (n = 114)	Nonrelative Foster Parents (n = 170)	All Foster Parents (N = 284)
Birth Family Facilitator	56.8	30.5***	41.1
	(SD = 26.0)	(SD = 16.9)	(SD = 24.7)
Assist with Social/Emotional Development	83.8	80.4*	81.8
	(SD = 11.8)	(SD = 10.6)	(SD = 11.2)
Agency Partner	37.4	31.4*	33.8
	(SD = 26.7)	(SD = 19.7)	(SD = 22.9)
Parenting	82.3	76.6***	78.9
	(SD = 12.5)	(SD = 13.3)	(SD = 13.2)
Spirituality	84.9	81.9	83.1
	(SD = 15.9)	(SD = 16.3)	(SD = 16.0)

*$p \le .05$
**$p \le .01$
***$p \le .001$

Development. These foster parents felt more of an obligation to working with youth in these areas, whether or not they were related to the child.

The third subscale, *Agency Partner,* included tasks that the foster parent might perform that relate not to the child in care but to the ongoing operation of the foster care agency. This subscale had the lowest rating for the foster parents as a group, with a mean of 33.8 and small but significant differences between the two groups (M for relatives = 37.4, M for nonrelatives = 31.4).

When the control variables were entered in a multivariate analysis, income level was a stronger predictor than relative status for the *Agency Partner* subscale. Thus, lower-income foster parents, irrespective of relative status, believed to a greater degree that their roles involved partnering with the agency in a variety of areas.

The fourth subscale, labeled *Parenting,* reflected tasks that are the general tasks of an adult caregiver for a child, such as deciding on discipline or working with teachers. The group mean was 78.9 on this subscale, with relative foster parents scoring significantly higher (M = 82.3) than nonrelative foster parents (M = 76.6).

Finally, the fifth subscale, *Spirituality,* includes items related to assisting the foster child to develop his or her spiritual life. The group mean on this subscale was the highest of all subscales at 83.1. There were no significant differences between relative (M = 84.9) and nonrelative foster parents (M = 81.9).

FOSTER PARENT ROLE CONCEPTION OF THE LOUISIANA SAMPLE

Louisiana Foster Parent Roles

Like their Casey counterparts, the Louisiana foster parents viewed training as a task that was not primarily their responsibility. As a group, the lowest mean score on the individual task items was "Training new foster parents," with a mean score of 36.8. "Training new social workers to work with foster families" was also rated low, with a mean of 37.3. The task items with the highest ratings by the Louisiana foster parents were "Shopping for a child's clothes," with a mean of 93.5, and "Working with teachers to help the foster child do better in school," with a mean of 92.4.

There were no major differences between the subgroup ratings for the highest- and lowest-ranked items (see Table 10.5). Both relative and nonrelative caregivers ranked "Shopping for a child's clothes" highest. Relative care givers ranked "Training new social workers to work with foster families" lowest, at only 30 percent their responsibility, while nonrelative caregivers ranked "Training new foster parents" lowest, at only 37 percent their responsibility.

Only four of the forty items showed statistically significant differences between the relative and nonrelative caregivers at the .05 level of significance.[11] These items, with the relative caregiver mean score listed first, are:

- Working with teachers to help the foster child do better in school (87.7, 93.3)
- Talking to child's counselor or therapist about the child's progress (82.9, 89.4)
- Deciding the best way to discipline a foster child (75.1, 84.5)
- Responding to medical emergencies at school (90.6, 92.6)

Louisiana Foster Parent Role Scales

In contrast to the Casey foster parents, the Louisiana foster parents showed no significant differences in the role scales resulting from their relative or nonrelative status. While a smaller sample size may have contributed to this result, none of the five scales showed differences greater than four points between mean scores for relative and those for nonrelative caregivers. Whereas in the Casey sample relative caregivers consistently scored higher on all scales than did nonrelatives, in the Louisiana sample nonrelative foster parents consistently had higher scores on all scales except the *Spirituality* scale; on that scale, relative and nonrelative caregivers had virtually the same mean score (see Table 10.7). It appears that the use of the role scales obscures some of the differences between the groups noted in the individual item analyses.

DISCUSSION

Practice Implications of Foster Parent Role Conceptions

Although there are many similarities between the two types of families, there are some significant differences in the role conceptions of relative and nonrelative foster families, particularly among the Casey families. First, relatives see themselves as having a strong role in maintaining the child's contact with

---

11. These statistical comparisons should be viewed as exploratory as no adjustments were made for multiple comparisons. Consequently, the experiment-wise error rate exceeds 5 percent.

TABLE 10.7
Role Scale Scores of the Louisiana Foster Parents

Subscale	Relative Foster Parents ($n = 35$)	Nonrelative Foster Parents ($n = 182$)	All Foster Parents ($N = 222$)[a]
Birth Family Facilitator	51.7	54.5	54.1
	(SD = 27.3)	(SD = 24.9)	(SD = 25.2)
Assist with Social and	82.3	83.7	83.6
Emotional Development	(SD = 13.8)	(SD = 12.7)	(SD = 12.7)
Agency Partner	40.1	43.6	43.2
	(SD = 29.8)	(SD = 27.9)	(SD = 28.4)
Parenting	76.9	80.7	80.0
	(SD = 18.1)	(SD = 14.1	(SD = 14.7)
Spirituality	81.5	81.9	81.9
	(SD = 17.6)	(SD = 17.2)	(SD = 17.1)

[a]Five foster families did not indicate whether they were relative or nonrelative foster parents. Thus, they are included in the total column, but not in the other columns. Total sample varied between 208 and 222 parents, with items marked having 5 or more missing cases.
*$p \leq .05$
**$p \leq .01$
***$p \leq .001$

his or her biological family, whereas nonrelatives rate that role as less their responsibility. Relative caregivers also feel that they have greater responsibility for helping children deal with issues of separation and loss and for facilitating visitation with birth family members.

These differences have implications for child welfare agencies as they try to maximize appropriate levels of birth family contact in the years ahead. Additional support must be provided to some nonrelative foster parents so that they can help the agency meet its responsibilities by incorporating some areas into their foster parent role. In addition, caseworkers may need to expand their roles with respect to facilitating contact with birth family members for children in nonrelative placements. (Certainly some of this is already occurring; nonrelative foster parents reported that the Casey social workers arrange as many visits with the biological family as the foster parents do. Data regarding this were not available for the Louisiana sample.)

Second, even though they care about a child's development, nonrelative foster parents see themselves as having less formal responsibility for helping the foster child with emotional problems, keeping a record of the child's progress while in care, and assessing the child's level of development. (In Louisiana the categories were working with teachers, talking to therapists about a child's progress, and responding to medical emergencies at school.) Implementing certain interventions to promote child development or address family crises may need to be tailored to the type of foster family involved. For example, relative family caregivers may more naturally monitor informal milestones of child development, whereas other foster parents may need special training or support to do this.

Third, the majority of foster parents in this study stated that their role was "the same as parents." Few foster parents, either relative or nonrelative, described their role as that of a "professional therapeutic caregiver," although many identified with tasks that may require specialized expertise, such as "helping foster child with emotional problems," "selecting the child's counselor or therapist," and "helping the child with issues related to being separated from his/her birth parents." It is important to avoid oversimplifying what these ratings portray. Most foster parents view their role as enhancing a child's growth and development, not as replacing the birth parent. In the cultures of many people of color, this form of child rearing is viewed as a part of a communal obligation to "care for our own" as a means of counteracting institutional racism and the lack of child supports in the larger community and society as a whole.

Social workers, however, are sometimes presented with challenging situation—foster parents who just want to be "parents" to a group of children who frequently require specialized care and treatment. When working with foster parents who are reluctant to attend extra training or unwilling to admit that a child needs more than "lots of love," social workers speak to the importance of validating what the parent is currently doing while at the same time educating the caregiver about the child's special needs. This is not an easy task. Perhaps the best approach is one of preparation, that is, ensuring that the prospective foster parents' first contacts with the agency emphasize realistically the type of children that might be placed in the foster home and the specific needs of the particular foster child.

Current efforts at Casey and elsewhere to involve prospective foster parents in ongoing support groups have been helpful and should be adopted by other agencies. Refinement of training approaches may be needed as well. Almost 40 percent of the Casey foster parents in this study felt that the preservice training did not sufficiently prepare them for the foster parent role. More information about the reason for this rating is needed. Foster parent training has evolved over time, and important questions remain to be addressed. For example, were the least satisfied foster parents those with the most experience, who started with Casey when the initial training was too brief to be helpful, or were they the more recently recruited foster parents? Initial orientation training may need to be reshaped to better fit the needs of relative and nonrelative foster parents.

As foster parent recruitment efforts become more difficult in certain communities and as the need for specialized treatment foster parents to work with children and their birth parents increases, certain role demands may become more crucial. The option of making foster parenting a paid career has become a recruitment and retention method for a small number of agencies. An example of this is the Continuum Program of Lighthouse Youth Services, which pays the foster parent who acts as the primary caretaker an hourly salary for special tasks such as transportation of other youth in the network, school advocacy, and crisis intervention (Gore, 1993). Foster care agencies may find it necessary to develop an array of child-caring options by working creatively with foster families and other social service agencies (e.g., state and tribal agencies).

Finally, foster parent training and support groups could also be refined to clarify areas of responsibility among foster parents and staff. The large standard deviation scores for a number of roles and the discussions held after the survey was completed in Louisiana by the trainer/researcher indicated that there is no clear consensus about who is primarily responsible for certain areas.

Other Practice Issues

Additional issues for both relative and nonrelative families include the fact that birth children of caregivers often feel separated from the foster children because of the services that the foster child receives. Creative ways of developing opportunities for birth children need to be devised and shared among staff members.

Participation in training may be different for different kinds of caregivers in terms of how people learn and how they respond to certain training and social events. In addition, sometimes the language on agency forms may exceed the reading level of some caregivers. Terms like "respite care" may not be understood. Agency forms such as foster parent applications, physical or mental health updates, and other paperwork may therefore need revision.

Family recruitment and selection may be complicated if the agency places a high priority on recruiting relative caregiver applicants where agency services and nonfinancial support will make a substantial difference, in addition to the monetary support. Although foster care payments are an important means of family support, many of the relative families were caring for these children before agency involvement and would have continued to care for these children without formal agency sponsorship. It is the support of the agency that, for them, makes the difference. One challenge is how to target services to the children who can most benefit from them. The implications for service delivery of these differences in foster parent compensation need to be considered further.

STUDY LIMITATIONS AND STRENGTHS

Generalizability

This study was limited to one private voluntary long-term foster care agency with 23 offices in thirteen states and to a group of foster parents served by a public foster care agencies in one southern state.[12] The findings, therefore, may not be generalizable to other long-term or short-term foster care agencies. For example, the Casey findings (particularly in the areas of foster parent role perception and motivation) may not generalize to a short-term foster care population (children for whom reunification is the placement goal) or to public or private agencies with much higher caseloads, different staff qualifications, more frequent staff turnover, and less access to supplemental services such as tutoring or psychotherapy. Yet the Louisiana sample is fairly representative of many public child welfare agencies produced some similar findings and increases generalizability for the overall study data.

---

12. This section has been adapted from Le Prohn (1993).

Cross-Sectional Design Limitations

This study presents a cross-sectional view of the foster families. Cross-sectional studies in foster care have been criticized for overrepresenting children with longer lengths of stay and underrepresenting children with shorter lengths of stay. Because this study intentionally included a group of children in long-term family foster care, the issue of exaggerating the length of stay may be less of a concern.

As a cross-sectional study, however, it is unlikely that each of the subsamples was "pure" in that the children in relative placements have been in relative placements *only* and the children in nonrelative placements have been in nonrelative placements only. Information on the *types* of prior placements the children had was not collected. Thus, similarities and differences between the groups of *children* may not accurately reflect similarities and differences between the two populations. Yet, in looking at the "life course" histories of the Casey children for this and other studies, we found that a high proportion of the children in the relative care group have been placed only with relatives.

Study Strengths

This combination of studies has several notable strengths. First, it provides some of the most complete descriptive data on a large group of relative foster parents to date. A comparison group was included, and detailed questions on roles and motivation were addressed.

Second, this study is one of the few studies of foster parents to collect data on both foster parents if there were two in the home. Typically, studies of foster families collect data from only one foster parent, usually the mother. The design of this study enabled foster fathers to have an equal voice and to present their views of foster parenting. Finally, this study collected both qualitative and quantitative data on the major concepts being measured. Although this chapter focuses on the quantitative data, the availability of the qualitative data from foster parents (Pecora & Le Prohn, 1993) and a postsurvey discussion with the foster parents in Louisiana allowed for a more comprehensive interpretation of the major findings.

CONCLUSION

This study represented a joint effort to gather the perceptions of relative and nonrelative foster parents from Casey offices in thirteen states and public child welfare foster parents in Louisiana. It is clear that relative and nonrelative foster families—both foster parents and foster children—have some distinct differences. Relative foster families are likely to have lower family incomes, to be headed by older single women, to have slightly younger foster children, and to be persons of color, in particular African American or Native American or, more recently, Hispanic or Latino. (In some states with a high proportion of people of color licensed as foster parents, we expect that this difference will be less, as was the case for the Louisiana sample.) Given these demographic differences and characteristics, the need for additional support and establishment of a plan for the child in the event of a death of one or both parents may be especially important.

Children in relative families are likely to have been in out-of-home care for more of their lives than have children in nonrelative placements. At the same time, relative placements tend to be more stable placements for children. By continuing to offer support, both financial and nonfinancial, to relative foster families, child welfare agencies are helping to maintain the stability of hundreds of children. In this sense, Casey and the State of Louisiana are providing a form of "Family Preservation Services" as mandated by these three major federal laws: the Indian Child Welfare Act (P.L. 95-608), the Adoption Assistance and Child Welfare Act of 1980 (P.L. 96-272), and the Family Preservation Services and Support Act of 1993 (P.L. 103-66).

Recent family preservation initiatives point to the importance of providing services to families in trouble. Kinship foster care can be viewed as a form of extended family preservation; original ties to the family are maintained, but under the close supervision and support of the social services agency. If we assume that kinship foster parents, who themselves are older, in more fragile health, and less financially stable, will be able to care for these very difficult children with fewer financial and concrete supports than foster parents, then our expectations are unrealistic. Until kinship providers with maltreated children are offered the same services, training, and reimbursement as foster parents, a fair assessment of quality can not be conducted. Indeed, it is incumbent on social service agencies (not on the kinship foster parents alone) to ensure quality of care for children (Berrick, Barth, & Needell, 1994, p. 59).

A number of important policy questions remaining to be addressed. First, criteria for assessing the appropriateness of the child's situation for agency-supported relative foster care need to be refined. For example, when is the major problem confronting a family primarily one of inadequate income (requiring income maintenance), and when does a child need a formal foster care arrangement with greater access to an array of specialized support services?

Second, what variations in licensing and other assessment criteria should be considered to best meet the full range of child needs without sacrificing certain minimum practice standards? This is a national policy issue with significant differences among states (Office of Inspector General, 1992a,b; Takas, 1993).

Third, a consensus about "best practice" with respect to establishing relationships with birth family members and monitoring child visits needs to be articulated, critically reviewed, and systematically disseminated. This core of practice could build upon the previous work of Maluccio and Sinanoglu (1981), Pine, Kreiger, and Maluccio (1993), Thornton (1991), and others.

Fourth, some aspects of permanency planning in the form of intensive family reunification services (e.g., Fraser et al., 1996), subsidized guardianship (Schwartz, 1993), and adoptions have not been fully explored for youth in kinship care.

Finally, our finding that role perceptions vary between relative foster parents, who see themselves as sharing more of the responsibility for helping children maintain contact with their birth parents and other family members, and nonrelative foster parents, who do not see themselves as having major responsibilities in these areas. This difference has implications for how easy or difficult it will be to promote birth family contact as part of future agency initiatives, because this depends upon the type of foster family involved with the child. Understanding the similarities and differences between kinship care and other forms of foster care should be an essential part of any foster care reform or services improvement effort. These findings add to the small but growing body of research in this area that is documenting the value of providing high-quality services to all types of foster families and their children.

References

Belsky, J. (1980). Child maltreatment: An ecological integration. *American Psychologist, 35*, 320–335.

Berrick, J. D., Barth, R. P., & Needell, B. (1994). A comparison of kinship foster homes and foster family homes: Implications for kinship foster care as family preservation. *Children & Youth Services Review, 16* (2), 33–63.

Berrick, J. D., Barth, R. P., Needell, B., & Courtney, M. E. (1993). Relative foster care and the preservation of families: What's the difference? In D. Haapala, V. Pina, & C. Sudia (Eds.), *Proceedings of the Sixth Annual Empowering Families Conference* (pp. 101–115). Cedar Rapids, Iowa: National Association for Family-Based Services.

Billingsley, A., & Giovannoni, J. M. (1972). *Children of the storm: Black children and American child welfare.* New York: Harcourt, Brace, Jovanovich.

Boyd-Franklin, N. (1989). *Black families in therapy: A multisystems approach.* New York: Guilford Press.

Carbino, R. (1980). *Foster parenting: An updated review of the literature.* Washington, D.C.: Child Welfare League of America.

Casey Family Program. (1994). *Child Care Report for December 1993.* Seattle: Casey Family Program, Research Department.

Dubowitz, H., Feigelman, S., & Zuravin, S. (1993). A profile of kinship care. *Child Welfare, 72* (2), 153–169.

Dubowitz, H., Feigelman, S., Harrington, D., Starr, R., Zuravin, S., & Sawyer, R. (1994). Children in kinship care: How do they fare? *Children and Youth Services Review, 16* (2), 85–106.

Eastman, K. S. (1982). Foster parenthood: A nonnormative parenting arrangement. *Marriage and Family Review, 5* (2), 95–120.

Essoyan, S. (1992, November 11). Hanai in the '90's: Is the traditional Hawaiian adoption custom slipping away? *Honolulu Weekly, 2*, (46), 4–5.

Fraser, M. W., Walton, E., Lewis, R. E., Pecora, P. J., & Walton, W. K. (1996). An experiment in family reunification: Correlates of outcome at one-year follow-up. *Children and Youth Services Review, 18* (4/5), 335–361.

Garbarino, J. (1981). An ecological approach to child maltreatment. In L. Pelton (Ed.), *The social context of child abuse and neglect* (pp. 228–267). New York: Human Sciences Press.

Garcia-Preto, N. (1982). Puerto Rican families. In M. McGoldrick, J. K. Pearce, & J. Giordano (Eds.), *Ethnicity & family therapy* (pp. 164–186). New York: Guilford Press.

Gore, C. A. (1993). *The Long-Term Network program evaluation report.* Cincinnati: New Life Youth Services (available from New Life Youth Services or The Casey Family Program Research Department).

Heighton, R. H. Jr., Jordan, C. E., & Gallimore, R. (1970.) Traditional and modern adoption patterns in Hawaii. In V. Carroll (Ed.), *Adoption in Eastern Oceania* (pp. 21–51). Honolulu: University of Hawaii Press.

Hill, R. (1972). *The strengths of black families.* New York: Emerson-Hall.

Inclan, J. E., & Herron, D. G. (1980). Puerto Rican adolescents. In J. T. Gibbs, L. N. Huang, & Associates (Eds.), *Children of Color: Psychological Interventions with Minority Youths.* San Francisco: Jossey-Bass.

Kadushin, A. (1980). *Child welfare services* (3rd ed.). New York: Macmillan.

Le Prohn, N. (1993). *Relative foster parents: Role perceptions, motivation and agency satisfaction.* Doctoral dissertation, University of Washington, School of Social Work, Seattle.

Le Prohn, N., & Pecora, P. J. (1994). *The Casey foster parent study—Research summary.* Seattle: Casey Family Program.

Maluccio, A. N., & Sinanoglu, P. A. (1981). *The challenge of partnership: Working with parents of children in foster care.* New York: Child Welfare League of America.

Office of Inspector General. (1992a). *State practices in using relatives for foster care.* Washington, D.C.: Department of Health and Human Services.

Office of Inspector General. (1992b). *Using relatives for foster care.* Washington, D.C.: Department of Health and Human Services.

Pecora, P. J., & Le Prohn, N. (1993). *The Casey foster parent study—Summary of foster parent comments.* Seattle: Casey Family Program, Research Department.

Pine, B. A., Krieger, R., & Maluccio, A. N. (1993). *Together again: Family reunification in foster care.* Washington, D.C.: Child Welfare League of America.

Scannapieco, M., & Jackson, S. (1996). Kinship care: The African-American response to family preservation. *Social Work, 41* (2), 190–196.

Schwartz, M. (1993). *Reinventing guardianship—subsidized guardianship, co-guardians and child welfare.* New York: Vera Institute of Justice.

Sena-Rivera, J. (1979). Extended kinship in the United States: Competing models and the case of *la familia chicana. Journal of Marriage and the Family, 41* (1), 121–129.

Sotomayor, M. (1991). *Empowering Hispanic families: A critical issue for the 90's.* Milwaukee: Family Service America.

Stack, C. (1974). *All our kin: Strategies for survival in a black community.* New York: Harper and Row.

Takas, M. (1993). *Kinship care and family preservation: A guide for states in legal and policy development.* Washington, D.C.: American Bar Association Center on Children and the Law.

Tatara, T. (1993). U.S. child substitute care flow data for FY '92 and current trends in the state child substitute care populations. *VCIS Research Notes, 9* (August). Washington, D.C.: American Public Welfare Association.

Thornton, J. (1987). *Investigation into the nature of the kinship foster home.* Doctoral dissertation, Yeshiva University, New York.

Thornton, J. L. (1991). Permanency planning for children in kinship foster homes. *Child Welfare, 70* (5), 593–601.

Wasson, D. L., & Hess, P. (1989). Foster parents as child welfare educators. *Public Welfare, 47* (4), 16–22.

Wilson, M. N. (1989). Child development in the context of the black extended family. *American Psychologist, 44* (2), 380–386.

Kin as a Family and Child Welfare Resource

The Child Welfare Worker's Perspective

JILL DUERR BERRICK, PH.D.
BARBARA NEEDELL, PH.D.
RICHARD P. BARTH, PH.D.

The emergence of kinship foster care into the domain of conventional child welfare services has changed practice, placement decisions, policy, and protocol in most jurisdictions across the country. While various states have instituted different policies in order to accommodate the incorporation of kin into child welfare services (Gleeson & Craig, 1994), the federal government recently stepped into the kinship care discussion with passage of the Personal Responsibility and Work Opportunity Reconciliation Act of 1996 (P.L. 104-193). That bill, which focuses specifically on reforming welfare in the United States, also included policy directives aimed at child welfare programs. The bill explicitly requires states to consider giving preference to adult relatives over non-related caregivers when considering foster placements for children. With this bill, the federal government has pushed the original provisions of P.L. 96-272, which required placement in the most family-like setting, to consideration of placement *with* family. The federal impetus to include kin in foster care decisions may result in a further expansion of kinship foster care.

The anticipated growth in kinship foster care follows a decade of rising kinship caseloads in a few large states. In California, the site of this study, kinship care is now the predominant placement setting, having surpassed foster family homes in the early 1990s (Needell, Webster, Barth, & Armijo, 1996). In that state, approximately 25 percent of the child welfare caseload resided with kin in 1985 (Hill, 1996). Ten years later, kin accounted for 46 percent of all placements.

In 1987 the California legislature codified its preference for kin when it passed Senate Bill 243 (Chapter 1485, California Welfare and Institutions Code, Section 300), a bill designed to implement several modest reforms in child welfare services. While placement with kin was considered preferential, neither regulations nor state guidelines were developed in order to guide counties and their staff in selecting kin caregivers. Funding for kinship caregivers followed a similar, loosely defined path. Many kin were deemed eligible for federal foster care board and maintenance payments if the child for whom they were caring came from a birth home that was AFDC-eligible at the point of removal, even though licensing requirements were waived. Unlike other states (e.g., Texas) that utilize kin within the formal child welfare system only when kinship caregivers become fully licensed foster parents, California did not specify such strict conditions. Absent licensing requirements and state guidelines for placement, each county developed separate approaches to implementing the preferential language of the bill. About half of the counties (out of a total of fifty-eight) recently developed formal assessment procedures for placement with kin (Children's Research Institute of California, 1996), and a few developed special training workshops for their staff. For the most part, however, the majority of county child welfare agencies did little to systematically address the new practice considerations initiated by the preferential policy.

The experience in California is not unique. Kinship foster care has developed so rapidly in many states that public child welfare practice has not kept up with the challenges of this new service delivery model. For example, a review of case records of kinship foster homes in New York City indicated that workers did not give these placements the level of placement supervision required by regulation, either because caseworkers felt that the child was safe and were uncomfortable intruding on family life or because they simply misinterpreted the rules (Meyer & Link, 1990). Other evidence suggests that many of New York City's kinship foster care cases have been supervised primarily by phone, though caseworkers are required to visit these families once a month (Manhattan Borough President's Advisory Council on Child Welfare, 1989, cited in Zwas, 1993). Kinship foster parents interviewed in a California study reported that they had less contact with social workers than did foster parents, and children in kinship foster care were seen by social workers less often than children in foster care (Berrick, Barth, & Needell, 1994). Twenty-nine percent of the kinship foster parents in a study by Dubowitz and associates (Dubowitz et al., 1990) in Baltimore had had no contact with a caseworker in the year preceding the evaluation, and one-fourth of the workers reported having seen the families fewer than four times in the past year, while less than one third of the workers had seen the child more than six times in the previous year.

In the opinion of some kinship foster parents and those who advocate for them, social service agencies consider them a low priority, treating them as though they were somehow less deserving than nonrelative family members (Minkler & Roe, 1992). When states were surveyed by the Office of the Inspector General (Kusserow, 1992) regarding their kinship care practices, the policy in the overwhelming majority of states was: "Relatives are not excluded from any social services which the State makes available to non-related foster parents" (p. 5). Nevertheless, the study showed that, while relatives were not systematically excluded from services, local child welfare offices often had the authority to limit services to kin and often did so.

Eugene F. v. Gross, a widely publicized 1986 lawsuit, provided many dramatic examples of New York City's failure to execute kinship foster care regulations (Zwas, 1993). The Legal Aid Society, on behalf of a group of children in kinship care, accused the city of failing to fulfill legal mandates regarding financial support, medical care, and health services. Compelling affidavits by kinship caregivers demonstrated that they often cared for too many children in inadequate housing and lacked necessities like beds, clothes, and school supplies for these children. Medicaid cards were delayed, and foster care stipends, along with day care assistance, were in some cases never received.

The families in Meyer and Link's (1990) sample received few services. Although approximately half of the cases were initiated because of a drug-exposed infant, none of these infants was receiving special attention, and there was no indication of cooperation between Child Welfare and Public Health Departments regarding neonatal follow-up after hospital discharge for these children. This study also found little in the way of service provision to birth parents of the children in kinship care, especially regarding adequate referral to drug treatment and assistance in locating housing.

Kinship caregivers in California (Berrick et al., 1994) were much less likely to be offered services such as respite care, support groups, and training than were traditional foster parents. Very few kinship foster or traditional foster parents received child care services, and many providers in both groups felt that additional services would be helpful, especially training, respite care, and child care.

Dubowitz et al. (1990) asked both caseworkers and kinship foster parents in his study what services had been provided. The number of relatives who reported having received such services as AFDC, medical assistance, case management services, and counseling and/or therapy was smaller than the number of caseworkers who reported receiving them. More than 40 percent of both caseworkers and caregivers felt that additional money was needed, few other services were considered lacking, especially by caseworkers. Considering the high prevalence of physical and mental problems in this sample, there appeared to be a critical gap between needs and services, despite what caseworkers and kinship caregivers reported.

Although practice with kin appears to be inconsistent across states, the advent of kinship foster care has been met with enthusiasm nationwide from child welfare leaders, practitioners, and communities of color (Child Welfare League of America, 1994; Wilson, 1991). Kinship care has been praised as an extended form of family preservation services, as a culturally congruent form of care, and as a potentially beneficial placement alternative for children who cannot remain with their parents (Berrick et al., 1994; Child Welfare League of America, 1994; Takas, 1993). The substantial benefit of family continuity brought about by kinship care is balanced, however, by some challenges to child welfare practitioners as workers sort through an array of issues related to family dynamics, economic hardship, and children's loyalties, to name a few. In order to learn more about the phenomenon of kinship care, we turned to child welfare workers for their expertise.

THE STUDY

This study was conducted in the state of California where, as described earlier, a high proportion of kinship caregivers are included in the child welfare system. Because the state is so large, we selected ten counties, including urban and rural sites, northern and southern California locations, and counties with widely disparate proportions of children residing in kinship care. Table 11.1 lists the counties and gives a sense of the range among counties in the use of kinship care as a placement alternative.

Whereas kinship care is used in about one-quarter of the cases in Butte County (a relatively rural setting) and in Solano County (a mix of rural and suburban communities), it is used in more than half of the placements in urban Los Angeles County. The differences in the rate of usage are great and are not necessarily related to rural status, Fresno County, for example, has a relatively high proportion of children in kinship care. We expected that our selection of diverse counties would bring a wide range of commentary from child welfare workers across the state, leading to a greater understanding of the multiple issues that arise in kinship foster care.

Two separate surveys were distributed to child welfare workers. The first was distributed to supervisors of intake staff—those working in Emergency Response, Dependency Investigations and in Court Investigations—with the request that the supervisors deliver the surveys to their staff for completion and direct return to the authors. These surveys focused solely on the placement process for those workers who have regular experience placing children in kinship homes. The second survey was distributed to supervisors of child welfare workers in continuing services, including family reunification and permanency planning. (The same procedures were followed.) This survey asked

TABLE 11.1
Percent of all Children in Care Residing with Kin on July 1, 1993

County	Percent
Alameda	40.9
Butte	27.0
Fresno	45.3
Los Angeles	53.6
Riverside	35.2
San Diego	35.1
San Mateo	38.1
Santa Clara	41.0
Solano	25.4
Stanislaus	36.4
STATEWIDE	44.9

a series of questions about the differences between working with kin and working with foster family parents.

Surveys were confidential (respondents were not asked their names and were provided self-addressed, stamped envelopes in which to return the surveys) and anonymous (U.C. Berkeley researchers were not involved in the distribution process among child welfare staff). Supervisors were sent two follow-up letters as reminders to encourage their staff to complete the surveys, along with additional forms, in case they were required. Supervisors were also called to encourage a higher response rate.

More than five hundred (n = 533) surveys were distributed to intake supervisors, and 1,091 surveys were distributed to continuing services supervisors (a breakdown of surveys distributed and returned is provided in Table 11.2). We do not know the proportion of surveys that was delivered to workers, the appropriate denominator for calculating a response rate. Assuming that all questionnaires were delivered to staff, the final minimum response rate for the survey was 45 percent for intake services workers and 27 percent for continuing services staff.

Instrumentation

The surveys were designed by the authors and included questions that had arisen through focus groups with child welfare workers (Berrick, Needell, & Barth, 1995). The survey designed for intake staff focused on the placement experience, the amount of time available to make adequate placement decisions, the quality of kinship homes, and the worker's support for kinship placements.

The questionnaire designed for continuing services staff included a series of questions concerning work with kin and nonkin, including the amount of

TABLE 11.2
Surveys Distributed and Returned by Type of Staff and County

County	Intake Staff[1]			Continuing Services Staff[2]		
	# Surveys Mailed to Unit Supervisors	# Surveys Returned	Minimum Response Rate (%)	# Surveys Mailed to Unit Supervisors	# Surveys Returned	Minimum Response Rate (%)
Alameda	23	14	60.9	72	27	37.5
Butte	33	17	51.5	27	14	51.9
Fresno	65	38	58.5	76	62	81.6
Los Angeles	100	27	27.0	300	46	15.3
Riverside	80	35	43.8	150	35	23.3
San Diego	70	44	62.9	145	49	33.8
San Mateo	30	6	20.0	74	5	06.8
Santa Clara	100	26	26.0	200	41	20.5
Solano	21	2	09.5	24	2	08.3
Stanislaus	11	11	100.0	23	11	47.8
TOTAL	533	220	41.3	1091	292	26.8

1. Intake staff refer to those staff who make initial placements (kin and nonkin) of children taken into custody.
2. Continuing services staff include welfare workers providing family reunification and/or permanency planning services to a mixed caseload of kin and nonkin.

time required by kin placements in comparison to nonkin placements, potential problems associated with delayed reunification efforts in kin and nonkin homes, and the kinds of services kinship foster homes required. This survey also asked workers about their views on a series of possible reforms to the child welfare system that might include changes in the payment structure for kin, the services and supports available to kin, and the responsibilities and standards asked of kin providers.

The questionnaire was pilot-tested with seven intake workers and ten continuing services workers from Merced County to determine the clarity of the questions and the appropriateness of the response categories. Comments from these staff were incorporated into a revised, final version of the questionnaire.

Results described in this chapter are derived primarily from the written survey. Where relevant, information from focus groups with child welfare staff, also conducted as a component in this larger study (Berrick et al., 1995), are presented.

Worker Characteristics

Intake staff respondents.   Staff (n = 220) had been working in the field of child welfare for an average of 7.4 years, sufficient time to participate in the significant shift in child welfare toward the utilization of kin. Their caseloads ranged from eight to one hundred, with an average of about thirty-five children. The majority (58%) had a master's degree (most of the others had a bachelor's degree). Approximately two-thirds of respondents were female (62%), more than half (59%) were Caucasian, one-fifth were Hispanic (21%), 9 percent were Asian or Pacific Islander, and 6 percent were African American. The average age of respondents was forty-one years.

Continuing services staff respondents.   As with the intake staff, continuing services workers (n = 292) also had strong backgrounds in child welfare, with the average length of service in the field at 5.9 years. Caseloads were somewhat higher among continuing services staff, with an average of forty children (minimum three, maximum seventy-one). Again, the majority of staff had a master's degree (62%), and women were more often represented among respondents than men (76% vs. 24%); the ethnic diversity of the staff was as follows: 62 percent Caucasian, 18 percent Hispanic, 11 percent African American, and 5 percent Asian/Pacific Islander. The average age of respondents was forty years.

KINSHIP CARE PLACEMENT DECISIONS

A significant number of children who in previous decades probably would have been placed in foster family homes are now being placed with kin. This shift in the use of kin has been a result of encouragement by legislatures and administrative officials. But if legal and administrative pressures were lifted, how often would intake staff place children with their relatives? Child welfare workers indicated that they would continue to place with kin in about 70 percent of cases, suggesting that the large majority of child welfare personnel are supportive of kin placements and generally embrace this placement alternative.

While many support kinship placements, child welfare staff in our focus groups showed a degree of concern regarding the quality of care provided in some kinship homes. Therefore, we asked survey respondents how often kinship placements were discovered to be substantially less adequate than the average foster family home. Respondents indicated that about 29 percent of kinship homes fell below the standards they regularly witnessed in average foster family homes.

Few child welfare workers had ever made placements that were so substandard they had concerns about the basic safety and security of the foster child. The number of respondents who had concerns about placements, however, was virtually the same for kin and nonkin placements (17% vs. 15%, respectively). Some of the problems child welfare workers had described in focus groups concerning the occasional inadequacy of kinship placements centered on the worker's inability to spend the time required to assess the kinship home. As one worker wrote, "If kin placement is done carefully, and appropriate time is taken, it works out 90% of the time. When pressured and rushed, the reverse is true."

When asked about the average length of time social workers spent assessing homes for the feasibility of placement, they indicated that nonkin homes took about 4.8 hours to assess, whereas kin homes took about 6.4 hours. These findings confirmed what we had heard in focus groups—that staff did not have much more time to work with kin than they had for foster families who might have been used for many previous placements.

Fewer than half of child welfare workers (41.6%) indicated that they had sufficient time to assess kinship foster homes adequately; slightly more staff felt similarly regarding the time available for assessment of nonkin homes (48.0%). The limited amount of time available for assessing homes might suggest that child welfare workers would welcome other initial placement resources for children. When asked if they would prefer that children routinely be placed in emergency foster homes or shelters to provide time for a more thorough preplacement assessment, child welfare workers indicated that they would support this notion most of the time or some of the time in 80 percent of kin placements (33.9% most of the time) and in 75 percent of nonkin placements (43.9% most of the time).

Because many child welfare workers do not currently have formal guidelines to follow in making kinship placements, we asked what particular characteristics of kinship caregivers or homes would clearly raise concerns regarding a kin placement. Responses from staff were fairly uniform and included:

- CPS history, criminal history, poor parenting skills, poor condition of home, drug/alcohol problems
- Lack of cooperation with department; too many people in the household
- Kin who have an agenda to obtain custody of a child, who have a personal vendetta, or who don't get along with parents; kin who are too soft with parents and allow unlimited access to the child

How do child welfare staff locate available kin? Focus group discussions with child welfare workers revealed that the majority of staff first asked the birth parent with whom he or she wanted the child placed. This began the selection process and was considered the best means of locating viable kin. If the relative made the allegation against the parent, the relative making the claim was first reviewed as a potential caregiver. Many workers also indicated that they asked the child where she wanted to live (when the child was old enough to discuss the matter), to ensure that the child's interests were also considered. The search for kin expanded beyond these basic confines only if the birth parent was reluctant to name family members or if the child expressed extreme displeasure over the stated relative. In these instances, child welfare workers followed a much more extensive process, asking about a wide range of possible kin.

In general, most staff indicated that they did not have time to be especially selective about kin. No staff in any county indicated that they had sufficient time or information to make well-considered decisions about kin.

EXPERIENCE WITH KIN AND NONKIN PLACEMENTS

Once children are placed in foster care, whether with kin or nonkin, continuing services staff play a significant role trying to assist the family toward reunification. Child welfare workers indicated that services to kin take more of their time, on average, than services to nonkin. Their work with kin is more time intensive in about 44 percent of cases. Additional time may be required to monitor progress toward reunification or to shore up aspects of the placement for the well-being of the child. For example, child welfare workers were more likely to report difficulties enforcing the child's case plan in kin placements due to the caregiver's relationship with the birth parent (37% of kin cases vs. 18% of nonkin cases, $t = 10.44$, $p < .001$). Similarly, staff suggested that kin were more likely than nonkin to be unable to provide adequately for the health and educational needs of the child (28% of kin cases vs. 15% of nonkin cases, $t = 10.61$, $p < .001$).

Kin were also somewhat more likely to delay reunification with the birth parent (29% of kin cases vs. 20% of non-kin cases, $t = 5.30$, $p < .001$). Delays in family reunification from kin placements were not always due to an inability or inadequacy on the kinship caregiver's part. When asked why delays occurred in kinship care, about one-quarter of respondents suggested that it was because the caregiver did not assist fully with the goal of family reunification. But more than half (57.9%) suggested that the primary reason was that the birth parent viewed the placement positively and had insufficient motivation to have the child returned home.

Another factor, raised by a significant number of child welfare workers during focus groups, is a potential disincentive effect brought about by higher payments to some kin. California has adopted a two-tiered payment system that provides AFDC-FC payments to families who meet certain eligibility conditions.[1] Families who do not qualify for AFDC-FC (as a result of the *Miller v. Youakim* decision) may receive AFDC payments instead. Empirical evidence from analyses of administrative data shows that children placed with kin who qualify for AFDC-FC have longer stays in foster care (Berrick & Needell, in press). Some workers' comments may clarify the family choices imposed by higher payments:

- AFDC-FC is a disincentive. Why not leave the kids with grandma and have increased money? Mom is often living in grandma's home, anyway. Or, if she isn't, grandma may be giving her money.
- Sometimes mom abandons the child, knowing that grandma will take the child, in order to get the *Youakim* money for the family. Mom can have supervised visits, and she knows it.
- If the family reunifies, they can't replace the *Youakim* money, so many parents leave the child with the extended family.

Family Dynamics

The added dimension of family dynamics overlaying the foster care placement with kin was pointed out as the greatest strength as well as the most significant challenge for child welfare staff. During focus groups, child welfare workers indicated that kin can act as great motivators for parents, and they can provide a natural support for children who are experiencing a period of great vulnerability. Workers described kinship foster parents as emotionally committed to children at a level that often exceeded that found in nonkin placements. Many kin caregivers stepped into the role out of their personal commitment to the child and the family, making their investment in the child's well-being all the greater.

Yet the strengths in utilizing family members for foster care are balanced by difficulties. There are unique intrafamilial dynamics that can arise in the kinship relationship between caregiver and parent that child welfare staff must be prepared to handle. For example, some problems associated with kinship care become apparent only several weeks into the placement. Caregivers who appear to be well adjusted during the initial phase of placement sometimes show later signs of dysfunction that are disconcerting to workers. Long-standing strains between relatives sometimes became more pronounced over time, including feelings of betrayal, resentment, and extreme anger. These dynamics often play out in efforts by kinship caregivers to sabotage the reunification

---

1. Some of these eligibility conditions include the following:

a. The child was removed from the home of a parent as a result of court involvement. (Children who were previously living with the relative caregiver, and where no removal was necessary, are not eligible for AFDC-FC payments.)

b. The child was receiving AFDC or was AFDC-eligible at the time of removal from the home.

c. The placement is the responsibility of the courts and the child welfare agency.

d. The home is generally considered licensable by the county (the home does not need to be licensed, nor does the home need to meet all of the licensing standards).

e. The relative must apply for AFDC-FC payments within six months of the child's placement in the home.

plan in myriad ways. In these instances, staff find their work especially complicated, demanding significant social work skills.

Some staff also pointed to the considerable emotional burden children experience when they try to shield the worker from some of their family secrets in kinship placements. If the parent is inappropriately visiting the child, or if the child has been informally moved into another relative's home, many workers find that the child is held responsible for maintaining these secrets from the social worker. Staff indicated that young children are particularly likely to tell family secrets and then experience guilt about their disclosure.

Just as children are afraid of social workers' responses to the reality of their circumstances, many kin caregivers are also reluctant to disclose information fully. Having seen the power of the system to take a child from his or her parent, kin caregivers are reluctant to share their own difficulties about a child or a placement for fear that they, too, may lose the child to a stranger's foster home. These dynamics make information sharing problematic in some kinship homes, and they require greater efforts by child welfare staff to become well informed about the child's well-being.

Placement-Related Services

Some child welfare workers indicated that kin homes required less time and that workers frequently requested that their supervisors exempt them from monthly visits. Others suggested, however, that because kin had not participated in training, they often required more social worker time. Kin who required more services were those who had strained relationships with the birth parents, who made efforts (conscious or unconscious) to sabotage family reunification, and/or who were unaware of their obligations as foster parents to the courts, to the child's educational progress, and to meeting the child's medical and mental health needs. Child welfare workers also indicated that kin were, on average, more resource-poor than foster parents and needed assistance locating housing, child care, transportation, and other services in order to accommodate their new family member.

Kin who required fewer services were found among families that were less stressed or dysfunctional or among families where the parent was essentially absent from the child's life (e.g., the parent was incarcerated or had abandoned the child). In these cases, many counties granted exceptions to the requirement for monthly visits, and child welfare workers contacted relative caregivers only once every three months.

The survey requested that staff members indicate what services or supports kin needed in order to best carry out their responsibilities to children. Although responses were mixed, they tended to fall into two groups. One worker clarified these differences:

> For most good relative placements, support groups and respite care programs would address most of the needs. For marginal relatives, the need is also for education (about following court orders; the need sometimes to limit contact with parents; that children sometimes need more than loving relatives, i.e., counseling or therapy).

These comments were echoed by other staff, who identified the following needs:

- Classes in parenting and nonphysical discipline
- Training to manage children's special needs; a list of expectations in regards to health, mental health, special needs; and service provider lists for housing, clothing, and money

Staff also were concerned that kin might need assistance reconciling their dual roles as children's protectors and as supports to the birth parent.

SPECIAL CHALLENGES

Child welfare workers are very specific about the nature of the kinship homes that they find most challenging. This is a positive sign, because it suggests that child welfare agencies can provide direction and support to their child welfare workers in defined areas of practice, rather than offering global suggestions for work with kin. The factors listed by child welfare workers in this survey point to challenges that many staff may face in working with kin, and they suggest areas of special training and support that all staff should receive in order to be prepared for child welfare practice. Among the potential problem areas identified by the workers are these:

- Inability to set limits with parents and unwillingness or inability to meet the educational, medical, or psychological needs of the child
- Tendency to blame the child for the situation
- Inappropriate motivation (e.g., some want only to keep child out of the foster care system but will return child to parent after termination of services)

These issues are difficult to assess prior to placement, and they are not easily addressed through caregiver training programs. They represent motivational and attitudinal concerns that require careful and proactive responses on the part of a skilled child welfare worker.

SYSTEMS CHANGES

In addition to the current service needs of kin and the importance of developing a skilled approach to dealing with the unique family dynamics that arise in these placements, staff also recognize the importance of developing systems changes in kinship care. First, the definition of kinship care in California currently pertains only to family members with close blood ties to the child. Many child welfare workers would like to see this definition expanded. About three-quarters (72%) of child welfare workers supported expanding the definition of kin to include more extended family (e.g., second cousins), and about 61 percent of staff supported the inclusion of fictive kin (e.g., godparents) as kinship foster parents. Sixty-three percent of staff supported changing current laws so that all kin would receive the same AFDC-FC payments as nonkin. But their support for a higher payment rate was coupled with strong support for changes that would bring the qualifications of kinship caregivers more closely in line with those of nonkin. For example, 91 percent of staff responded positively to the proposal that all kin be required to attend foster parent training or parallel kin caregiver training programs. Eighty-one percent also indicated that kin should be held to the same standards of care as foster family parents (except for standards associated with the space available in the home). One worker's comments were representative of several respondents to the survey:

> It is politically correct to talk of kinship and family placements, but we have not created sound guidelines for managing this obvious first choice for placement of minors. To be clear, we should continue in this momentum to value kin placements, however, we cannot be ostriches with our head in the sand ignoring the complexity of these placements.

Overall, the vast majority of staff were supportive of kin as children's caregivers in foster care but were highly critical of a system that placed children in homes that had not been adequately assessed or with caregivers who were not prepared to understand the complexities and requirements of the child welfare system and that offered fewer opportunities (in the way of services, supports, and financial reimbursement) for kin to provide the highest quality of care possible.

IMPLICATIONS FOR PRACTICE

Kinship foster care has rapidly developed as a preferred placement alternative for children in the child welfare services system, yet parallel developments in policy and guidelines for practice have yet to be initiated in several states. On the basis of the survey described in this chapter and of extensive focus groups with child welfare staff across California, we offer the following points for consideration.

Practice Points Regarding Placement Decisions

Child welfare workers should be aware that a significant number of kinship homes currently fall below the standards that are regularly seen in nonkinship care. As long as children remain under the jurisdiction of the courts, any placement away from a birth parent must be fully assessed for its adequacy and appropriateness. All states should develop assessment processes, whether informal (Scannapieco & Hegar, 1996) or formal (Berrick, Needell, & Barth, 1995), for addressing the nature and adequacy of care provided in kinship foster homes. Ensuring the quality of all kinship placements will be very important to the placement's ultimate success.

In order to make a thorough assessment of a potential kinship caregiver's home, child welfare staff must have adequate preparation and sufficient time to collect information on the kin caregiver and his or her environment. This may call for an emergency placement in another setting or a provisional placement with kin that can be abrogated if substantial concerns later arise.

Practice Points Regarding Services

During the first hours and days of placement, child welfare workers may need to spend additional time with kinship caregivers informing them about the requirements of the child welfare system, their role within the child welfare system, and the goals of permanency planning. Because of the low service use among kin, workers may need to be especially supportive to kinship foster parents to ensure that they regularly attend to children's physical and mental health and educational needs. Some kin may need services for themselves as well in order to support the child's placement. Staff should be prepared to offer referrals and to assist kin in locating additional support from local agencies for food, clothing, and other ancillary services, if necessary. Child welfare agencies should consider developing kinship training and support programs, customized for kin but similar to foster parent training, to prepare caregivers for their new role with their relative children.

Some of the challenges child welfare workers may face in coping with the unique family dynamics of kinship foster care may be best addressed by workers who become specialists in this area (Barth, Yeaton, & Winterfelt, 1994). This suggests the possibility specialized kinship care caseloads, although the risk with such caseloads is that different standards of care might become institutionalized. Whether specialized units are developed or all child welfare staff continue to carry mixed caseloads, it is clear that child welfare agencies have an opportunity to develop new protocols for training, guiding, and supporting staff in their work with kin.

Kinship care has developed very rapidly in the past decade, and now, with a large proportion of all children in out-of-home care residing with relatives, it is time to examine closely practice and policy. Kin care has developed with few guidelines for child welfare workers and little or no instruction or regulation for kinship caregivers. Kin are the most natural and appropriate caregivers for children who cannot reside with their parents, and, with the reduction in the number of foster family parents available to care for children, kin have also become a critical component of the child welfare system. But without more careful attention to this placement resource, child welfare agencies may one day experience significant criticism from the public for their role in allowing a second tier of foster care to develop without sufficient standards, supervision, or control. Proactive efforts to strengthen and safeguard kinship foster care present a challenge for the next decade so that children may remain with family whenever possible.

References

Barth, R. P., Yeaton, J., & Winterfelt, N. (1994). Psychoeducational groups with foster parents of sexually abused children. *Child and Adolescent Social Work Journal, 11,* 405–424.

Berrick, J. D., & Needell, B. (In press). Recent trends in kinship care: Public policy, finances, and outcomes for children. In P. Curtis (Ed.), *The foster care crisis: Translating research into practice and policy*. Lincoln: University of Nebraska Press.

Berrick, J. D., Barth, R. P., & Needell, B. (1994). A comparison of kinship foster homes and foster family homes: Implications for kinship foster care as family preservation. *Children and Youth Services Review, 16* (1/2), 33–63.

Berrick, J. D., Needell, B., & Barth, R. P. (1995). *Kinship care in California: An empirically-based curriculum*. Unpublished manuscript. Berkeley: California Social Work Education Center, School of Social Welfare, University of California at Berkeley.

Children's Research Institute of California. (1996). *Kinship care in California: The challenges and opportunities facing relatives and the children placed in their care*. Sacramento: Author.

Child Welfare League of America. (1994). *Kinship care: A natural bridge*. Washington, D.C.: Author.

Dubowitz, H., Feigelman, S., Tepper, V., Sawyer, R., & Davidson, N. (1990). *The physical and mental health and educational status of children placed with relatives: Final report*. Baltimore: University of Maryland at Baltimore, Department of Pediatrics.

Eugene F. v. Gross. 1125/86 (New York Supreme Court 1986).

Gleeson, J. P., & Craig, L. C. (1994). Kinship care in child welfare: An analysis of states' policies. *Children and Youth Services Review, 16*, 17–31.

Hill, E. G. (1996). *Child abuse and neglect in California*. Sacramento: Legislative Analyst's Office.

Kusserow, R. P. (1992). *State practices in using relatives for foster care*. Dallas Regional Office: Office of the Inspector General.

Manhattan Borough President's Advisory Council on Child Welfare. (1989, July). *Failed promises: Child welfare in New York City, 3*.

Meyer, B. S., & Link, M. K. (1990). *Kinship foster care: The double edged dilemma*. Rochester, N.Y.: Task Force on Permanency Planning for Foster Children.

Miller v. Youakim. 440 U.S. 125 (1979).

Minkler, M., & Roe, K. M. (1992). *Grandmothers as caregivers: Raising children of the crack cocaine epidemic*. Newbury Park, Calif.: Sage.

Needell, B., Webster, D., Barth, R. P., & Armijo, M. (1996). *Performance indicators for child welfare services in California: 1995*. Unpublished report. Berkeley: Child Welfare Research Center, School of Social Welfare, University of California at Berkeley.

Personal Responsibility and Work Opportunity Reconciliation Act of 1996 (Public Law 104-193).

Scannapieco, M., & Hegar, R. L. (1996). A nontraditional assessment framework for formal kinship homes. *Child Welfare, 75*(5), 567–582.

Takas, M. (1993). *Kinship care and family preservation: A guide for states in legal and policy development*. Washington, D.C.: American Bar Association Center on Children and the Law.

Wilson, M. N. (1991). The context of the African American family. In J. E. Everett, S. S. Chipungu, & B. R. Leashore (Eds.), *Child welfare: An Africentric perspective* (pp. 85–168). New Brunswick, N.J.: Rutgers University Press.

Zwas, M. G. (1993). Kinship foster care: A relatively permanent solution. *Fordham Urban Law Journal, 20*(2), 343–373.

Behavior Problems of Teens in Kinship Care

Cross-Informant Reports

RAYMOND H. STARR, JR., PH.D.
HOWARD DUBOWITZ, M.D.
DONNA HARRINGTON, PH.D.
SUSAN FEIGELMAN, M.D.

American children and youth have high rates of emotional and behavior problems; estimates of the percentage of youngsters, with problems range from 6 percent to 37 percent (Gould, Wunsch-Hitzig, & Dohrenwend, 1981). Nationally, more than 13 percent of children have emotional or mental health problems by age seventeen (Zill & Schoenborn, 1990).

Some groups of children, including those who live in poverty (McLoyd, 1990; Zill & Schoenborn, 1990) and those placed in foster care (Fanshel & Shinn, 1978; Kavaler & Swire, 1983; Landsverk, 1992; McIntyre & Keesler, 1986), are at greater risk for behavior problems. Impoverished children are more likely to display externalizing disorders such as aggression and delinquency, while children in foster care manifest an array of behavior problems (Fanshel & Shinn, 1978; McIntyre & Keesler, 1986). Many factors contribute to these difficulties, including abuse and neglect experienced prior to placement (Youngblade & Belsky, 1990), the trauma of being separated from biological parents, and inadequate preplacement and postplacement services (Dubowitz, Tepper, Feigelman, Sawyer, & Davidson, 1990; Kavaler & Swire, 1983).

While adolescence is no longer seen as a time of "sturm und drang" (storm and stress) (Josselson, 1980), it is still a major social and psychological transition point between childhood and adulthood (Marcia, 1980). Adolescent behavior problems may be a continuation of difficulties that began during childhood (Loeber, 1982; Petersen & Hamburg, 1986), or they may first appear during adolescence (Zill & Schoenborn, 1990). Regardless of when problems are identified, the type of difficulty an adolescent has may change during the teen years (Forehand, Neighbors, & Wierson, 1991; Links, Boyle, & Offord, 1989).

THE VALUE OF CROSS-INFORMANT JUDGMENTS

The diagnosis of behavior problems is complex. Like the fable of the blind men each of whom had a different perception of what an elephant was, we all have our own perspective on the people in our world. There are similarities across and differences between individuals.

A common approach to assessing behavior problems is to question the parent or caregiver of a child or youth. It is important to realize that such reports present only one person's view and may be biased by a number of factors (Landsverk, 1992). For example, depressed mothers report more behavior problems in their children than do nondepressed mothers (Webster-Stratton & Hammond, 1988), while physically abusive parents perceive more problems in their children than do nonabusive parents (Reid, Kavanagh, & Baldwin, 1987). When observer bias was removed by using neutral observers who did not know whether a child had been abused, the behavior of the two groups of children was seen as similar.

While some have suggested that foster parents may overreport behavior problems in children in care (Landsverk, 1992), other factors may also play a role. For example, foster parents might initially have a "savior mentality" that could contribute to reports of problems at the initial stages of placement, with problem reports declining over time. Alternatively, they could be poorly prepared to care for a child who has mild separation-related problems and perceive relatively normal behaviors as problematic. In addition, reports given by youths themselves may be biased. They may respond in ways that are socially desirable and report less depression and anxiety (internalizing symptoms) and, for males, more aggressive and delinquent acts (externalizing problems) as a result of peer group pressure.

The possibility of respondent bias and such factors as limitations on a parent's knowledge of a child's behavior and emotions and child reporting bias have led to a recent emphasis on the use of multiple informants to evaluate child behavior problems rather than rely on information from one respondent (Achenbach, 1991a; Achenbach, McConaughy, & Howell, 1987). Indeed, one study combined the findings of a number of other studies of behavioral and emotional problems and concluded that there was wide variation in the types of problems that different respondents perceived (Achenbach et al., 1987). The mean correlation between parents' reports of their child's problems and children's and adolescent's self-reports was only .25, indicating relatively poor agreement.

Few studies have used both Achenbach's Child Behavior Checklist (CBCL; Achenbach, 1991b), a parental report measure for assessing child and adolescent behavior problems, and the Youth Self-Report (YSR; Achenbach, 1991c), a parallel self-report measure of behavior problems for teenagers, to evaluate parent and adolescent perceptions of youth behavior. Only one study has evaluated cross-informant reports in a foster care sample (Madsen, cited in Landsverk, 1992). As expected, both caregivers and youths reported a high level of behavior problems, with more caregivers (48%) reporting youths as having clinically significant total behavior problem scores than youths (24%). However, the correlation between caregiver and youth reports was .41, higher than would be expected (Achenbach et al., 1987). Similar correlations were reported for both internalizing and externalizing behavior problems.

A number of factors such as culture, child gender, and the problem area examined may influence the degree to which parental and child reports of behavior problems agree. One comparison of cross-informant reports in Puerto Rican and mainland families found that, compared with Puerto Rican parents and youth, mainland parents reported fewer behavior problems on the CBCL, while mainland youths reported more problems on the YSR (Achenbach, Bird, Canino, Phares, Gould, & Rubio-Stipec, 1990). Another study found that child gender, respondent knowledge of the child, and type of behavior assessed influenced cross-informant agreement (Achenbach et al., 1987).

In summary, as Achenbach (1991a) has advocated, there is a need for more information about perceptions of problem behavior provided by multiple informants. In addition, as Landsverk (1992) indicates, more information is needed about factors that influence perceptions of behavior problems. Behavior differs across contexts, and this difference underlies at least some of the differences across informants. Such information must be obtained in order to adequately interpret the responses of multiple informants. Until then, the perception that an individual has a problem is important clinically regardless of the accuracy of the perception.

KINSHIP CARE

Children in need of substitute care are increasingly being placed in kinship care—the homes of relatives—in accordance with federal law mandating the use of the least restrictive placement (Adoption Assistance and Public Welfare Act of 1980, P.L. 96-272). Although national data are not available, regional statistics indicate that from half to two-thirds of African American children placed by public agencies in out-of-home care, usually following maltreatment, are placed with relatives (National Black Child Development Institute, 1989).

Kinship care has been advocated as a desirable form of out-of-home placement for a variety of reasons. Out-of-home placement is known to have negative effects on children (Fanshel & Shinn, 1978; Landsverk, 1992; McIntyre & Keesler, 1986), and these effects may be minimized through placement with relatives (Takas, 1991). In addition, relatives are likely to have the child's best interests at heart, and contact with the biological parents is likely to be maintained. Kinship care has been increasingly adopted across the country despite the absence of research demonstrating its effects on children in out-of-home care.

The limited data concerning children in kinship care suggest that, like children who have been placed in regular foster care, they are at a high risk for behavior problems (Dubowitz, Zuravin, Starr, Feigelman, & Harrington, 1993). Dubowitz et al. found 42 percent of boys and 28 percent of girls had behavior problem levels in the clinical range (that were clinically meaningful), compared to 10 percent of children in the general population. Boys were also significantly more likely than girls to have internalizing and externalizing problems in the clinical range.

To date, no studies have used multiple informants to examine the nature and prevalence of emotional and behavioral problems among adolescents living in kinship care, the degree to which the informants agree about the presence of behavior problems, and factors that relate to the extent of the disagreement. The present study was designed to provide such information. It was hypothesized that:

1. Kinship caregivers would report significantly more behavior problems in the "clinical" range than would the youths themselves.

2. In spite of such differences, kinship care provider and youth reports of broad categories of behavior problems would show a low but statistically significant level of correlation.

3. Significant gender differences would be found on both the CBCL and the YSR, with boys having more problems than girls when compared with their same gender normative data.

Two additional areas were explored in order to more fully understand the nature of cross-informant reports and differences between informants. First, we examined the degree of agreement across respondents at the individual item level in order to assess agreement across respondents for specific behaviors, rather than categories of problems. Second, teacher responses concerning behavior problems were examined in relation to CBCL and YSR scores.

METHOD

Study Background

Nationally, there has been concern about the status of children, including their mental and physical health and the possibility of maltreatment while in care, in out-of-home placements. Children's advocates filed a class action law suit against the State of Maryland in 1984 in which the plaintiffs alleged that the care of foster children was inadequately monitored. Four years later a consent decree led to a detailed evaluation of children in out-of-home placements, with information being collected on about 82 percent of the 524 children in Baltimore in kinship care on March 15, 1989. This report is an outgrowth of this larger study (Dubowitz et al., 1990).

Sample

Data for this chapter were obtained from sixty-six of the 144 eleven- to eighteen-year-old youths and their kinship care providers. While efforts were made to obtain data from the entire sample, fifty-three youths were not evaluated because the caregiver or adolescent did not wish to participate or the teen had returned to the biological home or had moved out of state. Seven youths attended the clinic but were incapable of completing the YSR. Thus, YSR data were available for eighty-four (58.3%) of the 144 eligible youths. No CBCL was available for eighteen youths who came to the clinic without their kinship caregivers. The sixty-eight youths for whom both CBCL and YSR data were available were significantly younger than those for whom we lacked complete data ($F = 10.26$, $p < .0001$), but there were no differences in duration of kinship care, gender, race, or relationship to the caregiver. The final sample was largely (92.4%) African American with a mean age of thirteen years ($SD = 1.63$, range = 11 to 18 years) and had been in care for a mean of 3.0 years ($SD = 2.4$ years) with all having been in care for at least one year. Approximately half (45%) of the sample was male.

Procedure

Data were collected during a clinic visit from the youths and from their accompanying caregivers. Most of the caregivers and the youths were able to complete the CBCL or YSR independently, although questions were read to them when necessary. Informed consent was obtained prior to data collection using procedures approved by the Institutional Review Board at the University of Maryland at Baltimore.

Measures

Measures included the CBCL (Achenbach, 1991b), the YSR (Achenbach, 1991c), and a project-developed teacher questionnaire. Both the CBCL (Achenbach, 1991b) and the YSR (Achenbach, 1991c) are widely used standardized measures. Each lists 118 behavior problems scored as occurring frequently, sometimes, or not at all. Scoring is based on T scores found by questioning a cross-section of children and assigning the average child a score of 50 with a standard deviation (SD) of 10. The scales provide scores for a number of dimensions: a composite measure of Total Behavior Problems; two broad-band scales: Externalizing (e.g., Aggressive and Delinquent Behavior) and Internalizing (Withdrawn, Somatic Complaints, and Anxious/Depressed); and eight narrow-band scales: Withdrawn, Somatic Complaints, Anxious/Depressed, Social Problems, Thought Problems, Attention Problems, Delinquent Behavior, and Aggressive Behavior. Both instruments have good reliability and validity (Achenbach, 1991b, 1991c).

Score interpretation is identical for both instruments. For the Total Behavior Problem and the broad-band scales, scores less than one standard deviation above the norm are considered normal ($T < 60$) while scores of 60–63 are classified as borderline and those above 63 (the 90th percentile) are classified as "clinical," indicating the likelihood of a clinically significant behavior problem. More stringent criteria are used for the narrow-band scales. Scores less than 67 (the 95th percentile) are considered normal, those of 67–70 are borderline, and scores above 70 (the 98th percentile) are clinical. We classified borderline problem levels as nonclinical in all analyses of clinical vs. nonclinical status in this chapter.

The teacher questionnaire included seven questions related to CBCL and YSR items (Dubowitz & Sawyer, 1994). Five were virtually identical to Externalizing items, and two were Internalizing items from the CBCL. Reliabilities for these scales were satisfactory (coefficient alpha = .82 for Externalizing and .71 for Internalizing behaviors).

RESULTS

The results of the present study confirm the high degree of behavior problems among youths placed in kinship care, regardless of who provides the information. Almost a third of the caregivers and more than a fifth of youths reported Total Behavior Problems in the clinical range. These findings that are similar to those reported for children placed in nonrelative foster care (Fanshel & Shinn, 1978; Kavaler & Swire, 1983).

The first hypothesis, that caregivers and youths would differ in their reports of behavior problems, was only partially confirmed (see Table 12.1). Compared to the youths, caregivers reported significantly more Externalizing problems, more problems on the two narrow-band scales that constitute the Externalizing scale (Delinquent and Aggressive Behavior), and more Attention Problems. There were no differences in reporting of total problems, Internalizing problems, and five of the eight narrow-band scales (Withdrawn, Somatic Complaints, Anxious/Depressed, Social Problems, and Thought Problems).

TABLE 12.1
Comparisons of Youth and Caregiver Reports of Behavior Problems

Scale	CBCL Mean (SD)	YSR Mean (SD)	t^* (p)	CBCL % Clinical	YSR % Clinical
Total Problems	55.2 (13.0)	52.9 (10.8)	1.33 (NS)	32%	21%
Broad Band Scales					
Internalizing Problems	52.8 (11.9)	53.2 (11.6)	−.26 (NS)	21%	17%
Externalizing Problems	56.2 (12.1)	50.4 (11.3)	3.52***	27%	9%
Narrow-Band Scales					
Withdrawn	56.3 (7.9)	54.9 (6.9)	1.22 (NS)	3%	2%
Somatic Complaints	57.0 (7.9)	57.0 (8.5)	.00 (NS)	4%	6%
Anxious/Depressed	55.2 (7.3)	54.4 (6.8)	.70 (NS)	4%	2%
Social Problems	57.3 (8.1)	56.8 (9.0)	.37 (NS)	6%	8%
Thought Problems	57.0 (7.9)	56.6 (6.9)	.31 (NS)	0%	2%
Attention Problems	57.8 (10.3)	53.5 (5.7)	3.21**	8%	2%
Delinquent Behavior	59.8 (8.6)	56.0 (8.1)	2.95*	12%	4%
Aggressive Behavior	57.9 (9.4)	54.0 (7.1)	3.68***	9%	4%

*Dependent t test.
*$p \leq .004$
**$p \leq .002$
***$p \leq .001$

Results support the second hypothesis of low but significant correlations between the CBCL and YSR scores for Total Behavior Problems and the broad-band Internalizing and Externalizing behavior problem scales (see Table 12.2). Caregiver and youth reports of Total Behavior Problem, Internalizing, and Externalizing problem scores were all significantly correlated. However, caregiver and youth reports on only two of the eight narrow-band, specific-problem-area scores were significantly correlated: Somatic Complaints and Aggressive Behavior.

Caregiver-youth response patterns were next examined by analyzing whether they agreed or differed on each individual CBCL/YSR item. To calculate a percentage agreement score, items were rescored on a two-point scale (problem behavior present or absent), and the number of items the caregiver and the youth agreed on were summed; the percentage was calculated as the ratio of the number of items agreed on to the total number of items. For example, if a given caregiver and a youth both reported that the youth had eighteen behavior problems and did not have fifty-six problems, they agreed on seventy-four of the total of 118 problems, or 63 percent of the items.

There was extensive variability in level of agreement across caregiver-youth dyads for all scales. For example, agreement on Total Behavior Problems ranged from 16 percent to 98 percent, with a mean agreement level across all of the sixty-six caregiver-youth dyads of 64 percent. Mean agreement for Internalizing and Externalizing scales was slightly lower (59% and 62%, respectively). Mean agreement on the eight narrow-band scales was 60 percent, with a range of 45 percent for Withdrawn to 67 percent for Somatic Complaints.

Results partially support the third hypothesis that boys would show more clinical behavior problems than girls. Overall, eight of twenty-two O^2 analyses were statistically significant. Boys had more problem behaviors than girls in all cases. On the CBCL, they were described as having significantly more Internalizing Problems ($O^2 = 5.87$, $p = .05$), Social Problems ($O^2 = 8.49$, $p = .01$), Thought Problems ($O^2 = 6.36$, $p = .01$), Attention Problems ($O^2 = 6.51$, $p = .04$), and Somatic Complaints ($O^2 = 10.92$, $p = .004$). For the YSR, boys

TABLE 12.2
Cross-Respondent Correlations for the CBCL and YSR

Scale	r	p
Total Problems	.29	<.05
Broad-Band Scales		
Internalizing	.30	<.01
Externalizing	.34	<.01
Narrow-Band Scales		
Withdrawn	.17	NS
Somatic Complaint	.26	<.05
Anxious/Depressed	.14	NS
Social Problems	.16	NS
Thought Problems	.24	NS
Attention Problems	.16	NS
Delinquent Behavior	.20	NS
Aggressive Behavior	.46	<.001

reported themselves as having more Total Behavior Problems ($O^2 = 6.73$, $p = .03$), being more Withdrawn ($O^2 = 7.92$, $p = .02$), and having more Social Problems ($O^2 = 8.49$, $p = .01$).

A final set of analyses was performed to determine the relationships among teacher responses to questions ask about youth mental health and caregiver CBCL and youth YSR responses. Because of missing teacher data, complete data were available for only forty-seven youths. Teacher total problem reports correlated significantly with CBCL Total scores ($r = 0.32$; $p < .05$) and with CBCL Externalizing scores ($r = 0.30$; $p < .05$). Teacher externalizing scores correlated significantly with CBCL Total Behavior Problem scores ($r = 0.30$; $p < .05$) and with CBCL Externalizing scores ($r = 0.29$; $p < .05$). Teacher internalizing scores did not correlate with any CBCL scores. There were no significant correlations between teacher scores and any YSR scale scores ($r = .17$ for Total Problems, .00 for Internalizing, and .18 for Externalizing).

DISCUSSION

The results of this study suggest that informants differ in their evaluation of externalizing problems; there is modest congruence in reporting across informants; and the caregivers of boys and the boys themselves tend to report a higher level of problem behavior than caregivers of girls or the girls themselves.

The most dramatic finding is that more than a quarter of the caregivers characterized the teenager in their care as having an Externalizing problem, while only 9 percent of the youth reported a problem. Since the norms for the tests indicate that 10 percent of the youths have T scores in the clinical range for Externalizing problems, the youths' self-reports do not suggest increased externalizing disorders. Similar conclusions hold for the three narrow-band scales—Attention Problems, Delinquent Behavior, and Aggressive Behavior—on which the caregivers and the youths responded differently. Caregivers report problem frequencies above the 2 percent level found in the overall population while the youths do not report elevated problem levels.

Cross-Informant Responses

Five reasons may underlie the present finding of behavior problem rating differences between the kinship care providers and the youths who are in their care. First, responses of parents and youths may be more discrepant when a high degree of clinical problems is present. Studies of adolescents in a psychiatric hospital (Thurber & Hollingsworth, 1992) and in foster care (Madsen, cited in Landsverk, 1992) found elevated parent/caregiver scores on the CBCL compared to the YSR. Second, the pattern of responses in the present study may be related to the high percentage of low-income African American subjects in the sample. While Achenbach (1991b, 1991c) contends that the impact of income and ethnic differences on the two scales is minimal, it has been suggested that this may not be the case for the CBCL, particularly for males

(Sandberg, Meyer-Bahlburg, & Yager, 1991). Indeed, the finding of differences between mainland U.S. and Puerto Rican CBCL-YSR response patterns in another study (Achenbach et al., 1990) may have been due to cultural differences between the two samples.

Landsverk (1992) has suggested two additional possibilities that may underlie the present cross-informant differences. First, parents of abused children rate their children as more aggressive than do neutral observers (Reid, Kavanagh, & Baldwin, 1987). Kinship caregivers' perceptions of misbehavior may be biased by such factors as reports by biological parents and their knowledge of the particular youth's history of maltreatment. Second, children may underreport externalizing behaviors. A number of studies have found underreporting of behavior problems in children and youths (e.g., Ivens & Rehn, 1988; Treiber & Mabe, 1987), although interpreting results in this area can be quite difficult, and research incorporating appropriate control groups is needed (Landsverk, 1992). Finally, caregivers and youths have different life experiences and different worldviews, which are evidenced in different perceptions of what constitutes problematic behaviors. Caregivers need to maintain order and to minimize problem behaviors and are therefore more likely to see everyday, developmentally appropriate behaviors as problematic, whereas youths in their care minimize the degree to which they perceive their own behaviors as problematic.

The second hypothesis of a low but statistically significant relationship between behavior problem reports across respondents was supported. Significant correlations were found for Total Behavior Problems, Internalizing, Externalizing, and two of the eight narrow-band scales. The .29 correlation between caregivers and youths for Total Behavior Problems found in this study is similar to the .25 mean correlation found across a number of studies (Achenbach et al., 1987) but is lower than the .39 correlation for boys and the .42 correlation for girls reported for a large, varied U.S. sample (Achenbach, 1991a). The present cross-informant correlations for Externalizing and Internalizing behavior problems, while significant, are also lower than the correlations reported by Achenbach (1991a): .32 for boys and .48 for girls on Internalizing and .46 for boys and .42 for girls on Externalizing problems.

With the exception of Aggressive Behavior ($r = .46$), all of the correlations between the responses of youth and their caregivers for the narrow-band behaviors in the present study were lower than those reported by Achenbach (1991a). He reported correlations of .39 for boys and .40 for girls for Aggression. The high correlation for Aggressive Behavior in the present sample may be related to the high level of maltreatment in the present sample and a lack of caregiver control over the youth's behavior. For example, maltreated youths have high rates of delinquent and aggressive behaviors (Starr, MacLean, & Keating, 1991). Aggression and related externalizing problems are more observable than many internalizing behaviors examined by the CBCL and the YSR and other, similar measures (Hodges, Gordon, & Lennon, 1990). When high problem levels are present, as is the case in the sample studied, caregivers have more opportunity to note the behavior, and this leads to a higher degree of cross-informant agreement.

There is only limited correspondence between the degree of cross-informant agreement on overall behavior problem scores and the data for agreement on individual items on the CBCL and YSR. In some cases, such as Aggression, there was relatively good agreement, with a 60 percent agreement level at the item level and a .46 cross-respondent correlation. In other cases, such as the Anxious/Depressed narrow-band scale, agreement was high (64%), but the cross-respondent correlation was low (.14). This lack of correspondence may be due either to different patterns of within-scale responding or to the procedures used to derive the percentage agreement score. The percentage agreement was based on an analysis of responses to each CBCL/YSR item, rather than a summary score. Thus, item-level disagreements are not reflected in the T scores. Furthermore, both the CBCL and the YSR are scored on a dimension of problem severity, whereas the agreement percentages for individual items were derived by using a dichotomous yes/no procedure that ignored problem severity.

To summarize, the relatively low level of overall cross-informant correspondence in our study may be due to several factors. First, the caregivers probably did not know the youths as well as the parents knew their teens in the Achenbach (1991a) sample. That this knowledge effect may exist is supported by both the present data and other reports concerning teacher-youth comparisons showing lower correlations than those for parent-youth self reports (Achenbach, 1991a). Second, cross-informant correlations decline from childhood to adolescence (Achenbach et al., 1987). Third, the maltreatment and subsequent placement experienced by the present sample may have led to a distrust of adults and institutions and consequently to a reluctance to fully disclose behavior problems. In addition, sample characteristics and different response biases may limit the degree of agreement in unknown ways. Finally, caregivers and youths may have different worldviews, leading to genuine differences in what is perceived to be problematic behavior.

Gender Differences

The significant gender differences for five CBCL and three YSR scales partially support the third hypothesis. Studies of children in nonrelative foster care have typically not examined gender differences in behavior problems (e.g., Fanshel & Shinn, 1978; Landsverk, 1992). Findings for gender differences in the few studies that have examined them are mixed; one study (Fanshel, Finch, & Grundy, 1990) did find differences, with boys having more conduct and behavior disorders and displaying more defiance to caregivers, "bizarre behavioral symptoms" (p. 61), and self-injurious behaviors, whereas girls had more sexual behavior and weight problems. Other studies have found no gender differences (McIntyre & Keesler, 1986; Rowe, Cain, Hundleby, & Keane, 1984). It must be noted, however, that the gender differences reported in the present study are for standardized scores for each gender compared to norms for that gender, not for the rates of problem behaviors compared across genders. They therefore may underestimate the extent of differences across genders.

Similarly, studies of maltreated children typically have not examined gender differences in the reaction to abuse and neglect. Some studies fail to find gender differences (e.g., Pfouts, Schopler, & Henley, 1981) while other evidence suggests that maltreated boys may be at greater risk for mental health problems than are maltreated girls. For example, Kaufman (1991) found that maltreated boys, including a number in out-of-home placements, tended to be more depressed than girls ($p < .10$), a finding that supports our finding of higher rates of anxiety and depression in the boys.

Teacher Responses

The greater correspondence between teacher behavior ratings and caregiver ratings than between teacher ratings and youth ratings was expected on the basis of Achenbach's (1991a) normative data. While different behaviors are seen in such settings as in the home and in school, adults tend to perceive behaviors in ways that are similar independent of the setting than do adults and youth.

Limitations of the Present Study

The present study is an initial effort to evaluate behavior problems among youths in kinship care. Our sample was limited in terms of size (66 cases) and diversity, with its largely low-income, African American sample. The generalizability of the present findings can be ascertained only through replication with other samples.

IMPLICATIONS

Clinical Work

Caregivers describe youths in kinship care as being at high risk for overall and Externalizing behavior problems and at slightly lower risk for Internalizing problems. These results support the findings of other research on caregiver judgments of behavior problems of children and youths placed in foster care. While the youths surveyed in the present study reported somewhat fewer problems than their caregivers perceived, the rates of Internalizing and Total Problems were both considerably higher than the expected rate of 10 percent based on the CBCL and YSR norms. Therefore, screening of youths *and* caregivers should be a routine part of monitoring children's status at the start of care and progress during out-of-home placement.

Given the similarity between caregiver ratings and those obtained using a set of seven questions asked of teachers, it may be useful to ask teachers to complete the questions used here or the Teacher Report Form (TRF, Achenbach, 1991d), an instrument parallel to the CBCL and the YSR. Indeed, some have advocated the use of multiaxial, empirical assessments across parents or caregivers, teachers, and children and youth in order to arrive at the best understanding of overall behavior problems (e.g., McConaughy, 1993).

However, opinions vary concerning how best to use multiple-informant data. Thus, Bird, Gould, Rubio-Stipec, Staghezza, and Canino (1991) suggest that parental reports are more valid indicators of behavior problems than are child reports, particularly in adolescents. Alternatively, Bird and his colleagues have more recently advocated considering a behavior to be a problem if it is listed by at least one of the informants (Bird, Gould, & Staghezza, 1992).

Regardless of the approach used to compare cross-informant reports, it is important to obtain YSR data for youths in out-of-home care, particularly since caregivers are often not sufficiently acquainted with the youths at the start of the out-of-home placement when many programmatic decisions are being made. It is important to recognize, however, that, even when caregiver responses are available, youths' descriptions of problems in the clinical or even in the borderline range should be explored using a more detailed clinical evaluation.

Multiple-informant responses are useful in planning clinical interventions, since they provide an index of the caregiver's and the youth's worldviews and how they resemble and differ from each other. Behaviors and emotions that both the caregiver and the youth agree are problematic should be more readily amenable to intervention, while clinicians will need to explore areas of disagreement with both parties. Clinical work in these areas should then focus on the differing perceptions, helping each participant to understand the other's perspective and reconciling different worldviews with the goal of increasing understanding and open communication.

Research

More research is needed on the factors that relate to the relative validity of parent/caregiver and youth self-reports of behavior problems. While the need for cross-informant information is often emphasized (e.g., Achenbach, 1991a), little research has been done on how best to integrate findings of different informants and on the factors that lead to discrepancies in the description of behavior problems. Clinical research dealing with these issues will be of great value in such areas as determining the best approach for screening for behavior problems.

There is also a need to examine the usefulness of different ways of presenting the results obtained using the Achenbach measures. For example, studies differ in their definition of behavior problems. The present paper uses the criteria recommended by Achenbach in terms of how Total Behavior Problems and narrow-band problems are defined, but, as is the case in most studies in the literature, it does not use his criteria for defining clinical Internalizing and Externalizing problems. Achenbach (1991b, 1991c, 1991d) advocates describing a child as having a broad-band behavior problem only if there is a T score difference of at least ten points—one standard deviation— for one respondent or five points across two respondents for Internalizing and Externalizing. Few studies have applied these criteria; most investigators use broad-band scale scores independent of the difference between the scores on the two broad-band dimensions. However, other scoring problems are present in the CBCL literature. For example, some authors use a clinical score on any one narrow-band scale as a cutoff for determining if a child has a clinical behavior problem, rather than using the more inclusive Total Behavior Problem and broad-band scores (McIntyre & Keesler, 1986). The advantages of using the same assessment measure across studies is diminished without greater agreement on scoring methods and their interpretation. Research needs to address how to best assess behavior problems in youth.

SUMMARY

Behavior *should* be assessed using reports from multiple informants to develop the most comprehensive portrait of a child and to plan appropriate interventions. Problems of subjectivity and bias are inherent in any assessment approach. Within a multiple-informant assessment context, any report of a behavior problem by any respondent needs to be addressed, regardless of the eventual accuracy of the report. Finally, if an in-depth clinical assessment can give a "gold-standard" answer about the presence or absence of clinically important behavior problems, research is needed on how to compare individual reports of problems to the findings developed using the "gold standard."

Regardless of the procedure used to diagnose behavior problems in youths, it is important to recognize that both caregivers and youths reported high levels of problems. Youths in out-of-home placements must receive appropriate monitoring at regular intervals and, when indicated, remedial services.

References

Achenbach, T. M. (1991a). *Integrative guide for the 1991 CBCL/4–18, YSR, and TRF profiles.* Burlington: University of Vermont Department of Psychiatry.

Achenbach, T. M. (1991b). *Manual for the Child Behavior Checklist/4–18 and 1991 Profile.* Burlington: University of Vermont Department of Psychiatry.

Achenbach, T. M. (1991c). *Manual for the Youth Self-Report and 1991 Profile.* Burlington: University of Vermont Department of Psychiatry.

Achenbach, T. M. (1991d). *Manual for the Teacher's Report Form and 1991 Profile.* Burlington: University of Vermont Department of Psychiatry.

Achenbach, T. M., Bird, H. R., Canino, G., Phares, V., Gould, M. S., & Rubio-Stipec, M. (1990). Epidemiological comparisons of Puerto Rican and U.S. mainland children: Parent, teacher, and self-reports. *Journal of the American Academy of Child and Adolescent Psychiatry, 29,* 84–93.

Achenbach, T. M., McConaughy, S. H., & Howell, C. T. (1987). Child/adolescent behavioral and emotional problems: Implications of cross-informant correlations for situational specificity. *Psychological Bulletin, 101,* 213–232.

Bird, H. R., Gould, M. S., Rubio-Stipec, M., Staghezza, B. M., & Canino, G. (1991). Screening for childhood psychopathology in the community using the Child Behavior Checklist. *Journal of the American Academy of Child and Adolescent Psychiatry, 30,* 116–123.

Bird, H. R., Gould, M. S., & Staghezza, B. (1992). Aggregating data from multiple informants in child psychiatry epidemiological research. *Journal of the American Academy of Child and Adolescent Psychiatry, 31*, 78–85.

Dubowitz, H., & Sawyer, R. J. (1994). School behavior of children in kinship care. *Child Abuse & Neglect, 18*, 899–911.

Dubowitz, H., Tepper, V., Feigelman, S., Sawyer, R., & Davidson, N. (1990). *The physical and mental health and educational status of children placed with relatives—Final report.* Baltimore: Author.

Dubowitz, H., Zuravin, S., Starr, Jr., R., Feigelman, S., & Harrington, D. (1993). Behavior problems of children in kinship care. *Journal of Developmental and Behavioral Pediatrics, 14*, 386–393.

Fanshel, D., Finch, S. J., & Grundy, J. F. (1990). *Foster children in a life course perspective.* New York: Columbia University Press.

Fanshel, D., & Shinn, E. G. (1978). *Children in foster care: A longitudinal investigation.* New York: Columbia University Press.

Forehand, R., Neighbors, B., & Wierson, M. (1991). The transition of adolescence: The role of gender and stress in problem behavior and competence. *Journal of Child Psychology and Psychiatry and Allied Disciplines, 32*, 929–937.

Hodges, K., Gordon, Y., & Lennon, M. P. (1990). Parent-child agreement on symptoms assessed via a clinical research interview for children: The Child Assessment Schedule (CAS). *Journal of Child Psychology and Psychiatry, 31*, 427–436.

Ivens, C., & Rehn, L. (1988). Assessment of childhood depression: Correspondence between reports by child, mother, and father. *Journal of the American Academy of Child and Adolescent Psychiatry, 27*, 738–741.

Josselson, R. (1980). Ego development in adolescence. In J. Adelson (Ed.), *Handbook of adolescent psychology* (pp. 188–211). New York: Wiley.

Kaufman, J. (1991). Depressive disorders in maltreated children. *Journal of the American Academy of Child and Adolescent Psychiatry, 30*, 257–265.

Kavaler, M., & Swire, F. (1983). *Foster-child health care.* Lexington, Mass.: D. C. Heath.

Landsverk, J. (1992, May). *Assessment of mental health needs of children in the child welfare system.* Paper presented at the Workshop on Mental Health Services to Children in the Child Welfare System: Setting an Agenda, Bethesda, Md.

Links, P. S., Boyle, M. H., & Offord, D. R. (1989). The prevalence of emotional disorder in children. *Journal of Nervous and Mental Disease, 177*, 85–91.

Loeber, R. (1982). The stability of antisocial and delinquent child behavior: A review. *Child Development, 53*, 1431–1446.

Marcia, J. E. (1980). Identity in adolescence. In J. Adelson (Ed.), *Handbook of adolescent psychology* (pp. 159–187). New York: Wiley.

McConaughy, S. H. (1993). Evaluating behavioral and emotional disorders with the CBCL, TRF, and YSR Cross-Informant Scales. *Journal of Emotional and Behavioral Disorders, 1*, 40–52.

McIntyre, A., & Keesler, T. Y. (1986). Psychological disorders among foster children. *Journal of Child Clinical Psychology, 15*, 297–303.

McLoyd, V. C. (1990). The impact of economic hardship on black families and children: Psychological distress, parenting, and socioemotional development. *Child Development, 61*, 311–346.

National Black Child Development Institute. (1989). *Who will care when parents can't: A study of black children in the child welfare system.* Washington, DC: Author.

Petersen, A. C., & Hamburg, B. A. (1986). Adolescence: A developmental approach to problems and psychopathology. *Behavior Therapy, 17*, 480–499.

Pfouts, J. H., Schopler, J. H., & Henley, H. C., Jr. (1981). In R. J. Hunner & Y. E. Walker (Eds.), *Exploring the relationship between child abuse and delinquency* (pp. 79–99). Montclair, N.J.: Allanheld, Osmun.

Reid, J. B., Kavanagh, K., & Baldwin, D. V. (1987). Abusive parents' perceptions of child problem behaviors: An example of parental bias. *Journal of Child and Adolescent Psychology, 15,* 457–466.

Rowe, J., Cain, H., Hundleby, M., & Keane, A. (1984). *Long-term foster care.* New York: St. Martin's Press.

Sameroff, A., & Chandler, M. J. (1975). Reproductive risk and the continuum of care-taking casualty. In F. D. Horowitz (Ed.), *Review of child development research* (vol. 4, pp. 187–244). Chicago: University of Chicago Press.

Sandberg, D. E., Meyer-Bahlburg, H. F. L., & Yager, T. J. (1991). The Child Behavior Checklist nonclinical standardization samples: Should they be utilized as norms? *Journal of the American Academy of Child and Adolescent Psychiatry, 30,* 124–134.

Starr, R. H., Jr., MacLean, D. J., & Keating, D. P. (1991). Life-span developmental outcomes of child maltreatment. In R. H. Starr, Jr., & D. A. Wolfe (Eds.), *The effects of child abuse and neglect: Issues and research* (pp. 1–32). New York: Guilford.

Takas, M. (1991, December/January). Kinship care: Developing a safe and effective framework for protective placement of children with relatives. *Zero to Three, 11,* 12–17.

Thurber. S., & Hollingworth, D. K. (1992). Validity of the Achenbach and Edelbrock Youth Self-Report with hospitalized adolescents. *Journal of Clinical Child Psychology, 21,* 249–254.

Treiber, F. A., & Mabe, A. P., III. (1987). Child and parent perceptions of children's psychopathology in psychiatric outpatient children. *Journal of Abnormal Child Psychology, 15,* 115–124.

Webster-Stratton, C., & Hammond, M. (1988). Maternal depression and its relationship to life stress, perceptions of child behavior problems, parenting behaviors, and child conduct problems. *Journal of Abnormal Child Psychology, 16,* 299–315.

Youngblade, L. M., & Belsky, J. (1990). Social and emotional consequences of child maltreatment. In R. T. Ammerman & M. Hersen (Eds.), *Children at risk: An evaluation of factors contributing to child abuse and neglect* (pp. 109–146). New York: Plenum.

Zill, N., & Schoenborn, C. A. (1990, November 16). Developmental, learning, and emotional problems: Health of our nation's children, United States, 1988. *Advance data from vital and health statistics* (No. 190). Hyattsville, Md.: National Center for Health Statistics.

The Adult Functioning of Former Kinship and Nonrelative Foster Care Children

Susan J. Zuravin, Ph.D.
Mary Benedict, Ph.D.
Rebecca Stallings, Ph.D.

Foster care is not a solution in and of itself. It is an interventive process that has two goals, child-saving and permanency planning. The former translates into providing a safe and temporary living arrangement for children who can no longer remain with their caretakers because they are at risk for maltreatment or because the child has experienced a catastrophe such as the death, incarceration, or illness of a parent. The latter translates into finding a care situation other than foster care—for example, reunification or adoption—that will provide the child with a sense of durability and constancy. Regardless of which goal child welfare professionals advocate, "ultimately, the use of foster care must be evaluated according to its long-term effects on the recipients of care" (McDonald, Allen, Westerfelt, & Piliavin, 1993, p. 20). As McDonald and colleagues so well note:

> Do we provide children a valuable service when we offer out-of-home care, or do we make a bad situation worse? Assessment of these effects may begin while the child is in care but eventually it necessitates an examination of the adult lives of former foster children, with a particular interest in their ability to function as productive members of their communities. For this is what we ask of families, including substitute families: that they produce adults who are willing and able to live stable, relatively independent, reasonably happy lives and who can contribute to society as a whole.

The purpose of the study presented in this chapter was to examine the young adult functioning of two groups of former foster children—those who lived in kinship care and those who lived in nonrelative care at some point during their growing-up years.

The importance of continuing attention to the adult functioning of former foster children stems from considerations other than developing an evaluative body of knowledge about substitute care as an intervention. First, the number of children needing this intervention has been increasing and is projected to continue to escalate. At the end of 1985, 276,000 children were in care. By 1994, nine years later, this number had risen to 462,000 (Tatara, 1992, 1995), an increase of 67 percent. Given the costliness of substitute care as an intervention and the severe cutbacks in available funding for program resources, poor outcomes for foster children as adults would at the very least signal us to be cautious regarding wholesale use of out-of-home care. Second, and notwithstanding efforts to make permanent plans for foster children, many children spend years in out-of-home care, and a good proportion "ages out" of the system. To adequately care for as well as plan for the independence of these long-term foster children, it is crucial to have information about the range of problems they encounter as adults.

BACKGROUND

This section focuses not on reviewing the findings from specific studies of adult functioning but rather on summarizing results from these prior efforts and critiquing their methodology for the purpose of providing direction for future research. Specific examination of findings for each study is obviated by the existence of several excellent literature reviews (Festinger, 1983; Maluccio & Fein, 1985; McDonald, Allen, Westerfelt, & Piliavin, 1993; Pecora, Kingery, Downs, & Nollan, 1996), which together include all but two very recent studies (Benedict, Zuravin, & Stallings, 1996; Widom, 1991).

Since 1920 at least twenty-seven published articles and unpublished reports (see the suggested literature reviews for information) have addressed some aspect(s) of the adult functioning of individuals who spent time in out-of-home care during their growing-up years. Though the majority have appeared since 1975, remarkably few have addressed this topic in the 1990s. Generally, this group of studies can be divided into three categories by purpose: studies whose primary purpose was to examine the adult functioning of former out-of-home care recipients; studies whose purpose was to identify predictors of adult functioning from among an array of characteristics, including type of maltreatment, child and family of origin factors, and foster care experiences; and studies that focused on examining some pressing social problem and either found out-of-home care during childhood to be a significant discriminating factor or found former foster children to be overrepresented among individuals with a particular social problem (i.e., homelessness).

Methodological Problems with Former Studies

Despite the relatively large size of this body of literature, extreme caution must be exercised when drawing conclusions about areas of adult functioning and their predictors/antecedents (Maluccio & Fein, 1985; McDonald et al., 1993). Studies are diverse in purpose, as noted, vary with regard to design features, and are compromised by an array of methodological problems. These various differences and problems impede both the interpretability of findings from individual studies and integration of results across studies. The three broad areas discussed in this section not only suggest methodological and substantive directions for future research but also provide a context for viewing the design of the study reported in this chapter.

Presence of a comparison group(s).   Studies vary tremendously with regard to design. The primary problem with the majority of efforts that examined adult functioning is their failure to include a comparison of subjects. This obvious design flaw and the consequent inability to employ inferential statistics ensures that findings can not be interpreted. In other words, without an appropriate comparison group it is impossible to determine whether former foster children are as well off or have more problems than other's in today's world. Unfortunately, even for those studies that did use comparison groups, findings are difficult to interpret because of questions about the appropriateness of the comparison group and problematic to integrate across studies because of differences among the groups from individual studies—that is, some used normative data, others data from national surveys, and still others specific comparison groups. With regard to the former problem, failure to match comparison and case groups at a bare minimum on age at time of data collection, gender, ethnicity, and socioeconomic status can lead to spurious results.

Sample and sampling issues.   Various sample and sampling-related issues hinder the generalizability, interpretation, and integration of findings across studies. Four issues create particular problems. First, the use of convenience samples of former out-of-home children that do not represent the population of one agency or any particular jurisdiction compromises the external validity of several studies. Second, high attrition rates from the original sample, with the consequent introduction of bias, jeopardize internal validity. In other words, findings may paint a more positive picture of adult outcomes than actually exists because the better functioning individuals may be more likely to consent to an interview. Third, and also compromising internal validity, is the failure of many studies to sample subjects from a specific population. In other words, many studies aggregate into one study group adults who resided as children in family foster care, group homes, institutions, or with relatives/friends. As a result, it is impossible to determine if outcomes differ by type of surrogate care. Given the greatly increasing proportion of children recently entering and remaining in kinship care, this design feature ensures that we will not develop a body of knowledge about long-term outcomes for this portion of the foster care population vis-à-vis others. Fourth and last, failure to adjust for differences in characteristics or experiences either statistically or by selection or to take them into account when analyzing the data leads to interpretational difficulties. For example, large differences in age among cohort members can lead to false impressions about outcomes because of differential periods of risk; differences in time in care or number of moves can lead to spurious findings about foster care in general because outcomes are likely to be dependent on these characteristics.

Adult characteristics examined and data collection methods.   The main data collection method for the vast majority of studies was interviews, either in person or over the phone. Some research efforts supplemented this data with information from archival records such as police, school, and other public records.

A wide array of adult characteristics has been examined. Although the list of characteristics is long, for ease of discussion the group of outcome variables can be divided into four categories (McDonald et al., 1993): (1) adult self-sufficiency (education, employment and economic well-being, housing); (2) behavioral adjustment (criminality and substance use); (3) family and social support (marriage and cohabitation rates and outcomes, parenting outcomes, family support, and general social support); and (4) personal well-being (physical health, mental health, and life satisfaction). As might be expected and is so common among a body of research, operational definitions of concepts differ widely across studies, and some have been studied much more widely and in depth than others. Consequently, findings regarding the same concepts from different studies are not always easy to integrate, and it is easier to draw tentative conclusions about some characteristics than others. Those that have been examined most frequently with a comparison group include educational achievement, employment, criminality, and mental health (McDonald et al., 1993). Those that have been examined less frequently or without comparison groups include substance use, parenting outcomes, family and friend support, physical health, and personal well-being (McDonald et al., 1993).

Summary of Findings

Because of the factors already noted, conclusions about individual areas of functioning for even the most well-studied characteristics must be viewed as highly tentative. Bearing this in mind, findings suggest the following about outcomes relative to education, employment, homelessness, criminality, and mental health:

1. For the majority of former foster children, educational accomplishment is below that of comparison group members.

2. Males appear to have higher rates of unemployment than comparison group members, and for many former foster children, employment is in low-paying and unsteady jobs.

3. Former foster children have consistently been overrepresented among studies of the homeless (e.g., Hardy et al., 1996).

4. For males in particular, arrest and convictions rates are higher than those for the general population (McDonald et al., 1993).

5. The vast majority of the studies that examined mental health found former foster children to be doing quite a bit worse than their comparison group counterparts.

Conclusions

Several recommendations for future investigations of adult functioning flow from the above methodological examination of prior efforts. First comes the need for the use of case cohorts that are (a) representative of a population of individuals who experienced some specific type of surrogate care (i.e., family foster care, kinship care, group care), (b) not characterized by high rates of attrition from the sample, and (c) homogeneous with regard to age and stage of the life cycle. Second is the very obvious need for studies that incorporate an appropriate comparison group. The question, of course, is what constitutes an "appropriate" comparison group. While studies that employ normative data or use comparison cohorts from large studies can identity how foster children fare compared to the average citizen, results are likely to be confounded by ethnic and socioeconomic status, since both ethnic minorities and low-socioeconomic-status individuals are overrepresented among the population of former foster children. Also likely to result in spurious findings are comparison groups that are not matched on age, since older individuals have had a longer period of time to develop any problem or outcome. Thus, at the very minimum, it seems that a reasonably adequate comparison group needs to be well matched to the case group on age, ethnicity, and socioeconomic status. Third is the need to control by selection or use of statistics for factors, such as the length of time in care and the number of moves, that are likely to affect and as a result confound the interpretation of outcomes. Fourth, and last is the necessity of replicating extant findings with better designed studies as well as examination of concepts that have either received little attention or attracted no or negligible regard in the context of a case-comparison study.

Study Objectives

The specific objective of this study was to compare the functioning of young adults who spent time in kinship foster care and those who spent time in non-relative foster care to that of a matched group of adults who did not spend time in out-of-home care. This study differed from many of the earlier efforts in three ways. First, it employed specific comparison groups that were matched for age, gender, and ethnicity to the two groups of former foster children. Second, the samples of former foster children were restricted to those who had been in family foster care only, as opposed to those who had been in an array of different out-of-home custodial arrangements (i.e., family foster care, group care, residential care). Third, a broader array of outcomes domains and operational definitions, including physical health, was examined than is found in many past studies.

STUDY METHODOLOGY

Overview

The findings reported in this chapter come from the second phase of a two-phase study of children who lived in family foster homes licensed by the Baltimore City Department of Social Services (BCDSS) between 1984 and 1988. Phase I, a case comparison study, focused on identifying characteristics of foster homes and foster children that are associated with maltreatment of children while they are in family foster care custody (Benedict & Zuravin, 1992a; Benedict et al., 1994; Zuravin et al., 1993). Data were obtained from case records. Included in the study cohort were 652 children divided into two groups. The case group included 423 children—every child who had been reported as maltreated while in care during the period 1984 to 1988 regardless of whether the report was substantiated upon investigation. The comparison group included 229 children randomly selected from family foster homes that provided care to children during the same four-year period and that had never been reported for maltreatment of any child in their home.

Phase II, also a case-comparison study (Benedict & Zuravin, 1992b), focused on (a) assessing the adult functioning of adults who had spent time in family foster care as children and (b) identifying predictors of adult functioning. Data were gathered during one in-person interview with each subject. The sample of case subjects included all the children from Phase I (n = 322) who were eighteen years or older at the time of the study interview (July 1993 to October 1994) and no longer residing in out-of-home care. Of the 322 adults in the sample, 214 were interviewed, for a completion rate of 66.5 percent. Comparison subjects were drawn from two different survey studies (Zuravin, DePanfilis, & Masnyk, 1994) that were conducted around the same time as the Phase II study.

Samples and Sampling Procedures

The case-comparison study reported in this chapter was conducted on 284 adults. The seventy-one case subjects (former foster children) are a subset of the 214 participants of the Phase II study described earlier. This group includes every participant in the study who was age twenty-five through thirty-one at the time of his or her interview. Of the seventy-one, thirty-one spent time in kinship foster care and forty in nonrelative foster care or a mixture of nonrelative and kin care. The 213 comparison subjects are a subset of 1,758 participants of a study conducted by Dr. Janet Hardy and colleagues (1996). They are matched for age, gender, and race to the seventy-one former foster children; none ever spent time living away from their natural parents. The matching and random selection involved (1) stratifying by gender, age group (27–28, 29–31), and race all of the Hardy study participants who were between twenty-seven and thirty-one at the time of their interview (twenty-seven is the bottom age because there were no younger respondents in this study) and (2) randomly selecting from the appropriate comparison group cell three different matched subjects for each kinship and each nonrelative subject. The selection methodology yielded a three-to-one comparison-to-case match and different comparison subjects for the each of the two groups of case subjects (kinship care cases and nonrelative care cases).

Kinship care definition.   The literature has reported several definitions of kinship care related to funding, relationship of caregiver to child, and agency supervision policies (Child Welfare League of America, 1994; Gleeson & Craig, 1994; Hegar & Scannapieco, 1995). Two issues are pertinent to the definition established for the current study. First, the caregivers of all children in this sample were licensed foster parents, and kinship care in this situation closely approximates Gleeson and Craig's (1994) definition as applied to families receiving federal or state foster care payments for the care of their relative children. To receive federal foster care board payments, all the kinship caregivers had gone through the same licensing and approval process as the nonrelative caregivers and theoretically were guided by federal and state foster care policies with the attendant permanency planning goals (Gleeson & Craig, 1994). The kinship care studied here is distinct from the type provided by the Baltimore City Department of Social Services (BCDSS) and described by Dubowitz and colleagues (1993, 1994). The latter included participants who were receiving AFDC payments for the care of relative children. These families were supervised by the Services to Extended Families with Children program (SEFC) within BCDSS (Scannapieco & Hegar, 1994).

A second consideration in definition emerged during the course of the present investigation. Many of the children in our sample did not remain in one setting for their entire out-of-home care experience but spent time in several types of settings, including group homes and nonrelative foster homes. To be part of the kinship care group for this study, more than 50 percent of the child's stay in out-of-home foster care had to be with relatives. Also included in the kin group were a few children who lived with godparent caregivers.

Data Collection Procedure and Measures of Adult Outcomes

Data for this chapter come from the interview. This document was used in Phase II of the study to gather self-report information about subjects' experiences during the growing-up years as well as their current and recent status and level of functioning in a number of domains. To assure comparability of data, specific questions, items, and scales were identical to a portion of those from the Hardy and colleagues' (1996) and Zuravin and colleagues' (1993) interview schedules.

Specific measures used for this particular examination of adult functioning were those developed and used by Hardy and colleagues. They index constructs from the four domains identified by McDonald and colleagues (1993) in their review of adult functioning outcomes. The McDonald (1993) domains include self-sufficiency, behavioral adjustment, family and social support, and mental health. The variables that define each domain are listed with findings in Tables 13.1 through 13.4 and described in the narratives that detail results for each domain. The majority are operationalized by single questions taken verbatim by Hardy and colleagues (1996) from various national-level surveys.

Data Analysis

Since this is basically an exploratory study with gender, race, and age controlled by matching, the analytic approach is bivariate in nature. Three analyses are conducted for each variable: the first compares the total group of former foster children (n = 71) to the total comparison group (n = 213), the second compares the kinship foster care children (n = 31) to their matched comparisons (n = 93), and the third compares the nonrelative foster children (n = 40) to their comparisons (n = 120). While findings are indicated as significant if $p < .05$, it is extremely important to caution that when so many analyses are being performed, some may be significant by chance. It is also important to note that findings regarding differences between outcomes for kinship versus nonrelative foster care children should be considered suggestive rather than definitive because no statistical comparisons are being performed between these outcomes. Statistical procedures were dictated by each variable's level of measurement and included chi squared, t-test, and the Kruskal-Wallis Test.

FINDINGS

Self-Sufficiency

The self-sufficiency domain, one that indexes, at least to some extent, preparation for the "harder" skills necessary for independent living, is operationally defined by four variables and one scale. The variables are "number of years of school completed at the time of the interview," "employment status week prior to interview," "homelessness status ever" (did not have a regular place to stay), and "ever receive any type of public welfare assistance, including SSI, food stamps, Aid to Families of Dependent Children, or General Public Assistance." The scale indexes their material level of living at the time of the interview. Its six items ascertain possession of various material items and other relevant effects, including a telephone, checking account, car/truck/motorcycle, credit card, and savings account. Responses are summed across the six items; the higher the scale score, the higher the material level of living.

Examination of findings (see Table 13.1) reveals rather impressive differences between former foster children as a group and their comparisons as well as kin care and nonrelative care children. Of the five variables, former foster children differ from their comparisons on four. At the time of the interview they were less likely to be employed and likely to have a lower material level of living. They had completed fewer years of school, had a lower level of living, were less likely to have been employed, and were more likely to have been homeless. In addition, for every single convenience in the material-level-of-living scale, they were less likely than their comparisons to have the item. For example, they were approximately 50 percent less likely to have a car or savings account and 25 percent less likely to have a telephone. Worthy of par-

TABLE 13.1
Findings for Self-Sufficiency Variables

Variable	Kin Comp Case		Nonkin Comp Case		Kin and Nonkin Comp Case	
Years of schooling						
Mean	12.3	11.4	12.5	11.8*	12.5	11.6***
SD	(2.4)	(1.8)	(2.0)	(1.6)	(2.2)	(1.7)
Ever homeless						
Percent yes	3.3%	32.3***	7.5%	25.0**	5.7	28.2***
Currently employed						
Percent yes	60.2	64.5	75.8	47.5***	69.0	54.9*
Material level of living scale						
Mean	2.9	1.8**	3.4	1.8***	3.2	1.8***
SD	(2.1)	(1.9)	(2.3)	(2.2)	(2.2)	(2.0)
Received public assistance during last year						
Percent yes	30.3	25.8	15.0	37.5**	21.5	32.39

*$p < .05$
**$p < .01$
***$p < .001$.

ticular note because of their magnitude are the results with regard to homelessness. Overall, former foster children are approximately five times more likely than their comparisons to have experienced at least one period of homelessness.

Comparison of findings with regard to kin care and nonrelative care former foster children suggests a consistent pattern of poor self-sufficiency for the nonrelative subjects compared to the kin care subjects. Of five possible differences, nonrelative subjects differed from their comparisons with regard to all five, while kin-care subjects differed with respect to only two. They were more likely to have been homeless, and their current material levels of living were lower than those of their comparison subjects.

Family and Social Support

The family and social support domain, one that indexes, at least to some extent, preparation for the "softer" skills necessary for independent living, is operationally defined by four variables. The variables are "frequency of visits with neighbors during the week preceding the interview," "current number of close friends," "current number of voluntary group memberships," and "current status with regard to being married or cohabiting with a meaningful other."

Examination of findings (Table 13.2) does not reveal consistent and pronounced differences between the former foster children and their comparisons. Of the four variables, only one is associated with former foster child status—marital status. While neither the foster children nor their comparisons are very likely to be married or cohabiting, when they are involved in one of the two types of relationships, former foster children are more likely to be cohabiting, while the comparison subjects are more likely to be married. Conceivably, this difference with regard to marital status may account, at least in part, for the difference in material level of living between the comparison subjects and the former foster children.

TABLE 13.2
Findings for Family and Social Support Variables

Variable	Kin Comp Case		NonKin Comp Case		Kin and Nonkin Comp Case	
Frequency of visits with neighbors						
Median	2	1	1	1	1	1
Range	(0–20)	(0–11)	(0–41)	(0–20)	(0–41)	(0–20)
Number of close friends						
Median	5	3**	4	3	4.5	3
Range	(1–25)	(0–20)	(0–40)	(0–25)	(0–40)	(0–25)
Voluntary group memberships						
Median	0	0**	0	0	0	0
Range	(0–4)	(0–2)	(0–8)	(0–3)	(0–8)	(0–3)
Marital/cohabitation status (in percents)						
Married	25.8	19.4	33.3	12.5*	30.1	15.5**
Cohabiting	14.0	25.8	11.7	22.5	12.7	23.9
Neither	60.2	54.8	55.0	65.0	57.3	60.6

*p < .05
**p < .01

While comparison of the kin/comparison and nonrelative/comparison results fails to show a pronounced and highly consistent pattern of differences similar to those shown for the self-sufficiency domain, they do suggest that the former kin-care foster children may be more socially isolated than their nonrelative care counterparts. They have fewer close friends and belong to significantly fewer voluntary groups than their comparisons. Also noteworthy is the finding that they do not appear to demonstrate the same marital-cohabitation pattern as their nonrelative-care counterparts, that is, they are not significantly more likely to be cohabiting than living in a legally sanctioned relationship.

Behavioral Adjustment

The behavioral adjustment domain is divided into two subdomains, substance use/abuse and deviant activity. The former subdomain is operationalized by four variables and the latter by two variables and a scale. The scale taps the domain "deviant activities." Its items ascertain whether the respondent has ever perpetrated any of six acts, such as stealing $50 or more, hitting or threatening to hit someone, selling drugs, or stealing a vehicle. Responses are summed across the items; the higher the score, the greater the number of deviant acts.

Findings (see Table 13.3) with respect to comparisons between the full group of former foster children and their nonplaced counterparts rather consistently show no differences between these two groups with regard to the behavioral problem indicators. Seven of eight findings are not significant. Although noteworthy differences between the groups are not present, the magnitude of various individual results merits comment. Of particular interest is the high rate of drug use for recreational purposes. Sixty-four percent of the full group of subjects had used a drug for recreational purposes, 50 percent had used a drug six or more times, and 35 percent of those who had used a drug six or more times had ever used a drug every day for two weeks. Also of interest is the high rate of participation in deviant acts.

TABLE 13.3
Findings for Behavioral Adjustment Variables

Variable	Kin Comp	Kin Case	Nonkin Comp	Nonkin Case	Kin and Nonkin Comp	Kin and Nonkin Case
Ever drink alcohol						
Percent yes	94.6	87.1	93.3	82.5*	93.9	84.5**
Ever use drugs for recreational purposes						
Percent yes	67.7	61.3	63.3	62.5	65.3	62.0
Ever use any drug 6+ times						
Percent yes	52.7	51.6	47.5	50.0	49.8	50.7
Ever use any drug every day for two weeks if used 6+ time						
Percent yes	41.7	25.0	36.8	20.0	39.1	22.2
Crime scale	1.2	1.7	1.2	1.2	1.2	1.4
	(1.4)	(1.7)	(1.4)	(1.2)	(1.4)	(1.4)
Ever booked, charged, or arrested						
Percent yes	28.0	32.3	26.7	41.0	27.2	37.1
Ever convicted of crime						
Percent yes	17.2	16.1	15.8	25.6	16.4	21.4

*$p < .05$
**$p < .01$

The average subject reported committing 1.3 deviant acts, 30 percent of the full group reported being arrested for a misdemeanor (other than a minor traffic violation) or felony, and 18 percent reported having been convicted of a crime.

Similar to the results for the comparisons of the total group of foster children and their controls are those for the kin and nonrelative former foster children. There, too, no consistent pattern of significant and meaningful differences between the two groups was demonstrated. High rates of recreational drug use and deviancy are common for both groups of foster children and for their comparison counterparts.

Mental Health

The mental health domain is operationalized by three variables and one scale. Two of the variables are self-rating items; one asks respondents to rate themselves on a scale from 1 to 7 (terrible through delighted) regarding "how you feel about your life as a whole" and the other asks them to rate their current mental health on a scale from 1 to 5 (excellent to poor).

The third variable asks respondents if they have ever had an emotional or mental breakdown. The scale, the General Health Questionnaire (Bridges & Goldberg, 1986) is a twenty-eight-item measure developed to detect nonpsychotic psychiatric illness. Subjects are instructed to answer each item no or yes with respect to their mental/emotional state "over the past few weeks." A full-scale score is developed by summing across items; the higher the score, the greater the psychiatric symptomatology. The cutpoint recommended for clinical significance is 12 (Bridges & Goldberg, 1986).

Examination of findings (see Table 13.4) does not reveal easily interpreted patterns for either the full group of foster children and their comparisons or

TABLE 13.4
Findings for Mental Health Variables

Variable	Kin Comp Case		Nonkin Comp Case		Kin and Nonkin Comp Case	
General Health Questionnaire						
Median	38.7	38.9	38.9	39.2	38.8	39.1
Ever had emotional or mental breakdown						
Percent yes	4.3	16.1*	7.5	17.5	6.1	16.9**
Self-rating of current mental health status[1]						
Median	2.0	2.0	2.0	2.0*	2.0	2.0
Range	(1–5)	(1–5)	(1–5)	(1–4)	(1–5)	(1–5)
Self-rating life as a whole[2]						
Median	5.5	6.0	6.0	5.0	6.0	5.0
Range	(1–7)	(2–7)	(1–7)	(2–7)	(1–7)	(2–7)

1. Responses range from 1 through 5 where 1 is excellent and 5 is poor.
2. Responses rate from 1 through 7 where 1 is terrible and 7 is delighted.
*$p < .05$
**$p < .01$

for the kinship and nonrelative subjects. The former two groups differ with respect to one variable—former foster children were more likely to report having had a mental breakdown than were their comparison counterparts. The latter two groups differ in opposite ways with regard to two variables: (1) nonrelative care subjects rate themselves better on current mental health status than their comparisons, whereas kin foster care subjects do not, (2) kin foster care children are more likely to report having had a mental breakdown than their comparisons, whereas nonrelative children are not.

Possibly more illuminating and more important than the very unclear pattern of differences between the groups is the large magnitude of the General Health Questionnaire median for all of the various groups. Such a large value, one so much over the cutpoint of 12, suggests that many of the subjects are experiencing emotional symptoms that are clinically significant.

DISCUSSION

This chapter presents findings from research that focused on (a) describing and comparing the young adult functioning of former foster children and a matched group of adults who had not spent time in foster care and (b) determining if the functioning of former kinship foster care children differs from that of their nonrelative care counterparts. Before summarizing results, placing them in the context of findings from earlier efforts, and exploring their implications for policy and program formulation as well as future research, it is important to identify and discuss the effect of design limitations on interpretation of findings. First, small sample size may have led to false negative findings for some of the variables, particularly those involving former kin-care foster children and their matched counterparts. Power to detect small and medium-size effects was less than .80. Second, restriction of subjects to ages twenty-five through thirty-one, while enhancing internal validity, is likely to compromise the generalizability of findings. Third, use of single-item indicators may have resulted in under- or poor representation of study constructs and thus decreased the interpretability of results. And, finally, the descriptive nature of the study and the exclusive use of bivariate analyses obviates interpreting findings as the end result of living in foster care or a particular type of foster care. To begin to determine the etiology of observed outcomes, it is necessary to determine if foster care status is associated with functioning independent of other possible causal factors, such as various growing-up experiences, and characteristics of the foster care experience, such as length of time in care and number of different homes.

Bearing in mind these limitations, the most impressive and telling findings are those pertinent to self-sufficiency. Two conclusions seem reasonable and worthy of note: (1) overall, former foster children appear to be less self-sufficient than their nonfoster care counterparts, with homelessness being one of the more remarkable types of problems, and (2) former kin foster care children appear to be somewhat more self-sufficient than their nonrelative foster care counterparts. With regard to the remaining three domains, those pertinent to behavioral adjustment—drug use and deviant acts—are sufficiently consistent to suggest one conclusion: neither type of behavior is more characteristic of former foster children than of their nonfoster care counterparts.

Consideration of findings in the context of those from earlier comparison group efforts finds much support for some but not for others. Like earlier studies, ours, too, reveals former foster children to have completed fewer years of school and, not unexpectedly given the deficits in education, to have higher rates of unemployment than their counterparts who did not spend time in care. Moreover, our study, the first comparison-group effort to examine homelessness among former foster children, also supports findings from the large body of homelessness literature, which shows former foster children to be overrepresented among this population. Unlike prior work, we did not find arrest and conviction rates to be higher than those for the comparison group. However, it is possible that this finding reflects our inability to separately analyze the data by gender. Earlier efforts found arrests and conviction rates to be higher, particularly for men. And finally, contrary to earlier efforts, our mental health findings fail to provide consistent support for the notion that former foster children are worse off than their counterparts. While they were more likely to report having had an emotional or mental breakdown, they were not likely to report clinically significant symptomatology on the General Health Questionnaire.

While it is not possible to interpret differences in functioning as due to differences in foster care status, recommendations for policy and program changes and enhancements are not barred. Findings, like those of earlier studies, underscore the importance of special services to prepare youngsters who are aging out of foster care for independent living and federal initiatives like P.L. 99-272: Section 477 (Transitional Independent Living Program for Older Foster Children). Clearly, educational remediation is paramount. Not only has it been found to be highly correlated with employment, well-being, and interpersonal relationships, but Festinger's foster care respondents "rated it as one of the three most important areas for agencies to stress in discharge planning" (McDonald et al., 1993). While it is not clear precisely why former foster children are way overrepresented among the homeless population, weak family ties are likely to be one of the reasons. This, in turn, suggests how important it truly is to help foster children maintain contacts with natural family members. Another possible reason, one underscored by a study completed by Barth (1990), is failure to offer assistance in finding a place to live to the youngster leaving care. Barth (1990) found that only 26 percent of those interviewed reported that they had been offered help in this area.

Future research on the adult functioning of former foster children will be valuable for two reasons: (1) building theoretical and empirical knowledge about the long-term outcomes of foster care, and (2) guiding foster care policies and programs targeted to children aging out of care. Research in the near future should be guided by the following two key questions, both of which should be addressed by each study.

1. How does the functioning/functional status of former foster children differ from that of their matched counterparts?
2. What accounts for the variation in functioning seen among former foster children?

Pursuit of the first question is important for two reasons. First, and as noted in the introduction, few of the at least twenty-seven existing studies have used an appropriate comparison group; consequently, findings are difficult if not impossible to interpret. Second, ongoing research on outcomes will allow child welfare program and policy professionals to monitor the outcomes of "Transition to Independent Living" programs. To date, the second point has received little attention compared to the first, even though it is very important for helping to identify those adolescent foster children who are likely to have problems once they become independent. Potential mediating variables or areas to investigate include (1) characteristics of the foster care experience, such as type of care (e.g., family foster care, group care, residential care), length of time in care, number of placements, and age at first placement, (2) circumstances surrounding placement and experiences in the natural family, and (3) the child's problems while in care.

References

Barth, R. (1990). On their own: The experience of youth after foster care. *Child and Adolescent Social Work, 7* (5), 419–440.

Benedict, M., & Zuravin, S. (1992a). *Factors associated with maltreatment by family foster care providers.* Final report submitted to DHHS, ACF, NCCAN, Grant #90-CA-1367. Washington, D.C.: Clearinghouse on Child Abuse and Neglect.

Benedict, M., & Zuravin, S. (1992b). Grant proposal for "Foster children grown up: Social, economic, educational, and personal outcomes." DHHS, ACF, Children's Bureau, Grant #90-CW-1076.

Benedict, M., Zuravin, S., Brandt, D., & Abbey, H. (1994). Types and frequency of child maltreatment by family foster care providers in an urban population. *Child Abuse and Neglect, 18,* 577–585.

Benedict, M., Zuravin, S., & Stallings, R. (1996). Adult functioning of children who lived in kin versus nonrelative family foster homes. *Child Welfare, 75* (5), 529–549.

Bridges, K., & Goldberg, D. (1986). The validation of the GHQ-28 and the use of the MMSE in neurological in-patients. *British Journal of Psychiatry, 148,* 548–553.

Child Welfare League of America. (1994). *Kinship care: A natural bridge.* Washington, D.C.: Author.

Dubowitz, H., Feigelman, S., Harrington, D., Starr, Jr., R., Zuravin, S., & Sawyer, R. (1994). Children in kinship care: How do they fare? *Children and Youth Services Review, 16,* 85–106.

Dubowitz, H., Feigelman, S., & Zuravin, S. (1993). A profile of kinship care. *Child Welfare, 72,* 153–169.

Festinger, T. (1983). *No one ever asked us . . . A postscript to foster care.* New York: Columbia University Press.

Gleeson, J., & Craig, L. (1994). Kinship care in child welfare: An analysis of states' policies. *Children and Youth Services Review, 16,* 107–122.

Hardy, J., Shapiro, S., Mellits, E., Skinner, E., & Astone, N. (1996). Self-sufficiency at age 27–33 years: Factors present between birth and 18 years predictive of educational attainment among children born to inner-city families. *Pediatrics, 99*(1), 80–87.

Hegar, R., & Scannapieco, M. (1995). From family duty for family policy: The evolution of kinship care. *Child Welfare, 74,* 200–216.

Maluccio, A., & Fein, E. (1985). Growing up in foster care. *Children and Youth Services Review, 7,* 123–133.

McDonald, T., Allen, R., Westerfelt, A., & Piliavin, I. (1993). *Assessing the long-term effects of foster care: A research synthesis.* Institute for Research on Poverty, Special Report #57-93. Madison: University of Wisconsin, Institute for Research on Poverty.

Pecora, P., Kingery, K., Downs, C., & Nollan, K. (1996). *Examining the effectiveness of family foster care: A select literature review.* Unpublished manuscript. Seattle: University of Washington School of Social Work and the Casey Family Foundation.

Scannapieco, M., & Hegar R. (1994). Kinship care: Two case management models. *Child and Adolescent Social Work Journal, 11,* 315–324.

Tatara, T. (May, 1992). Characteristics of children in substitute and adoptive care—A statistical summary of the VCIS national child welfare data base. *VCIS Research Notes, 3,* 1–4. Washington, D.C.: American Public Welfare Association.

Tatara, T. (August, 1995). U.S. child substitute flow data for FY '93 and trends in the state child substitute care populations. *VCIS Research Notes, 11.* Washington, D.C.: American Public Welfare Association.

Widom, K. (1991). The role of placement experiences in mediating the criminal consequences of early childhood victimization. *American Journal of Orthopsychiatry, 61,* 195–209.

Zuravin, S., Benedict, M., & Somerfield, M. (1993). Child maltreatment in family foster care. *American Journal of Orthopsychiatry, 63,* 589–596.

Zuravin, S., DePanfilis, D., & Masnyk, K. (1994). *Teen motherhood: Its relationship to child abuse and neglect.* Final report submitted to DHHS, ACF, NCCAN, Grant #90-CA-1376/02. Washington, D.C.: Clearinghouse on Child Abuse and Neglect.

PART IV

Conclusion

Kinship Foster Care
The New Child Placement Paradigm

REBECCA L. HEGAR, D.S.W.

Earlier in this book, I trace cultural roots of kinship care reaching into ancient and traditional societies in many parts of the world (see chapter 2). It may at first seem contradictory that this final chapter presents kinship foster care as the new child placement paradigm. Any conflict is more apparent than real. A paradigm, as a model governing thought and practice, is inherently linked to acceptance within a professional community. It is its recent embrace by the child welfare field, social work, and public policy that transforms kinship care from a cultural artifact into a new paradigm for professional practice.

Thomas Kuhn, who introduced the concept of the scientific paradigm in 1962, defined paradigms as "universally recognized scientific achievements that for a time provide model problems and solutions to a community of practitioners" (1970, p. viii). A paradigm shift or "scientific revolution" begins with "extraordinary investigations that lead the profession at last to a new set of commitments ..." (1970, p. 6). The rise of a new paradigm, often begun, in Kuhn's view, by a new discovery, invention, or theory, "requires the reconstruction of prior theory and the re-evaluation of prior fact, an intrinsically revolutionary process that is seldom completed by a single man and never overnight" (1970, p. 7). As a new paradigm arises, and before an older one is discarded, a professional community finds itself in a period of paradigm conflict, which can last for an extended period of time.

Kuhn explicitly questioned whether paradigms existed in the social sciences, though he acknowledged that they might develop (1970, pp. 15, 21). His reservations have not stopped those in nonscientific fields from appropriating the construct for their own use, however. Obviously, adapting a scientific concept to the social sciences or professions requires some tailoring. The emergence of paradigms in social work and related fields may be less dependent on invention and more related to the publication of seminal ideas and theories. For example, it is easy to see Freud's (1938) conceptualization of the unconscious mind as the beginning of a paradigm shift. In the child placement field, Goldstein, Freud, and Solnit's (1973) construct of psychological parenthood might also qualify.

Paradigm shifts in a social discipline also may be initiated by changing social conditions that demand adaptation, such as shifts in family composition or population mobility. In fact, multiple factors may have to coincide for a profession to embrace a new paradigm of practice. That has been the case in the history of child welfare, as medieval clerical management of poverty and dependency shifted to public responsibility under the Poor Laws, as Poor Law solutions gave way to specialized institutions, as institutions declined with the advance of free foster homes and boarding homes, and now as traditional foster care increasingly is replaced by kinship foster care. This chapter traces those shifts in the dominant paradigm for child placement practice, with heaviest emphasis on the rise of kinship foster care.

New paradigms bring new insights and solutions, but they also expose previously unrecognized questions and problems. This chapter includes an analysis of some unintended and unforeseen consequences of policy and practice under the newest child placement paradigm. In that analysis, it draws from some of the research findings, practice models, and policy conclusions presented in the earlier chapters of this book. A final section of this chapter looks forward to the state of child placement practice at the turn of the millennium, posing the question: Will kinship foster care meet the needs of the next century?

PUBLIC RESPONSIBILITY FOR DEPENDENCY: POOR LAW SOLUTIONS

European antecedents of American social welfare policy include a long period of church responsibility for ameliorating poverty and dependency. Church doctrine was congruent with long-standing Jewish teaching that to give to the poor was a duty and to receive when in need a right (Trattner, 1994). Later, Americans would pioneer the conviction that church and state should be separate entities, but in medieval Europe the two overlapped in numerous ways. One of these was the compulsory nature of the tithe, or church tax. Both religious and secular authorities had roles in determining what proportion of church revenues, including the tithe, supported poor relief. An early and typical mandate was that a fourth be set aside for the relief of poverty, although in England from 1014 C.E. the proportion was a third (Tierney, 1959).

The three church institutions that carried out the work of poor relief were the parish, the monastery, and the hospital, which at the time denoted an institution that cared for either a specific or general group of dependent individuals. Children in need of care were assisted by all three institutions, and some hospitals resembled early orphanages (Tierney, 1959; Trattner, 1994).

Church responsibility for poor relief persisted on much of the European continent even after the Protestant Reformation, but in England a new paradigm emerged. Tierney (1959) poses the question:

> If ecclesiastical poor law worked tolerably well in thirteenth-century England, why did it become so relatively ineffective in the later Middle Ages that, from the mid-fourteenth century on, the secular government became increasingly preoccupied with problems of poor relief? (p. 109)

Many of the forces that led to state responsibility for the poor in England are connected to the end of feudalism and the rise of mercantilism and an economy based on trade. Social and economic conditions changed dramatically during the fourteenth century, as more people became independent of agriculture, the population fell precipitously due to the bubonic plague, and personal mobility increased (Tierney, 1959; Trattner, 1994). Somewhat later, the shift from farming to sheep raising and wool production displaced many feudal tenants, and the dissolution of monasteries as the English Reformation took hold forced others to wander in search of livelihood (Trattner, 1994).

The Poor Laws were a series of statutes that culminated in the final and most famous Act of 1601. Children made up one of three classes of dependent individuals the Act specifically addressed. The Act of 1601 extended family responsibility in cases of dependency, and grandparents became legally obligated to provide support for needy grandchildren (Jansson, 1997). After family and private charity were exhausted, the chief Poor Law solution for dependent children was apprenticeship or indenture, although children also found their way into almshouses, especially if they were disabled or too young to work. Later in England's American colonies, a few orphaned children were among those boarded at public expense in private homes, although most observers believe their number to be insignificant (Folks, 1902; Guest, 1989).

One might question whether a law that includes such a range of solutions is indeed a single paradigm for care of dependent children. Although the principle of public responsibility is less specific and ideological in nature than later child placement paradigms, the English Poor Laws resulted from the same kind of revolutionary inventiveness in the face of changed circumstances that Kuhn (1970) describes as a paradigm shift. The shift came about because experts in church law "failed to display the intellectual vitality that was needed to devise new legal remedies for the new problems that arose" (Tierney, 1959, p. 110).

THE INSTITUTIONAL IDEAL: ORPHANS' ASYLUMS AND HOMES

Aspects of the English Poor Laws were codified soon before the establishment of England's American colonies, and although their influence was strong in some parts of America (Folks, 1902; Guest, 1989), it was less or absent in other parts of what became the United States. It is not surprising that the first orphanage established in American territory was founded by Ursuline sisters in New

Orleans, then part of French Louisiana (Gates, 1994; Trattner, 1994); French territories in 1727 still operated under the principle of church responsibility for the dependent. During the same period, Spanish missions in the American Southwest served many of the roles of monasteries and hospitals in Europe.

It took another century before the English colonies really abandoned Poor Law solutions in favor of specialized institutions for dependent individuals, including children in need of care. Indenture and forced apprenticeship fell into disfavor first, in part because of similarities to slavery but primarily because of economic changes associated with the beginnings of the Industrial Revolution, which lessened the need for skilled craftsmen trained under the apprentice system (Trattner, 1994). Next, reformers targeted almshouses that took in a range of dependent people, arguing that children in such settings were neglected and suffered from the poor examples set by mentally ill adults and other residents.

Other forces also led to the founding of institutions, some of them similar to those that had underpinned the Poor Laws. The country was expanding to the west, and older social structures were disappearing:

> Americans regarded the ceaseless social and geographic mobility as a threat
> to familiar routines and restrictions that helped assure responsible conduct.
> They thought an erosion of family discipline was producing not just willful children, but vagrant and criminal adults. (Crenson, cited in Keiger, 1996, p. 36)

Keiger summarizes: "In response, this new and agitated society embraced the idea of asylums; take people who were at risk or who were causing harm to society, and isolate them" (1996, p. 36). Although a handful of asylums for children appeared in English America before 1830 (Folks, 1902; Smith, 1995), it was during the age of the "institutional ideal" that they proliferated, to some six hundred by 1890 (Trattner, 1994, p. 115–116). During the subsequent thirteen years, an additional four hundred were established (Smith, 1995).

The "institutional ideal," as Trattner (1994) calls it, is an apt label for the new paradigm that directed the founding, not just of orphan asylums and children's homes, but also of mental hospitals, residential schools for the blind, deaf, and retarded, and other specialized institutions. Particularly during the second half of the 1800s, the use of Poor Law solutions for poverty and dependency declined dramatically as reformers campaigned for hygiene, specialization, and isolation within self-contained "total institutions" for individuals with a range of personal needs. The final decline of the orphanage in the United States has been placed as late as the period after World War II (Jones, 1993), although after 1900 it was increasingly supplemented, then supplanted, by the rise of a newer child placement paradigm.

PLACING OUT: FREE FOSTER HOMES AND BOARDING HOMES

As with the earlier paradigm shifts, the movement toward "placing out" involved a long period of advocacy and reconsideration. In Trattner's words, "The nineteenth century, which began with attempts to get needy children into institutions, ended with attempts to get them out of those institutions" (1994, p. 123). Smith (1995) reports that:

> The decline in the use of institutions was preceded by at least 60 years of debate, and the conclusion, after the first 40, that family care was preferable to institutionalization. The debates began during the last third of the nineteenth century, and by 1886 were well under way. (p.132–133)

The 1899 National Conference of Charities and Corrections went on record as favoring placement in families over institutional care (Folks, 1902; Hacsi, 1995), a position echoed at the original White House Conference on Children in 1909 and reiterated at the 1919 White House Conference in the statement "The carefully selected foster home is for the normal child the best substitute for the natural home" (Smith, 1995, p. 134).

Once again, the push for a new paradigm of child placement took its momentum from social and economic changes in the broader society (Holt, 1992; Nelson, 1995). The three decades from 1880 to 1910 were characterized by the second great wave of European immigration, increased urbanization and growth of tenement districts, and exploitative working conditions in many industries. These same pressures and abuses that fueled the whole Progressive Movement influenced child advocates. In the face of spreading urban squalor, much of late-nineteenth-century America idealized its rural and more homogeneous past. Nativist sentiment was common, and Hacsi concludes that "placing-out was based on an anti-urban, anti-immigrant ideology" (Hacsi, 1995, p. 163). Nelson (1995) goes further in labeling it a response to fear of civil disorder and urban revolution, a position that appears to be supported by the writings of some of the major figures of the placing-out movement (e.g., Brace, 1872).

Although a few children had been boarded with families under the Poor Law, and infants were frequently "farmed out" for nursing even during the age of the institutional ideal, placing children with families began in a major way after Charles Loring Brace founded the New York Children's Aid Society in 1853. It ultimately placed at least 150,000 children in foster and adoptive homes, primarily in rural areas of the Midwest, the Plains states, and the West Coast (Cook, 1995; Holt, 1992). The reality that most midwestern and western farm families were Protestant led to charges of forced assimilation of Catholic and Jewish children relocated from the big population centers. In response, non-Protestant communities sometimes clung to the older institutional paradigm, as well as beginning their own placement services (Cook, 1995; Keiger, 1996; Folks, 1902; Hacsi, 1995; Trattner, 1994). Not all placement agencies sought to remove children from their home cities and states. Folks (1902) reports that, at one point in the 1870s, Massachusetts supervised approximately one thousand children placed with families.

Although Brace's "orphan trains" form the best known image of the early placing-out movement (Holt, 1992), Homer Folks (1902) was among its strongest advocates at the turn of the century. He foresaw a time when an increase in hard-to-place children and a decrease in the need for farm labor would make it necessary for state agencies "to place certain of their children in fam-

ilies with payment for board" (1902, p. 243). This was not a new idea or practice (Hacsi, 1995), but Folks correctly identified the forces that would lead to
foster boarding homes becoming the linchpin of child placement for close to
a century. Free foster homes largely disappeared by the end of the 1930s
(Jones, 1989, 1993).

KINSHIP FOSTER CARE: THE RISE OF THE NEWEST PARADIGM

The theme of chapter 2 of this book is that kinship foster care is rooted in ancient cultural practices. There is nothing new about grandparents taking responsibility for children when parents cannot. That was mandated by the Poor
Law and, in addition, was a cultural pattern in many traditional societies and
American subcultures (Billingsley, 1992; Delgado & Humm-Delgado, 1982;
Shomaker, 1989; Timberlake & Chipungu, 1992). But until recently, kinship
fostering was a phenomenon that remained outside the formal mechanisms
for providing substitute care to children. In exploring why kinship foster care
has become the newest paradigm for child placement, it is necessary to examine demographic trends, social attitudes, and policy instruments, as well as
other possible explanations.

Trends in Demographics

Just as the Poor Laws arose to deal with labor shortages and population mobility, the "institutional ideal" responded to the decreased need for skilled labor
and the problems of westward expansion. Placing out was fueled in part by
immigration and urban crowding, along with the demand for labor in the West.
The adaptation of boarding care grew when demand in the West decreased
and farm families became fewer. Boarding out evolved into what we think of
today as traditional foster care: placement with unrelated foster parents who
receive payment to cover the expense of caring for one or more foster children. Changes in employment patterns, family composition, and other demographic shifts contributed to a decline of almost a third in the number of active
foster families between 1987 and 1991 (Merkel-Holguin, 1993). Contributing
factors probably include many of the social trends of the past thirty years: the
increase in the number of married women and mothers who work outside the
home; the practice of limiting family size; the increased rates of divorce and
single parenthood; greater mobility in employment and geography; and the
erosion of middle-class incomes. Much as free foster homes became incompatible with the economic conditions of the early twentieth century, traditional
foster care is an increasingly poor match for the conditions at century's end.
    Other factors also contribute to the inadequacy of traditional foster care
to meet contemporary needs. While the number of foster homes has declined,
the number of children needing placement has increased (31.1% between 1987
and 1991) (Merkel-Holguin, 1993). At the same time, the relative successes of
the permanency planning and family preservation movements have left a
harder-to-place foster care population with greater needs and problems (Hacsi,
1995; Wulczyn & Goerge, 1992). Finally, racial differences between the popu-

lation of children needing placement and the traditional population of foster families have become increasingly difficult to manage.

The Relationship Between Race and Kinship Care

Concern when children are placed outside of their own culture is nothing new, as was apparent from the response of immigrant Catholic and Jewish communities to early placing-out programs. More recently, the long pattern of placing Native American children in boarding schools and foster homes outside their tribes and culture provoked opposition that led to the passage of the Indian Child Welfare Act of 1978 (Mannes, 1995; Matheson, 1996). That act became the first U.S. policy document to express a preference for kinship foster care. In striking parallel to the nineteenth-century example, it prioritizes placement in Indian-run institutions above placement in families from nonnative cultures.

The biggest racial challenge facing foster care today is that, while the population of children in foster care is disproportionately African American (Brown & Bailey-Etta, 1997), the population of traditional foster families is disproportionately white. In 1972, the National Association of Black Social Workers went on record opposing out-of-race adoption for black children (Jones, 1972), which worked to decrease the number of transracial placements for some years. Placing agencies, which had systematically excluded African American families for decades, responded with limited efforts to recruit black foster and adoptive families (e.g., Washington, 1987).

Since 1972, foster families have become preferred adoptive resources for children in their care, and this change has moved some of the controversy over transracial placement into the foster care arena. Most recently, a few states have addressed the controversy surrounding transracial placements by passing legislation to prohibit consideration of race in adoption and, in some cases, in foster care (McRoy, Oglesby, & Grape, 1997). On the federal level, the Multiethnic Placement Act of 1994 denies federal child welfare funds to agencies that rule out placements solely on the basis of race, although race may be considered along with other factors.

Supplementing limited efforts to make traditional foster care and adoption responsive to the needs of African American children, kinship foster care has become a solution that many observers see as congruent with African American family patterns and cultural preferences (Danzy & Jackson, 1997; Scannapieco & Jackson, 1996). Although no national figures break down the population of children in kinship foster care by race, Scannapieco's (see chapter 9) review of the research reveals disproportionate placement of African American children in kinship foster care in a number of large city and state jurisdictions (Benedict, Zuravin, & Stallings, 1996; Berrick, Barth, & Needell, 1994; Gebel, 1996; Iglehart, 1994; see also chapter 3 by Gleeson and chapter 10 by Pecora, Le Prohn, and Nasuti).

Given the long-standing use of informal kinship caregiving in African American communities, some observers question whether the current influx of children of color into kinship foster care does not simply incorporate many who formerly were or would have been living in the homes of kin without state license, subsidy, or both. In a few cases, this incorporation hypothesis has been documented. For example, when New York put into effect new regulations for approving relative homes in 1985, New York City's Child Welfare Administration faced the task of approving five thousand existing kinship placements not previously reflected in its foster care statistics (Task Force, 1990). Individual cases in the literature also illustrate how caregiving relatives sometimes become involved in the foster care system (Kurtz, 1994).

Policy Instruments Promoting Kinship Care

In addition to the Indian Child Welfare Act mentioned earlier, other social forces and instruments of policy also have influenced the rise of kinship foster care. In chapter 3, Gleeson details policy developments in Illinois that led to the U.S. Supreme Court decision in *Miller v. Youakim* (1979), which held that for purposes of federal foster care funds, relative homes that met foster home licensing standards were eligible for the same reimbursement as nonrelative homes. However, as Gleeson points out, states have interpreted and implemented this ruling in different ways. These different approaches help explain the range of state kinship foster care programs presented by Scannapieco in chapter 5. Other court cases have also addressed the financing of kinship care, but they have tended to affect individual states, and they are not reviewed here (see CWLA, 1994). Although the extent of its contribution is hard to judge, passage of the Adoption Assistance and Child Welfare Act of 1980, with its emphasis on placement within the most family-like setting, probably has contributed to increased use of kinship foster homes.

Welfare deregulation will pose the next policy challenge for kinship foster care (Kamerman & Kahn, 1997). Passage of the Personal Responsibility and Work Opportunity Reconciliation Act of 1996 ensures the continuation of wide state-to-state variability in how kinship foster care is funded. Undoubtedly, cutting previously eligible recipients of Aid to Families with Dependent Children (AFDC) from the rolls of the new Temporary Assistance for Needy Families (TANF) program will force more children into state custody and kinship foster care (see Gleeson, chapter 3; Lawrence-Webb, 1997).

Informal kinship care will also be affected. Mullen (1996) addresses how subsequently adopted provisions of the Act will affect kinship caregiving by grandparents, particularly. She notes the possibilities of restricted eligibility or waiting lists for cash grants or Medicaid, elimination of child-only grants (often paid to caregiving relatives), and the question of how work requirements will be applied to caregiving grandparents and other older relatives. Brown and Bailey-Etta (1997) raise provocative questions about whether the kind of child welfare movement that marked the Progressive Era will reemerge to confront obvious present-day injustices to poor children and their families, especially since the population of children in care in some jurisdictions is now heavily African American.

UNFORESEEN ISSUES IN KINSHIP CARE

Like earlier child placement paradigms, kinship foster care has evolved from complex social changes and political forces. Unlike some of the earlier paradigms, it is hard to trace its origin in social policy to the advocacy of an individual, group of reformers, or publication. After its emergence as a paradigm to be reckoned with, a number of individuals and groups voiced support for kinship care as a form of formal substitute care for children in state custody (e.g., CWLA, 1994), and certainly the editors of and the contributors to this volume may generally be counted as supporters. However, as a largely unforeseen shift in the way substitute care is delivered in the United States, kinship foster care raises troubling issues. Some of these issues are posed as a series of controversial questions in chapter 1: Is kinship foster care out-of-home care or family preservation? Where would children in kinship foster care otherwise be living? Should kinship foster homes meet the same licensing requirements as other homes? Should children in kinship foster care live in poverty? What kind of efforts should states make to end kinship foster care placements? What do families risk or lose when they opt for kinship foster care? Is a two-tiered, racially segregated system of foster care developing?

The last of these questions is among the most provocative and troubling to arise out of the new child placement paradigm. Gleeson reports in chapter 3 that 87 percent of Illinois children in formal kinship care as of March 1995 were African American (see also Bonecutter & Gleeson, 1997). This, along with other research discussed earlier that shows that African American children are placed disproportionately in kinship care, raises clear cause for concern. Racially, ethnically, and religiously separate services have also been features of earlier placement paradigms (CWLA, 1995; Stehno, 1988), but much of that history occurred before racial integration and civil rights appeared on the U.S. policy agenda.

A related concern is that kinship foster care may bring into the formal child welfare system children who have been, or would have been, in informal kinship care. The potential exists for an even greater influx of children into kinship foster care, particularly if poverty rates rise (Hornby, Zeller, & Karreker, 1996). This probability touches an issue at the core of the debate about kinship foster care: Do the children require protection from their parents because of abuse or neglect, or do they primarily need support from the state due to poverty?

Under the older child placement paradigms, from church responsibility and Poor Law solutions through institutional placement and placing out, many poor children needed and found economic support, stability, and structure. Recognition of that need was reflected in the language of many older statutes giving juvenile courts jurisdiction over "dependent and neglected" children who, due to the absence, incapacity, actions, or omissions of their parents, depended on the state for sustenance. Later, in the middle decades of this century, came the conviction that children should not be placed solely because of poverty, the rediscovery of child abuse, much more specific statutory language

governing juvenile court adjudication, and an emphasis on "protective services" as the point of entry into the child welfare system.

Kinship foster care blurs the already fine distinction between some of those
who need protection from their parents or guardians and those who need support from the state due to poverty. Eligibility for services hinges on that distinction, although the overlap between the two groups makes their separate
treatment a shaky basis for social policy. In recent decades, child welfare and
foster care programs (including federal AFDC foster care funds) were targeted
on those in need of protection, while the AFDC program (including child-only
grants to relative payees) served those in need of support. The distinction between the two groups of children becomes even harder to maintain when some
caregiving relatives receive no financial help, some child-only AFDC or TANF
grants outside the child placement system, some AFDC or TANF grants in-
side it, some an intermediate level of reimbursement designed for kinship foster homes, and some the state's full foster care board rate. Because of the
range of state approaches to paying for their support, kinship foster care not
only takes some children out of poverty; it leaves others in it (Berrick, Barth,
& Needell, 1994; Gabel, 1992; Task Force, 1990). The nonsystem of funding
and serving those in kinship foster care has the earmarks of a class-action suit
waiting to be filed, as has in fact occurred in New York and Maryland.

A related area of shortcoming is revealed by research showing that the
training, monitoring, and services provided to kinship foster parents and the
children in their homes are less than to those involved in traditional foster care
(Berrick, Barth, & Needell, 1994; Dubowitz, Feigelman, & Zuravin, 1993;
Gebel, 1996; Iglehart, 1994; Scannapieco, Hegar, & McAlpine, 1997; Thornton,
1991). Finally, kinship care placements tend to last longer than traditional foster placements (Berrick et al., 1994; Gabel, 1992; Scannapieco, Hegar, &
McAlpine, 1997; Task Force, 1990; Thornton, 1991; Wulczyn & Goerge, 1990).
While this may meet the immediate needs of children, their parents, and extended family caregivers, it may also reflect lack of energy on the part of agencies to effect reunification of the original family or to achieve other permanency
planning.

When the differences between kinship and traditional foster care are ag-
gregated, it is hard to escape concluding that a two-track system of substitute
care is emerging in the United States. The older foster care paradigm continues to serve many children. They tend to come from areas of the country outside its major central cities, and they may be less likely to be labeled
"hard-to-place." They are also more likely to be white. Their foster homes have
more family resources, and, in many places, those homes receive higher levels of state support. Another, growing group of children is disproportionately
urban and minority. These children tend to be placed in the care of relatives
or fictive kin who are predominately single older women with lower levels of
education and home ownership than are found among traditional foster parents (Scannapieco, Hegar, & McAlpine, 1997; see also chapter 9 by
Scannapieco). In many places, they receive lower levels of state support. As
the editors of this book noted several years ago, "This difference in personal
and social resources highlights one of the most disturbing aspects of the kin-

ship care picture: children living in poverty or near-poverty, lacking adequate financial and social support from the state that assumed responsibility for their care" (Hegar & Scannapieco, 1995, p. 212). Brown and Bailey-Etta (1997) recently summed up the situation this way:

> The perceived virtue of these arrangements [kinship foster care] and the desire of kin not to be treated like "foster parents" by the system, should not be allowed to obscure the fact that many of the families providing kinship care are often poor, and that they often have some of the same needs for supportive services as the biological parents. Kinship care arrangements should not be pursued by child welfare agencies as a cost-effective way to avoid providing supportive services to children and families in need. African American children in kinship care tend to receive fewer services that do children in nonrelative family foster care, and fewer services than their Caucasian counterparts in kinship care. (p. 76)

KINSHIP CARE 2000: CHALLENGES FOR THE FUTURE

In a conservative era, marked by reductions in public social programs, what, if anything, makes kinship foster care something other than a residual solution that returns to family members responsibility for children in need of placement (see Wilensky & Lebeaux, 1965)? Three things could prevent kinship foster care from being the most residual feature of the already residual child welfare system: (1) the state role in safeguarding the rights of parents, children, and relatives who provide kinship foster care; (2) adequate state funding; and (3) state oversight to assure quality of care and provide supportive services.

Legal Security for All Parties

The first criterion for a less residual solution, a state role in ensuring that children, their parents, and caregiving relatives have legally respected statuses and claims, appears on the surface to be the easiest to achieve. After all, the legal processes of adjudication, foster care review, and termination of parental rights involve legal rights to notice, counsel, and other guarantees of due process. Also, while a foster child is in agency custody, contracts with foster parents and family team conferences with parents and, sometimes, other relatives are designed to make mutual expectations clear to all parties. In contrast to informal kinship caregiving, kinship foster care no doubt does protect children, their parents, and caregiving relatives from each others' unpredictable or endangering behavior. On the other hand, families do pass a significant degree of control from themselves to the state when they participate in formal kinship foster care.

In two case studies of permanency planning run amok, Kurtz (1994) emphasizes the autonomy and control over the placement that extended families lose when its members become agency foster parents. She is concerned about two different types of outcomes: unnecessary termination of the rights of noncustodial parents in the interest of guaranteeing "permanence" with kinship caregivers and failure of agencies to give established kinship placements the same consideration due nuclear families when problems arise or reports of abuse or neglect are received. Kurtz (1994) writes:

> Kinship foster care was not designed to result in unnecessary excising parents from the familial network of their children, but the thoughtless application of foster care laws to these situations . . . can create just that result (1994, p. 1499). . . . The current scheme denies kinship caretakers who become foster parents any assurance that the state will work with them and support the relationship between them and their relative foster children if problems arise. . . . Ensuring that these family arrangements are better protected from unnecessary permanent destruction during their times of difficulty will serve all members of the family. (p. 1517–1518)

It is difficult to estimate the prevalence of the types of permanency planning problems that Kurtz has observed in a New York legal clinic. However, it is possible to respond to such concerns on two levels: that of the agencies and families involved in providing kinship foster care, and that of family law and social policy that might change the current framework for practice. At minimum, agencies must communicate clearly and honestly with families about where the responsibility for future decisions about placement and permanency planning rests. It is essential that those involved in kinship foster care understand the respective roles of foster parents, parents, the agency, and the court. However, clear communication is not a sufficient safeguard against mistakes by agencies or poor decisions by judges.

Also needed are new protocols for making placement changes for children in kinship care. Perhaps kinship foster parents should be regarded as immediately eligible for administrative hearings when they contest agency decisions to move children out of their care into other substitute placements (but not back to parents). Such hearings, which are sometimes afforded to foster parents after a child has spent a given period of time in their care, are designed to protect established relationships. Obviously, hearings in kinship foster care cases, even placements of short duration, would serve to protect the relationships of children and their caregivers. The Supreme Court ruled in *Smith v. OFFER (1977)* that the right to such hearings is limited because foster families lack the degree of liberty interest in family privacy enjoyed by natural families (see Hegar, 1983). However, some commentators argue that kinship foster families have liberty interests similar to those of nuclear families (Killackey, 1992; Kurtz, 1994). The next time a foster care case similar to *Smith v. OFFER* reaches the appellate courts, it is likely that the foster parents will also be grandparents or other close relatives of the children in care.

Kinship foster parents might also be given statutory legal standing to intervene in court proceedings concerning the children in their care, which would afford them an opportunity to contest plans to terminate parental rights or return children to parents or other actions they believe detrimental to the children. Kinship adoption without termination of parental rights (as proposed in chapter 4 by Takas and Hegar) would also provide a way to strengthen and preserve the rights of parents, the claims of kinship caregivers, and the interests of children.

Adequate State Funding

The issue of how kinship foster care should be funded is among the most difficult in contemporary child welfare policy. It goes to the heart of the basic question we raise in chapter 1 of this book: How should formal kinship foster care differ from informal kinship care arranged by families themselves? It is clear that the present mixed system of child-only AFDC or TANF grants, intermediate subsidies, and foster care payments provides the least support to those most in need and leaves many children in state custody living in poverty. On the other hand, it frequently offers caregiving relatives more financial help than parents can obtain. It is also clear that welfare reform will give states even more lattitude to make their own rules about support for children in the homes of both parents and relatives (see Kamerman & Kahn, 1997).

There appears to be no short-term solution to the inequity and, in some places, the inadequacy of foster care funding. Nor are related problems, such as the incentive that kinship foster care may offer poor parents to allow their children to be placed, likely to be solved until the United States takes a broader approach to the problem of the cost of child rearing. When family poverty leads to child dependency and placement, whether with unrelated or kinship foster parents, the ultimate challenge is to address family poverty, not to tinker with foster care board rates. To repeat here what the editors of this book have written elsewhere:

> In the United States, care of children is not a social utility carrying publicly sponsored benefits (e.g., child-rearing allowances, health coverage, respite care) for whoever performs the task. If parents, kinship caregivers, and foster parents were equally eligible for such benefits and services, many troublesome questions about kinship care leading to unnecessary state custody or leaving foster children in poverty would be moot. (Hegar & Scannapieco, 1995, p. 213)

Until the country is ready for more fundamental remedies for lack of economic opportunity and for childhood poverty, contradictions and tensions surrounding the funding of kinship foster care are likely to remain.

State Oversight and Services

It is apparent from the research reviewed and presented in earlier chapters and discussed in this one that various state services are delivered less often in cases of kinship foster care than in traditional foster care. These missing services range from training and monitoring home visits to concrete and professional services to help ameliorate individual and family problems. Most observers note this gap as a serious problem, though there also are those who believe that kinship foster families should be treated as more autonomous than other foster families (Kurtz, 1994). Still, leaving kinship foster families to carry out their role alone, with minimal state oversight and services, contributes to the conclusion that kinship foster care is a residual service designed to minimize the use of public resources.

A new emphasis is beginning to emerge in the literature that undoubtedly will be the theme of much future work concerning kinship foster care. This new theme is that kinship foster care requires substantially different practice approaches and services to families, not provision of the missing services documented in many research studies (see chapter 7 by Jackson; chapter 5 by Scannapieco; Bonecutter & Gleeson, 1997; Everett, 1995; Killackey, 1992; Scannapieco & Hegar, 1996). This new model or practice paradigm is still in the beginning stages of development, and there is still substantial disagreement about key elements of services to families and children in kinship care.

CONCLUSION

The next challenge to policy and practice under the kinship care paradigm will be to ensure the three things that can prevent kinship foster care from becoming a highly residual denial of public responsibility: legal safeguards, adequate funding, and needed monitoring and services. How that challenge is met will determine whether this period in child welfare history is regarded as the time when a new paradigm for child placement achieved successful dominance or as a time of crisis in child placement that ultimately led to a different solution.

References

Adoption Assistance and Child Welfare Act of 1980, Public Law 96-272.

Benedict, M. A., Zuravin, S., & Stallings, R. R. (1996). Adult functioning of children who lived in kin versus nonrelative family foster homes. *Child Welfare, 75*, 529–549.

Berrick, J. D., Barth, R. P., & Needell, B. (1994). A comparison of kinship foster homes and foster family homes: Implications for kinship foster care as family preservation. *Children and Youth Services Review, 16* (1/2), 33–63.

Billingsley, A. (1992). *Climbing Jacob's ladder: The enduring legacy of African-American families.* New York: Simon & Shuster.

Bonecutter, F. J., & Gleeson, J. P. (1997). Broadening our view: Lessons from kinship foster care. *Journal of Multicultural Social Work, 5*(1/2), 99–119.

Brace, C. L. (1872). *The dangerous classes of New York and twenty years among them.* New York: Wynkoop and Hallenbeck.

Brown, A. W., & Bailey-Etta, B. (1997). An out-of-home care system in crisis: Implications for African American children in the child welfare system. *Child Welfare, 76* (1), 65–83.

Child Welfare League of America. (1994). *Kinship care: A natural bridge.* Washington, D.C.: Author.

Child Welfare League of America. (1995). For God and children: The religious roots of U.S. child welfare before 1920. *Children's Voice, 4* (4), 24–26.

Cook, J. F. (1995). A history of placing-out: The orphan trains. *Child Welfare, 74* (1), 181–197.

Danzy, J., & Jackson, S. M. (1997). Family preservation and support services: A missed opportunity for kinship care. *Child Welfare, 76* (1), 31–44.

Delgado, M., & Humm-Delgado, D. (1982). Natural support systems: Source of strength in Hispanic communities. *Social Work, 27*(1), 83–89.

Dubowitz, H., Feigelman, S., & Zuravin, S. (1993). A profile of kinship care. *Child Welfare, 72,* 153–169.

Everett, J. E. (1995). Relative foster care: An emerging trend in foster care placement policy and practice. *Smith College Studies in Social Work, 65* (3), 239–254.

Folks, H. (1902, reprinted 1978). *The care of destitute, neglected, & delinquent children.* Washington, D.C.: National Association of Social Workers.

Freud, S. (1938). *The basic writings of Sigmund Freud.* New York: Random House.

Gabel, G. (1992). *Preliminary report on kinship foster family profile.* New York: Human Resources Administration, Child Welfare Administration.

Gates, D. (1994, December 12). History of the orphanage. *Newsweek,* 33.

Gebel, T. J. (1996). Kinship care and non-relative family foster care: A comparison of caregiver attributes and attitudes. *Child Welfare, 76* (1), 5–18.

Goldstein, J., Freud, A., & Solnit, A. J. (1973). *Beyond the best interests of the child.* New York: Free Press.

Guest, G. (1989). The boarding of the dependent poor in colonial America. *Social Service Review, 63* (1), 92–112.

Hacsi, T. (1995). From indenture to family foster care: A brief history of child placing. *Child Welfare, 74* (1), 162–180.

Hegar, R. L. (1983). Foster children's and parents' right to a family. *Social Service Review, 57* (3), 429–447.

Hegar, R. L., & Scannapieco, M. (1995). From family duty to family policy: The evolution of kinship care. *Child Welfare, 74* (1), 200–216.

Holt, M. A. (1992). *The orphan trains: Placing out in America.* Lincoln: University of Nebraska Press.

Hornby, H., Zeller, D., & Karraker, D. (1996). Kinship care in America: What outcomes should policy seek? *Child Welfare, 75* (5), 397–418.

Iglehart, A. P. (1994). Kinship foster care: Placement, service, and outcome issues. *Children and Youth Services Review, 16* (1/2), 107–121.

Indian Child Welfare Act of 1978, P.L. 95-608, 92 Stat. 3069.

Jansson, B. (1997). *The reluctant welfare state: American social welfare policies- past, present, and future* (3rd ed.). Pacific Grove, Calif.: Brooks Cole.

Jones, E. B. (1972). On transracial adoption of black children. *Child Welfare, 51* (5), 38.

Jones, M. B. (1989). Crisis of the American orphanage, 1931–1940. *Social Service Review, 63* (4), 613–629.

Jones, M. B. (1993). The decline of the American orphanage, 1941–1980. *Social Service Review, 67* (3), 459–480.

Kamerman, S. B., & Kahn, A. J. (eds.). (1997). *Child welfare in the context of welfare "reform."* New York: Columbia University School of Social Work.

Keiger, D. (1996, April). The rise and demise of the American orphanage. *Johns Hopkins Magazine,* 34–40.

Killackey, E. (1992). Kinship foster care. *Family Law Quarterly, 26* (3), 211–220.

Kuhn, T. S. (1970). *The structure of scientific revolutions* (2nd ed). Chicago: University of Chicago Press.

Kurtz, M. (1994). The purchase of families into foster care: Two case studies and the lessons they teach. *Connecticut Law Review, 26*(4), 1453–1524.

Lawrence-Webb, C. (1997). African American children in the modern child welfare system: A legacy of the Flemming rule. *Child Welfare, 76* (1), 9–30.

Mannes, M. (1995). Factors and events leading to the passage of the Indian Child Welfare Act. *Child Welfare, 74* (1), 264–282.

Matheson, L. (1996). The politics of the Indian Child Welfare Act. *Social Work, 41* (2), 232–235.

McRoy, R. G., Oglesby, Z., & Grape, H. (1997). Achieving same-race adoptive placements for African American children: Culturally sensitive practice approaches. *Child Welfare, 76* (1), 85–104.

Merkel-Holguin, L. A., with Sobel, A. (1993). *The child welfare stat book 1993.* Washington, D.C.: Child Welfare League of America.

Miller v. Youakim, 99 S.Ct. 957 (1979).

Mullen, F. (1996). Public benefits: Grandparents, grandchildren, and welfare reform. *Generations, 20*, 61–64.

Multiethnic Placement Act of 1994, P.L. 103–382.

Nelson, K. (1995). The child welfare response to youth violence and homelessness in the nineteenth century. *Child Welfare, 74* (1), 56–70.

Personal Responsibility and Work Opportunity Reconciliation Act of 1996, P.L. 104-193.

Scannapieco, M., & Hegar, R. L. (1996). A nontraditional assessment framework for formal kinship homes. *Child Welfare, 75* (5), 567–582.

Scannapieco, M., Hegar, R. L., & McAlpine, C. (1997). Kinship care and traditional foster care: A comparison within one Maryland county. *Families in Society, 78,* 480–488.

Scannapieco, M., & Jackson, S. (1996). Kinship care: The African American response to family preservation. *Social Work, 41* (2), 190–196.

Shomaker, D. J. (1989). Transfer of children and the importance of grandmothers among Navajo Indians. *Journal of Cross-Cultural Gerontology, 4*(1), 1–18.

Smith, E. P. (1995). Bring back the orphanages? What policymakers of today can learn from the past. *Child Welfare, 74* (1), 115–142.

Smith v. OFFER, 431 U.S. 816 (1977).

Stehno, S. M. (1988). Public responsibility for dependent black children: The advocacy of Edith Abbott and Sophonisba Breckinridge. *Social Service Review, 62*(3), 485–503.

Task Force on Permanency Planning for Foster Children. (1990). *Kinship foster care: The double-edged dilemma.* Rochester, N.Y.: Author.

Thornton, J. L. (1991). Permanency planning for children in kinship foster homes. *Child Welfare, 70*, 593–601.

Tierney, B. (1959). *Medieval poor law: A sketch of canonical theory and its application in England.* Berkeley: University of California Press.

Timberlake, E. M., & Chipungu, S. S. (1992). Grandmotherhood: Contemporary meaning among African American middle-class grandmothers. *Social Work, 37* (3), 216–222.

Trattner, W. A. (1994). *From poor law to welfare state: A history of social welfare in America* (5th ed.). New York: Free Press.

Washington, V. (1987). Community involvement in recruiting adoptive homes for black children. *Child Welfare, 66* (1), 57–68.

Wilensky, H. L., & Lebeaux, C. N. (1965). *Industrial society & social welfare.* New York: Free Press.

Wulczyn, F. H., & Goerge, R. M. (1992). Foster care in New York and Illinois: The challenge of rapid change. *Social Service Review, 66*, 278–294.

Index